Hooked Up

Jack Myers

Jack Myers is a Media Ecologist and Chairman of Media Advisory Group, which advises more than 250 media advertising, marketing, entertainment and financial services companies who subscribe to the weekly *Jack Myers Media Business Report*. Jack founded the Women in Media Mentoring Initiative and the *Newhouse Network* to support and advance diversity and the careers of young people. He speaks internationally on the impact of emerging media technologies on society, culture and business. He is a George Foster Peabody award-winning and Academy Award nominated documentary film producer and author of four books. His 1998 book, *Reconnecting with Customers: Building Brands and Profits in The Relationship Age*, is recognized as a leading edge primer that anticipated today's dramatic digital transformation. *Virtual Worlds: Rewiring Your Emotional Future*, published in 2007, focuses on the growing influence of social networks on young people. Jack is a Board Member Emeritus of the Newhouse School of Communications at Syracuse University. He served on the Advisory Board for the Steinhardt School of Culture, Education and Human Development at New York University. His career included management positions at CBS Television and ABC Radio and he co-founded the *Syracuse New Times*.

Other Books by Jack Myers:

- *Adbashing: Surviving the Attacks on Advertising*   1993

- *MEDIA 2005*   1997

- *Reconnecting with Customers:*   1998
  Building Brands and Profits in The Relationship Age

- *Virtual Worlds: Rewiring Your Emotional Future*   2007

Hooked Up

A New Generation's Surprising Take on Sex, Politics and Saving the World

By Jack Myers

YORK HOUSE PRESS

ShellyPalmerdigitalliving *series*

Library of Congress Control Number: 2012939587

ISBN: 978-0-9855508-0-6

York House Press
1266 E. Main St. 700R
Stamford, CT   06902

Dedication

Dedicated to the Women I Love,

Especially My Mom, Gert Myers,

Who Serves as an Inspiration to

All Internet Pioneers

Contents

Gert Myers:

Undoubtedly, the Internet is impacting every aspect of "Internet Pioneers'" lives, since they have been influenced by the Internet from birth. However, it also impacts in a truly wonderful way the life of this 90-year-old.

I, too, grew up with computers (obviously not from birth), starting with keypunch and programming lessons in the 1950s and actually working with the conversion of manual accounting systems to computerized systems, both in private and governmental accounting. The impact on my life was a challenging and fascinating systems accounting career over a forty year period.

But the greatest impact today for this 90-year-old great-grandma in Texas is the ability to see great-grandchildren from New Jersey on the computer screen, and actually hear the three-year-old say "Hi Grandma Gert". What a blessing for a "Non-Internet Pioneer."

Introduction:
Oh Wow! Oh Wow! Oh Wow!

"Oh Wow! Oh Wow! Oh Wow!" Those were the final words of Apple co-founder Steve Jobs. Considering his almost otherworldly life, we can believe that he had a hopeful and positive vision of the future — both his own and Apple's...and ours.

But hopes for a positive future are hard to come by as we progress more deeply into the second decade of the 21st century. A new century begins with hope. But for a generation entering their teen years early in the millennium, hope was marred by the 9/11 attacks, economic uncertainty, social unpredictability, civil unrest, political polarization, global chaos, climate crisis, technological disruption and cultural dispassion. What does the future hold for this generation, and how will this generation impact the future?

The answer lies in the minds and actions of the self-assured, self-aware and tech-savvy Internet Pioneers. This group of 21.2 million Americans, born between 1991 and 1995, is the first generation to grow up after the Internet browser Mosaic was introduced in 1993. To Internet Pioneers, online and mobile connectivity is an integral and integrated part of their everyday lives, yet they still relate to and understand the legacies of a pre-Internet society. They belong to the first generation born and raised in a culture in which the Internet and the cell phone have always existed. The influence of these technologies on Internet Pioneers is huge, truly redefining life in the 21st century. They represent the generation that will define how the Internet will serve society for hundreds of years into the future.

Who are these Internet Pioneers? What are the forces that have influenced them? What are they doing with their lives, and what are they thinking? What can we learn about the future from them? When we look at the future through their eyes, do we see an "Oh Wow" vision that truly gives us hope?

In June of 2011, as I sat at the high school graduation of my then 17-year-old stepdaughter, Izzy, I wondered how the Internet had influenced her life and future. How different were she and her classmates from past generations of graduates, even from last year's graduating class and the class or two before that? I was curious about the traits, beliefs, behaviors and attitudes that 17- to 21-year-olds might have in common. How will they impact society, culture, business, politics, education, the arts, sciences and the global community? Could their patterns of behavior and actions be predicted based on history? What could we learn from this group that would enable us to anticipate their future, our future and the future of generations to follow?

Those questions triggered an extensive study of Americans born from 1991 to 1995 — just before and after the Internet browser was introduced in 1993. Through the research company Ipsos/OTX, I surveyed one thousand high school and college students in this age group, asking more than one hundred questions about their opinions and attitudes toward a wide range of topics from politics to sexuality. Interviews were conducted with students on college campuses across the country along with interviews of educators, experts and professionals.

This is the story of what I discovered and a vision of the future through their eyes. It's a story that offers hope that the innovations and advances enabled by the Internet will foster economic stability, peace, security, and social harmony.

"I'm heartened and encouraged that there seems to be a basic desire among this generation to make a difference somehow. For some of them it's superficial like being famous, and for others it's getting a great job and being recognized for achievement. They have an opportunity to take their knowledge and skills and make a difference and do something good for the world. The tools are at their disposal. I think they are up for the challenge and I think they will figure it out."

~ Dean Lorraine Branham
S.I. Newhouse School of Communications, Syracuse University

The conclusions outlined in this book are informed by my research survey and interviews. But the overall conclusions and perspectives, as in any generational study, reflect broad generalities and my opinions. This book has been written not as an educational thesis, but rather as a cultural overview and informed guidebook for parents, educators, professionals and the Internet Pioneers themselves.

The book is best read as a continuum, but you can read the first three chapters focusing on Internet Pioneers and their importance during a period of rapid and radical societal and cultural transformation followed by specific chapters that interest you most: sexuality; feminism and women's rights; religion; politics; education; media and entertainment; globalism; communications and culture; privacy and piracy; jobs, careers, business and marketing.

You'll discover a generation that is fascinating, fun, relevant and important. Of course, not everyone born between 1991 and 1995 shares all the characteristics I've identified, but as members of the first generation born into the Internet Age, they carry the responsibilities and burdens of pioneers — the first to cross an unexplored frontier and settle in an unknown territory.

Chapter 1:
A Hooked Up Generation

Internet Pioneers are the small band of impatient, empowered, multi-tasking, curious, confident, confused, sexually liberated, sometimes binge-drinking and often fragile kids who were the first to be born into the Internet Age. They're the ones you see texting as they're walking and talking with their friends (and often texting the same friends they're walking with, holding conversations within conversations).

Unlike past generations that typically encompass a 20- to 30-year period, the Internet Pioneer generation spans only a 5-year period, encompassing those who were born between 1991 and 1995, with the older class graduating from college and the younger class entering college in 2012. They comprise more than 95 percent of current college students.

The Internet is the defining influence on Internet Pioneers, and they are hooked up to and dependent on the Internet for managing almost every aspect of their lives. They'll eagerly embrace the latest apps, innovations and technological advances that simplify and enhance their connectivity yet just as quickly reject products and services that are overtly marketed to them without demonstrating a clear value.

They've grown up with the Internet and the economic collapse of 1999; the impeachment of President Clinton; the Bush/Gore contested election and Bush presidency; 9/11; weapons of mass destruction and the Iraqi War; the Oklahoma Federal Building bombing; religious extremism; the war in Afghanistan; atrocities in Africa; the economic collapse of 2009 and subsequent 'bail out' debates; too big to fail; steroids; sex-related scandals; the election of the first African-American president and intensified political polarization. They're aware of current affairs: the Arab Spring and "Occupy" movements; debates over climate change, abortion, contraception, gay rights, health care, gun control, immigration and illegal aliens, education, unionization, states' rights and taxes. People who have dominated the news during their lives have included Paris Hilton, Britney Spears, Lindsay Lohan, Snooki, Michael Jackson, and

Janet Jackson with her "unintentional" 2004 Super Bowl flash. Internet Pioneers have also experienced unprecedented hurricanes, earthquakes and natural disasters in the United States and around the world.

As exciting as the vision of Steve Jobs and the technological advances spurred by the Internet have been, the economic, political, educational, social and cultural realities facing today's college-age generation are as negatively charged as any since the Great Depression and World Wars of the 20th century. This is the world that Internet Pioneers are inheriting.

Internet Pioneers will have a future full of "Oh Wow!" moments, even as they shed the baggage of the depressing realities with which they have grown up. This is the first generation that, to paraphrase Marshall McLuhan, has not been driving down the road of life looking in its rearview mirror. Members of this generation have had a television screen, an Internet-connected computer screen and a mobile screen throughout their lives through which they've been able to discover the past, connect to the present *and* invent the future.

The chasm between pre- and post-Internet generations is a wide one. Internet Pioneers, because they straddle both, are the special group that has grown up in the 21st century-connected world but remains encumbered by the baggage of the 20th-century world they are inheriting. Many of them will live to experience most if not all of this first century of the new millennium, and they will be the ones to define and write its story.

Internet Pioneers will be the inspiration, creative force, intellectual foundation, economic backbone and social conscience of the 21st century. They represent the generation that will lead America and the world into the most important and formative period of the 21st century.

Overloaded and Wary

Internet Pioneers are different from generations that came before them. They may be the most aware generation ever yet they're so overloaded from being on a life-long roller coaster of emotionally charged knowledge and experiences that they're inclined to with-hold voicing strong opinions. They are measured and controlled in their actions. They'll listen to both sides of an argument and, *if* they engage at all, will try to find common ground, even if they strongly agree with one opinion or the other.

Internet Pioneers are, in a word, wary: wary about having strong feelings or taking strong positions; wary about their future prospects, their plans, their ability to contribute to and influence the world. They're wary about the economy, politics, institutions, organizations, movements, trends and fads. That wariness extends to teachers, coaches, clergy, and celebrities. It encompasses privacy issues, spam, bullying and hazing.

Although they may mature in fits and starts, sometimes resentful of the responsibilities heaped upon them and confused by the chaos and conflicts in their lives, they are generally at peace with adults. They're slow to protest against the institutions they mistrust. They are socially connected far beyond relatives and friends, to friends of friends, organizations, brands and corporations. Internet Pioneers are fun-loving but hard-working, focused on their futures polarized on many issues but generally cohesive in their hopes and plans for the future.

News and information comes at Internet Pioneers 24/7; they're constantly engaged in online and mobile social interaction; they're media junkies who are more aware than any generation before them of the world and its realities as well as the day-to-day and even minute-by-minute realities within their own social circles. They have grown up with information at their fingertips. These students were the first to rely on the Internet for class projects as early as elementary school. From there, they quickly discovered the ease with which an Internet connection could open all kinds of doors. The Internet could provide them with information, friends, entertainment and much more. The online world became a kind of virtual home.

Internet Pioneers have grown up with instant gratification media and with the world outside their homes constantly and urgently intruding on their family and personal lives. What are the implications?

"Many have grown up in homes with their moms and dads spending more time looking at their Blackberrys and iPhones than at their kids. Their parents have been connecting to the world outside the home in such an urgent way via email they've created a sense of apprehension about the challenges of adulthood."

~ Dean Lorraine Branham
S.I. Newhouse School of Communications, Syracuse University

A childhood of tolerant parenting also defines this generation. They belong to the first generation to attend schools that maintain zero tolerance for punishment, with some students in classrooms that abolished grade point systems. Others joined sports leagues that gave trophies to every player on every team. Some students went to schools where everyone who wanted to be in the school play got a role, and where gay students could openly form their own clubs. And above all, Internet Pioneers have been able to connect with each other 24/7 with minimal parental interference or even awareness.

As the Internet Pioneers generation has matured, its members have evolved from media consumers to content creators.

Taught in an environment that promoted individual expression, these young adults aren't satisfied to sit back and let others tell them what to think or how to feel. They have voices and they want to use them. And an explosion in the world of social media has allowed them to do just that.

High school and college students have an arsenal of social networks available — Facebook, Twitter, Digg, Reddit, StumbleUpon, Tumblr, Google Plus, plus *Quepasa, WeeWorld* and Foursquare, in addition to hundreds more specialized networks and virtual worlds. Students with initiative and a love for the written word can broadcast opinions to the world with the help of Blogger, WordPress, Square Space or LiveJournal.

Internet Pioneers' social lives are centered around technology, but they're socially comfortable and more likely to hug and embrace each other than shake hands. Dating and relationships among college students reflect a new "hooked up" culture in which relationships are often developed via engaged texting and in which sex is often a casual one-time-only encounter. The wary attitudes Internet Pioneers have toward commitments and long-term relationships affect their politics, education, careers, religious beliefs, media and entertainment interests, and all aspects of their lives.

The Internet and social networks have enabled Internet Pioneers to explore new cultures and simultaneously be a part of multiple social circles in an inclusive and open social structure. The Facebook pages of Internet Pioneers often reflect more about their core self-image and interests than they might share even in a close relationship. These Facebook pages and updates identify their social networks, current relationships and passions, attitudes toward authority likes and dislikes, fashion tastes, and day-to-day activities. Facebook users might post their thoughts on whatever issues or challenges they're confronting, consumer brands they support, the games and apps they like, and their plans for the future. In other words, studying the Facebook page of an Internet Pioneer can reveal much about his or her current life as well as his or her long-term hopes, dreams and fears.

Chapter 2:
Why Are Internet Pioneers So Important?

The Internet itself is more than an invention or innovation; it is a transformational catalyst that is differentiating the 21st Century from all of history before it.

The advances we are experiencing within our lifetimes border on incomprehensible for many of us. But for Internet Pioneers, they are expected. On the near-term horizon are ubiquitous WiFi…cloud storage with unlimited memory…4G and Ultra-5G connectivity with exponentially increased Internet speed… mobile devices that are elegant extensions of home communications centers…organization of content from millions of sources into personalized and curated resource centers…collaboration, communication and even voting through social networks…handheld remote controls and keyboards replaced by motion and voice detection…wireless global communications and instant translation that further disrupt traditional boundaries and bring the world together into new social and political systems…chips literally being embedded in our bodies for control, monitoring, tracking and communications…our brains learning to discern, process and communicate digital signals…our bodies becoming our own personal energy sources…medical advances that could extend the lives of many for decades. The list of technological advances that are already developed or in development could go on and on. Technological advances are a day-to-day reality with which Internet Pioneers have grown up and which they have come not only to expect, but to rely on.

"Today, we anticipate continuous technical progress and the social repercussions that follow. But the future will be far more surprising than most people realize, because few observers have truly internalized the implications that the rate of change itself is accelerating."

~ Ray Kurzweil
Inventor

We're living in the midst of a transformational period comparable to the development of the Industrial Age in the mid-to-late 1800s and early 1900s. The impact of the Internet is as transformational as that of the wheel, sea navigation, the printing press, the steam engine, electricity and the automobile.

Transformational periods share a common pattern. They begin with a single break-through invention or technological advance — such as electricity and the Internet — which then leads to a period of massive innovation. This period of massive innovation has two stages: the first being a stage of jaw-dropping invention, disruption and evaluation; and the second stage being a period of application, implementation, advancement, infrastructure development, and monetization.

We saw explosive technological inventions in the first stage of the Internet Transformation between 1993 and 2010. The introduction of the iPad in 2009 marks the beginning of a transition into this second stage: *application.* Internet-based "apps" are in the early stages of contributing to the arts, business, education, science, social rights and families as well as to every other aspect of society you can imagine. We have only just begun to scratch the surface of the application of Internet-based technology.

As we move further into the application stage of the Internet Transformation, get ready for innovation to shift into high gear. Internet-based businesses have been advancing at high speed for the past two decades, but the rate of advance can and will accelerate. The advances and applications coming soon will far transcend those we have witnessed to date.

Because Internet Pioneers are the first generation to reach college age having grown up with the Internet, they are the key influencers and implementers of this shift.

As they gain influence and power over the next two decades, Internet Pioneers will become the most important contributors to the Internet gene pool. Internet Pioneers will be prepared and experienced to exploit the cloud, social networking, mobility and super-fast connectivity. They will innovate at ever-increasing speed — giving the marketplace a heavy and sustained course of steroids.

Internet Pioneers are the first generation whose full adult lives and careers will exist in a world of cloud networks with unlimited storage. Medicine and biological computing will be dramatically impacted, as human bodies will be wirelessly connected to networks via chips and implants embedded in their bodies, just as pacemakers are already connected through phone lines and WiFi. Communications, already instant and global, will foster new societal structures built not around geographic borders, but around cultural, religious, ethnic, political, social and educational patterns and preferences.

Education will transcend the classroom as the fundamental concept and context of education is radically restructured to an Internet-based curriculum. The typical printed newspaper page will be relegated to museums and libraries within just a few decades. Virtual real-time travel will make science fiction time-and-space-travel a cyber-reality. News, information and entertainment dissemination will be progressively more responsive to individual demands for anywhere, anytime, anyway. The automobile is already well on its way to becoming a computer on wheels. Soon all cars will have fully embedded Internet and mobile connectivity, giving the driver and each individual passenger independent online access and a complete communications, information and entertainment center.

Most of these advances will become a reality not only in the lifetimes of Internet Pioneers, but also within the lifetimes of many of their analog predecessors. To pre-Internet generations, the Internet is life-altering as it sweeps away businesses and business models, lifestyles and societal norms. Internet Pioneers view these advances as a normal progression, consistent with all they have experienced throughout their lives. They are prepared and preparing to ride the wave.

Sky Dayton, who founded Earthlink at the age of 23, believes "It's not content that's at the core of new media; it's communications. Being connected to a network of friends is the killer app." Mobile phones and tablets are being used for video conferences, school classrooms, for downloading and watching satellite television, blogging, taking and uploading photos, storing and listening to music, and even as charge cards. Most importantly, they are used for social connectivity with defined and discreet groups of friends, colleagues and family... and with the world.

Internet-connected mobile devices are enabling users to access the Internet every waking (and even some sleeping) moment of their lives. The Internet is and will continue to be integral to the functioning of social media and mobility. It is at the core of almost every aspect of society we can imagine in the future, and mobility is accelerating its role and relevance. There are nearly six billion mobile phone subscriptions among the seven billion people currently on earth. For nearly four billion of these people, their current mobile phones are the first they've owned. Their phones are changing their lives and collapsing the concept that communication is restricted by time, location or economic status. Mobile connectedness is not just enabling instant global communications.

"The early web was built around content — many websites of content connected to one another...But this is quickly being replaced with a web where content is broken down and aggregated in different ways for different people. It's a more personalized, and unique experience based on knowing who we are, who our friends are, and what our friends have liked or done. With the emergence of mobile, platforms and APIs across the web, content is now being disaggregated, broken down into it's smallest components, and being re-aggregated and reformatted in many other places."

~ Paul Adams
Facebook

Content is just particles of communications to be discovered and shared, and what you discover and share will help define who you are and what you're interested in having others share with you. Today hundreds of companies are developing programs to help individuals and organizations in recognizing, curating, storing and sharing the millions of fractional pieces of content that are floating in cyberspace.

Thousands of venture- and equity-funded companies are introducing — literally every day — new tools, programs, services, content, offers, and opportunities across a spectrum of Internet-based businesses. This economic ecosystem is the first ever that is consumer-led. The autocratic and often monopolistic rule that governments, corporations and institutions have had on society and economies throughout history is collapsing. The Internet is proving to be far more powerful.

Innovation and connectivity are advancing at accelerated rates, transforming almost every aspect of relationships, society, culture, business, politics, and global economics. We are building a completely new economic ecosystem on top of the economic system developed over the past 150 years of Industrial Age expansion.

Futurist David Houle, author of *The Shift Age*, believes that civilization will experience as much change in the next decade as was experienced in the thousand years from the year 1000 to the beginning of the new millennium in 2000. Ray Kurzweil, author of *The Singularity is Near*, believes "Because we're doubling the rate of progress every decade, we'll see the equivalent of a century of progress — at today's rate — in only 25 calendar years." But Kurzweil also points out that the rate of change is accelerating, arguing that we could see the equivalent of the past 100 years of change in the next decade.

Although the small generation of Internet Pioneers is just beginning to come to terms with its own importance, it is the generation that will lead us into this future. Because Internet Pioneers are spearheading the transformational period that is redefining the way we live, it is vital to understand what drives the members of this generation. Their attitudes, hopes, fears and actions are setting the agenda for the future.

Chapter 3:
The Internet Pioneer Psyche

Internet Pioneers are the first generation of Internet Natives and have scarcely known life without the Internet. Born between 1991 and 1995, most Internet Pioneers have graduated from high school. A few are starting families. Whether Internet Pioneers are in college, working or looking for work in a destabilized economy, they're facing unprecedented challenges. Many still live at home or will need to live at home after college.

There's no digital or technology divide among Internet Pioneers. Kids from the poorest neighborhoods have been early adopters of the latest mobile phones. They text, game, and use YouTube. Everyone has access to the same technology and everyone uses it in similar ways.

24/7 online and mobile connectivity is the norm for Internet Pioneers. They don't "go online;" their online and offline worlds converge into one "always on" reality. They *are* socializing almost all the time. As my 18-year-old stepdaughter, Izzy, said: "I don't think about the role or impact the Internet has on me and my life. It's just there."

To Internet Pioneers, computers have always been small enough, Google has always been a verb and cell phones have been in their hands for much of their lives. These students depend on technology in ways not previously seen in other age groups. *The 2011 Cisco Connected Technology Report* stated that "One of every three college students and young employees believes the Internet is as important as air, water, food, and shelter." The survey also found that two out of five college students ranked surfing the Internet above dating, hanging out with friends and even listening to music. This means that slightly less than half of Internet Pioneers are as happy to socialize online as face to face.

According to a survey sponsored by Pearson Foundation, many of today's college students consider a high-speed Internet connection more important than any single person on campus. Of 1,434 community college students surveyed in 2011, more than 70 percent believe that a high-speed Internet connection is essential for educational success.

My research further backs this up:

- 95% of Internet Pioneers are on Facebook and 50% update daily

- 47% "tweet"

- 40% use check-in apps like Foursquare and Facebook Places

- 44% write their own blog while 62% comment on the blogs of others

- 52% post their own videos to YouTube

- 58% engage with virtual worlds

- 83% play online and/or console games

- A whopping 90% shop online, with 52% using online coupons from Groupon, Living Social and other "sales deal" sites

Typical Internet Pioneers wake up in the morning, turn off the Smartphone alarm and immediately check for new texts or emails. In seconds, they can respond to messages from school and friends, accept an invitation to lunch, and wish friends a happy birthday via Facebook. Communication is as much a part of their routines as brushing their teeth.

Internet Pioneers: A Subset of the Millennials

Millennials, also known as Generation Y, are the larger generation that includes the subset of Internet Pioneers. Millennials are the last generation born in the 20th century and the first few years of the 21st — including everyone born between 1980 and 2005, a total in the United States of 105 million people. (In the addendum to this book is the Wikipedia description of Millennials.)

Whatever the purpose for analyzing this generation — sociology, political, marketing, urban planning — it's misguided to consider Millennials as a single cohesive generation. They comprise three (or more) overlapping but distinct and diverse subsets that have the computer and television as their common bond.

Younger post-Internet Millennials born *after* 1995, many of whom were born into homes with computers already connected to the Internet and AOL, will be dramatically different from those pre-Internet Millennials born from 1982 to 1991, whose first years may have included computer software and games but who were typically not online until well into their school years.

Internet Pioneers are the *Bridge Generation* between pre- and post-Internet Millennials. They make use of media far more actively than any generation before them. They are creating systems and platforms and new ways of integrating media in all aspects of their lives. They expect to be able to use technology and media to make their lives better. They assume technology will be there for dealing with things as simple as attending meetings via their cell phone, voting, teleconferencing with teachers, and controlling their home electronics. They are more likely to shop online, and their sophisticated understanding of privacy issues is greater than prior studies have suggested. They spend inordinate amounts of time in pursuits far, far different from those of generations before them.

Pre-Internet Millennials

The older Millennials (born 1980-1990) are more comparable to the younger Gen-Y cohort born in the mid-1970, the period when microprocessors were introduced.

"Computers began to invade everyday life with astonishing speed. It was more than sixty years between Watt's first rotary steam engine and the coining of the phrase Industrial Revolution, but it was clear that a computer revolution was under way less than a decade after the first microprocessor was produced. The first commercial products were handheld calculators that quickly sent the adding machine and the slide rule into oblivion. Word processors began to replace the typewriter in the mid-1970s. And microprocessors, unseen and usually unnoted, began to be used in automobiles, kitchen appliances, television sets, wristwatches and hundreds of other everyday items. Many new products — cordless phones, cell phones, DVDs, CDs, digital cameras, PDAs — would not be possible without them. By the 1990s they were ubiquitous ... Today tens of millions of children and adolescents have on their desks, and use constantly, computing power that would have been beyond the reach of all but national governments thirty years ago. Their developing brains are ... being wired to use computers as an adjunct of their own intellect."

~ John Gordon Steele
An Empire of Wealth: Rise of the American Economy 1607–2000

Second Wave Millennials

Internet Pioneers the second wave of Millennials, also have had their brains figuratively connected directly to the Internet, accounting for their informed perspectives on politics, social involvement, education, religion, sexuality, women's rights and many other issues.

The all-encompassing Millennial or Gen-Y group is also known as the MTV Generation. But the Internet Pioneer subset is better described as the Nickelodeon Generation. Think of the differences between MTV and Nick and you get the differences between older Millennials and Internet Pioneers. (Read more about this in Chapter 11.)

The five-year Internet Pioneer group born between 1991 and 1995 represents only 20 percent of total Millennials, yet they promise to be the most influential and important bloc not only among Millennials but one of the most influential of the next 100-plus years.

What is the Fundamental Nature of Internet Pioneers?

• They are confidently empowered, but do not consider themselves to be entitled.

• They are focused on themselves, but care deeply about their families and their friends, which is sometimes an imposing responsibility.

• They have opinions and respect the opinions of others, and have little patience or tolerance for uninformed viewpoints.

• They expect to be given the freedom and power to manage their lives, yet seek out and consider the advice of others.

• They are perfectionists who strive to achieve, assuming they have the ability and potential.

• They question the rules but mostly live within them.

• They accept and embrace diversity, not as an aspiration, but as an accepted reality.

- They are global in their vision and also embrace and value their local communities.

- They are spiritual and open to universal thinking about life after death and their responsibilities in this life.

- They celebrate and value both intelligence and fun.

- They're creative and love talented musicians, actors, writers, and artists, and they also embrace creativity in everyday activities.

- They have a sense of humor and embrace sarcasm. They're clear on the difference between being funny and being insensitive to others.

- They expect to marry and have families but are in no hurry. They're sexually active and accepting of different sexual lifestyles.

- They want the opportunity to achieve their goals and dreams as we all do; they understand that the world is a difficult and challenging place, and that they need to work hard to achieve these goals.

These attributes differ in many ways from those of the older Millennials.

How Do Internet Pioneers Spend Their Time?

Internet Pioneers watch more television than any generation before them, yet they find time to create and watch YouTube videos, blog and text non-stop, browse the web, endlessly play video and social games, listen to music, hold down paying jobs, spend time with their family, and somehow get their homework done. They take connectivity for granted, expect to have 24/7 access to each other, their families, information, shopping, music, movies and television.

We know they are active and engaged via technology, but how about Internet Pioneers' offline lives? Although they may be constantly texting, Tweeting or updating, all but a handful also spend quality time each day with their families and "in person" time with friends. They have personal hobbies and complete their homework. More than two-thirds play sports or participate in activities such as music, dance or drama. Seventy-five percent actually pick up a newspaper, magazine or book (including textbooks) in print format every day (a habit that connects Internet Pioneers to previous generations but an activity that will inevitably wane among future Internet Natives). Considering all this activity, a surprising number of Internet Pioneers claims to spend a few minutes each day awake but doing nothing. How do they find the time to do nothing at all? My guess is they're actually engaged doing something but just not defining it.

Most (64 percent) Internet Pioneers rarely see a live sporting event, concert, theater or other out-of-home entertainment, which certainly contradicts the perceptions of marketers who invest billions in on-site sponsorship of these events. Only 8 percent attend live events at least once weekly. Those who are college students are actively partying, but they're less likely than prior generations to date in the traditional context or to participate in organized social events. Even movies attract Internet Pioneers only once a month on average, with only 8 percent going out to the movies every week.

How much time do they spend daily *outside of school* on socializing, studying, sleeping and doing nothing at all? All in, with multi-tasking, they are active every minute of every day, spending six to seven hours in classes during the school year, and getting nearly seven hours of sleep nightly. A total of more than 36 hours of activity each 24-hour day. College students are doing all this while consuming an average of six alcoholic drinks per week, according to Mathimortician.com.

Internet Pioneers: Time Spent in all Activities
Source: Jack Myers/Ipsos-OTX Survey of 1,000 Internet Pioneers, August 2011 (Includes % spending no time on each activity)

	Hours : Minutes	% Who Engage In this Activity
Online Socialization:		
Texting	1:20	91%
On Facebook	1:12	91%
On Other Social Media, Blogs, etc.	: 46	72%
Video Calling (Skype, etc.)	: 27	54%
On Twitter	: 22	57%
TOTAL	4 hours, 7 minutes daily	

	Hours : Minutes	% Who Engage In this Activity
Personal Time with Friends & Family:		
In Person with Friends	1:43	94%
Spending "Quality Time" with My Parents	1:21	92%
Talking on the Phone	: 39	89%
TOTAL	3 hours, 43 minutes daily	
Activities:		
Homework & School Activities (during school year)	1:52	95%
Working at a Paying Job	1:43	62%
Working on Personal Hobbies/ Passions	1:00	89%
Console Gaming Like Xbox, Wii	: 54	68%
Virtual Gaming — Online & Apps	: 51	67%
Playing Sports, Musical Instruments, Drama, Dance, etc.	: 49	71%
Writing on My Own of Any Type	: 33	64%
TOTAL	7 hours, 42 minutes daily	
Media Time:		
Watching TV Content on TV, Computer, or Phone	1:25	89%
Browsing the Web for Interesting Things	1:18	94%
Listening to Music on iTunes or Any Online App	1:11	86%

	Hours : Minutes	% Who Engage In this Activity
Listening to Music on the Radio	: 47	82%
Watching YouTube	: 45	86%
Reading Newspapers, Magazines, Books in Print	: 36	77%
Listening to Music on CDs/TV	: 34	57%
Reading Newspapers, Magazines, Books Online or in Apps	: 31	72%
TOTAL	7 hours, 7 minutes daily	
Other:		
School	6:30	
Sleeping	6:58	
Spending Time Awake, but Alone, Doing Nothing	: 54	83%
TOTAL:	14 hours, 22 minutes daily	

Engaged Awake/Non-School:	22 hours, 33 minutes daily
Total Time Spent Daily:	37 hours, 5 minutes daily

Remodeling Our Experiences Around the Social Web

"We're moving from a web primarily built around content to a web primarily built around people."

~ **Paul Adams**
Facebook

Adams' perspective can be applied to pretty much *every* part of our lives. Fill in the blank in this sentence: "The world of [*families, relationships, news, entertainment, politics, arts, education, religion, television, transportation, science, medicine, cooking...*] will fundamentally change because of the emergence of the social web." The list can go on ad infinitum.

Internet Pioneers will inevitably want to integrate the social web more actively into their day-to-day experiences.

The platform they are likely to turn to is one they grew up with and understand: virtual worlds. For Internet Pioneers, virtual worlds mean programs and games like *Sims, Neopets, Club Penguin, WeeWorld, Quepasa, World of Warcraft, Call of Duty* and other second homes where they spent large chunks of their childhood. They are attracted to and understand how to navigate a parallel world in which their avatar, a graphical representation of the user, is their agent and representative.

The first major virtual universe, *Second Life*, broke through at the end of the 20th century as the "first great city in a new virtual world." Its popularity grew from an adult eagerness to be a part of a new wave of online technology. Developed by Linden Labs, *Second Life* was launched in 2003 and offered free programs that enabled users, called Residents, to interact with each other through avatars. Residents could explore the world, meet other residents, socialize, participate in individual and group activities, and create and trade virtual property and services with one another. As of 2011, *Second Life* still had about one million active users, but it never expanded beyond its original roots. Today it is used by several United States governmental departments such as NASA, by universities for educational and remote learning programs, and by businesses such as IBM and Cisco Systems for meetings and training.

While virtual worlds have taken a back seat to social networks, the two will inevitably merge. Immersive virtual worlds and games have been popular among Internet Pioneers since they were in their early childhood. Just as suburbs and shopping malls defined community in the second half of the 20th century, complex and absorbing cyber communities are on the horizon in the 21st century.

Personal avatars will move from network to network, from the television screen to the computer to the mobile device. Microsoft's Xbox, Ninendo's Wii and Sony's Playstation are already integrating avatars as an embedded part of their technologies. Xbox studies the physical characteristics of each player and develops representational avatars that look and act like their human counterparts. This functionality is in its infancy. Within the decade, Internet Pioneers will introduce avatars to their Facebook pages, social networks and gaming activities. Future avatars will be sophisticated, with a human voice and a physical presence, enhanced by motion and voice detection technology such as Apple's Siri and Microsoft's Kinect.

Representational avatars will take their places in virtual classrooms and at conference tables as the vision embodied in the original *Second Life* morphs to be more user-friendly. As avatars will be owned by their creators, they will travel from site to site, game to game, and app to app.

Summary

As developed as the Internet seems to us now, it is still largely undeveloped and unexplored. There is an endless quest ahead that will be exciting, challenging and fascinating.

Will Internet Pioneers be up to the task of applying the advances made possible by the Internet? Will they prove to belong to the most important generation of the 21st century? Will they be inventors and innovators? Are they likely to become an economic force, and will that force be positive or disruptive? Will their relationships and marriages be stable and healthy?

As with all generations, circumstances will have an impact on their opportunities and the realities they face. Yet this group of young people is unlike any that has come before. We cannot assume that the life lessons and experiences of previous generations will be very relevant to Internet Pioneers or to our understanding of them.

What does this generation expect from itself? And what can we expect from its members?

I know from my study that Internet Pioneers are social, engaged, active, immersed in media, gaming and online commerce. They have opinions on the leading social, political and economic issues of the day. Sexually, their attitudes, influences and values differ dramatically from earlier generations as well as from those who are just a few years older.

In the next several chapters, I look at Internet Pioneers' attitudes and formative influences on lifestyle choices from sexuality and women's rights to religion, politics and education. In subsequent chapters, I share the influences that have guided the development of Internet Pioneers and how the future is likely to evolve as they become dominant forces in society and culture for decades ahead.

Chapter 4:
Hooking Up: Relationships, Sex and Porn

It's ten p.m. Do you know what your college student is doing...or looking at... online? You might be surprised. Do you have a sense of what they're doing behind closed doors? In some cases, it's surprising *them*. And it just might be connected to what they're seeing online.

The topic at hand is sex. And relationships — or lack thereof. And pornography. And it's the ways that sexuality, social networks, and porn are increasingly intertwined across America. For Internet Pioneers, questions of what's acceptable, what's publicly acknowledged, what's socially *the norm* when it comes to sexual behavior, are changing. Nowhere, it seems, is this more apparent than on the college campus.

Dating and relationships among college students have changed dramatically in recent years, and continue to do so. Students now flirt with each other through text messages, announce commitments on Facebook, and relationships develop via engaged texting. But the changes go even deeper, affecting Internet Pioneers' overall view of commitment and long-term relationships. It's likely that the shifts in attitude among today's college students will be reflected in the attitudes and actions of future generations of Internet Natives.

It may seem to parents of Internet Pioneers that serial monogamy is extinct. To the casual observer on today's college campuses, the traditional dating relationship — and its accompanying string of monogamous relationships — may seem to have gone the way of the dodo bird. At colleges and universities across the United States, the weekend ritual of dinner and a movie seems to have largely been replaced by no-strings-attached, spontaneous sexual encounters commonly known as "hook ups."

However, though recent research reflects growing numbers of college students engaging in casual sex on a regular basis — in lieu of traditional dating relationships — studies also show increasing numbers of students who describe themselves as virgins or abstinent.

These conflicting results paint an ambiguous picture of college students' attitudes toward sexuality, as well as a shift in behavioral trends over time. The situation is further complicated by the influences of the Internet and social networking on cultural factors — such as gender, ethnicity and religious belief systems.

Shifting Attitudes and Behavior

College students can peer into each other's lives through Facebook, seeing revealing pictures and finding out what they did last weekend. Instead of waiting for the phone to ring, college students use texting as a mating ritual. Flirting is often done by text, and dates are set up through text messages. Internet Pioneers rarely make a phone call except to their parents. While many young professionals grew up on AOL Instant Messenger and MySpace, Internet Pioneers grew up on Facebook. This social media site opened to high school students in 2005 and to everybody in 2006, so most Internet Pioneers have had a Facebook account since they were young teens.

One area of the Internet that this cohort of college students hasn't really gotten caught up in is online dating. Student Torrey A. commented, "My mom found her second husband on an online dating website and that turned me off forever. In college, there are plenty of people my age to meet on campus, so I don't need online dating."

Her perspective is representative of the overall feeling of people her age, that real-world connections are a much better place to start when looking for a relationship or a hook up. College campuses provide plenty of connections that make it easy to meet someone.

Students interested in casual hook ups used to hang out exclusively at bars, nightclubs and house parties, a challenging environment to many. Today's students can supplement their dating opportunities by scoping out flings on the Internet. Websites such as CampusHook, LikeALittle, DateMySchool and Craigslist are used with the express purpose of finding consenting partners.

An alternative version of online dating is getting connected with people in the real world but allowing their relationships to unfold largely over the Internet. Students rarely become Facebook friends without having a trusted connection, being introduced by a mutual friend, or meeting at an event. Once they are "friends," the door opens up to having a relationship mediated by the Internet.

The traditional obstacle of exchanging phone numbers or email addresses has become moot, replaced by finding and "friending" a new acquaintance on Facebook. These relationships allow couples to get to know each other mostly online and start dating in person when they agree the relationship has potential. Today's college students find people with whom they are compatible without having to go on many in-person dates; however, this practice can also perpetuate relationships in which participants exhibit habits and mannerisms that aren't evident online.

Modern Courtship

This phenomenon of getting to know each other remotely is something that we once saw in couples who would be introduced and write letters back and forth as a form of courtship. The Internet is bringing it back in a different, more modern and accelerated form that includes photos and videos posted on Facebook and YouTube.

Advancements in technology have made a huge impact on the college dating scene. College students' casual approach to dating and reliance on easy-access technology to form connections has resulted in a generation that prefers short-term relationships to long-term commitments.

"These kids want a partner to be sexual with, romantic with and have fun with. But they are not looking for someone for the longer term right now."

~ Dr. Fran Walfish
Adolescent and Family Therapist, Beverly Hills, CA

The Internet and technology play a large role in this shift in attitudes. "The regular use of computers has taught these young adults to expect a fast result," said Dr. Walfish. "They have been trained to expect a fast response, a fast engaging and a fast everything."

College students consider themselves exclusive and in a committed relationship only when both partners make the relationship "Facebook Official" by changing their Facebook relationship status to announce their boyfriend or girlfriend. A first-year college student says, "Facebook makes it so easy for me to find out if a guy I have my eye on is available or not. As soon as we're Facebook friends, I can check out his status and even see photos of him with his girlfriend if he has one."

The relationship status feature on Facebook also forces a couple to clarify their relationship even if it's a confusing one. Couples can be "in a relationship," "in an open relationship," or the elusive "it's complicated" option. "Your Facebook relationship status really defines your relationship," said Caroline Radaj, a University of Wisconsin at Madison senior. "And there is huge pressure when you break it off with the person because it is now a very public thing."

Social networking and other online platforms can also be utilized to educate college students about the risks inherent in spontaneous sexual activity, especially when alcohol is involved. Social media presents an invaluable method of sex education , promoting the use of contraceptives and increasing awareness of date rape.

As a whole, U.S. culture has grown more open about sex since the 1970s according to a 2010 article from the Kinsey Institute. A 1997 survey of 1,752 college students found that 75 percent of both males and females were sexually active. In contrast, by 2009, 90 percent of college students were sexually active by the time they reached their senior year, according to the University of Connecticut's College Health Advisor.

Alcohol also figures prominently in many college students' sexual reality. A 2011 survey from the University of Montana indicated that drinking plays a role in sexual encounters, especially spontaneous hook ups. *Psychology Today*'s Suzanne Zalewski notes that the span between ages 18 and 24 is associated with both the highest increase in heavy alcohol consumption and the greatest number of sexual partners. She suggests that drinking is used to ease communication about sex; in fact, some studies show that simply holding a drink is perceived as an indicator of sexual availability.

Alcohol and casual sex seem to go hand in hand. According to the University of Connecticut, a study of 446 undergraduates revealed that 49 percent of female students had unplanned, spontaneous sex as a result of binge drinking as compared to 25 percent of non-binge drinkers. Events such as spring break, where college students gather and consume an average of ten alcoholic drinks per day tend to encourage sexual encounters as an integrated part of the social experience.

The Hook Up

Though college students commonly use the term "hook up," it doesn't have a clear definition. Students use "hooking up" to describe a range of behavior from kissing to intercourse, but a common factor in these spontaneous encounters is their short-term nature. In fact, the author of a 2011 study in *Health Communication* entitled "Talk About 'Hooking Up'" says the term is strategically ambiguous and notes that students use it so they can talk about sex without having to reveal too many details.

This deliberate ambiguity makes hooking up a difficult behavior to analyze. In an interview with *USA Today*, Leah, a 19-year-old sophomore at Harvard University, says that hooking up is intentionally vague and notes that it allows college students to satisfy sexual desires without entering into long-term, committed relationships.

Recent media reports and studies support the trend towards casual relationships among college students, especially hooking up. A 2011 research study by the University of Montana defined hooking up as "a sexual encounter between two people who are not in a dating or serious relationship and do not expect anything further." The study found that 54 percent of the students surveyed said that they had hooked up with someone outside of a relationship in the current school year.

A March 2011 *USA Today* article highlighted the trend toward hooking up replacing committed relationships, or at least preceding them, for many students.

"For the majority of students, they're not going to dinner and a movie unless they've hooked up with someone. Some physical interaction comes before the dating. Often dates happen after a relationship, rather than before."

~ **Justin Garcia**
Doctoral Fellow, State University of New York

The statistics surrounding college students' sexual behavior reflect a range of results. A Stanford University study of more than 17,000 students found that 72 percent of students had experienced at least one hook up by their senior year. Men had, on average, 9.7 hook ups while women had an average of 7.1.

Some college students mourn the loss of a more innocent time, but others enjoy the more laid-back approach to dating. In some ways, it's hard to call the present arrangement dating, for many students never actually go on dates. Some students find that the lack of dating translates to fewer burdens. They no longer have to scrape money together to take potential partners out on expensive outings. These students can get all the sex they want without financial sacrifice. They have more freedom to see whom they want, when they want, without worrying about clingy partners. And the availability of birth control means that students can have multiple sex partners without worrying about pregnancy or sexually transmitted diseases. Kate at the University of Nebraska says that her female friends prefer to participate in hook ups — not relationships — as a matter of choice and sexual inclination.

Goals vs. Relationships

In his 2010 book *Premarital Sex in America*, Mark Regnerus suggests that the increasing numbers of women who attend college — in 2011, nearly 58 percent of college students were female — has precipitated a shift in attitudes toward sex. The presence of more women on campus leads to more competition for men, which in turn results in briefer sexual experiences as well as increased tolerance for sexual encounters that take place outside of committed relationships.

Others suggest that college students may simply be focusing on goals rather than relationships. According to a *USA Today* report, many female college students concentrate on their careers and educations rather than on forming and maintaining romantic relationships. This necessitates a shift in the way young women approach sex.

Research points to long-term relationships as a marker of health in young adults and argues that the shift to more open and casual sexual behavior is an unhealthy trend. Lasting relationships are rarely formed overnight, and they typically require more than the casual sex and short-term dating that today's students are drawn to. "Relationships require a give and take along with being patient, which is not something these kids have learned," explains Dr. Walfish. The Internet enables people to connect and form online relationships that become sexual before they actually know much about each other.

In 2010, the International Association for Relationship Research (IARR) released a groundbreaking study on the physical and mental impacts of romantic relationships on college students. The study followed a sample of 1,621 single and romantically attached college students. Participants were asked to provide feedback on physical and mental health problems in the 12 months leading up to the study, as well as their current body mass index (BMI) at the time of the survey. They also reported recent incidences of risky behavior, including binge drinking and use of illicit drugs. The researchers predicted that students in committed relationships would "exhibit better mental and physical health than their single peers" and that they would be "less likely to engage in risky behavior." Although differences in physical health were negligible, the researchers' predictions proved correct in regard to mental health and risky behavior. It appears that the extra support of a long-term partner may be enough to prevent depression and other mental health issues prevalent on college campuses.

Many students are aware of the mental health benefits of long-term relationships, but they aren't willing to rush headlong into commitments for which they are ill-prepared. Some students shy away from relationships for lack of time. Erin Thompson certainly has found this to be the case. A junior at the University of Nebraska, she has not been in a committed relationship during her time at college. "I'm way too busy for a boyfriend. In addition to taking a full course load, I have to work full-time in order to pay my tuition. Between studying, working and attending class, there's no time left over for dating." Although she would like to be in a long-term relationship at some point, she does not expect to be committed in the near future. "I'm fine with being single for now. I'd rather be on my own and happy than in a relationship and miserable." This cavalier attitude toward dating departs from the traditions of earlier generations, when many women attended college in hopes of meeting eligible men.

Theories on marriage postponement vary widely from one circle to the next, with everything from birth control to the poor economy cited as the main culprit. Some researchers believe that young women, realizing the threat of the glass ceiling, are choosing to push back marriage and babies in hopes of pursuing successful careers.

Today's students are more interested in getting into graduate school and scoring productive jobs. That is not to say that young women have completely cast off family life. They are simply postponing these aspirations for later.

"Overall, most of my friends are waiting to get married and plan to do so in our late 20s. I'm not going to school for four years to not have a career right away.

~ **Caroline Radaj**
Senior, University of Wisconsin

This trend is reflected in current marriage statistics. In 2009, the United States Census Bureau reported an average first marriage age of 26 for women and 28 for men, and even in the past few years the median age for marriage has gotten older. This is well up from the average age of marriage in 1950, which was only 20 for women and 23 for men.

Erin Thompson counts herself among this group of high-achieving young women. Upon graduating from the University of Nebraska, she plans to attend graduate school and then pursue a career in project management. Marriage and children are not in her immediate plans. "It would be nice to have a kid while fertility is not an issue, but that would mean giving up on my career. I'd rather spend some time building my career before settling down."

As they graduate from college, Internet Pioneers generally believe that relationships and children will detract from their ability to fulfill the demanding requirements of their first few jobs. Having progressed through college with few — if any — sustained romantic relationships, Internet Pioneers are less eager than past generations to enter into these relationships post-graduation.

Dual Income Families and Stay-at-Home Dads

But most Internet Pioneers also expect that when they do eventually enter into relationships and have children, both parents will hold jobs. Some would still prefer to have a parent stay home with the children but are not necessarily opposed to leaving the homemaking duties to the father. Of the 66.3 million dads currently living in the United States, a total of 105,000 identify themselves as stay-at-home dads. While this number may be low, it marks a significant increase from the parenting statistics of years past.

Men and women alike see the possibilities of successfully earning income from home and being able to be more involved with children. The number of stay-at-home dads will continue to increase. (A survey of 236 students at the University of New Hampshire found that most students did not hold negative attitudes toward stay-at-home fathers.) The Internet opens doors to run businesses from home or to work remotely, allowing one parent to work at home and freeing the other to work outside the home without needing to pay for child care.

Because Internet Pioneers have grown up in a culture in which divorce has been a norm, they are far more aware than past generations of the challenges of maintaining healthy marriages. They are therefore more likely to delay marriage and, once committed be more focused on maintaining their marriage and proactively confronting and resolving marital problems.

Another indicator of the future divorce rate for college kids is a University of Pennsylvania's Wharton School's study, which found that one of the most important factors in predicting a marriage's success is the age at which people get married, with those marrying later having a higher success rate. And marriages in which both partners have college degrees have a lower divorce rate.

While having children is far from the minds of Internet Pioneers today, Dr. Walfish says the majority of these young adults are planning to have children. "No question, hands down. When I ask them if they want to be a mom or dad, almost every one of them says yes," she says, adding that most plan to start a family in their late twenties to mid-thirties.

Student Caroline Radaj said that she sees the same trend on her campus. "Most of us want kids, just not now." Another factor is that current culture is much more accepting of children born out of wedlock than previous generations. Radaj says that many of her female friends have a backup plan of having a child as a single parent if they don't find the right person to marry.

Abstinence and Virginity

To complicate the picture of college student sexuality even further, increasing numbers of students describe themselves as "virgins" or "abstinent." A National Center for Health Statistics survey found that almost 12 percent of 20- to 24-year-old women and 13 percent of men indicated that they'd never had sex, as compared to 8 percent of both men and women in 2002. These findings stand in stark contrast to other statistics that indicate a shift toward casual sex.

Students who choose abstinence may do so out of religious beliefs, the influence of the abstinence-only movement or a better understanding of the risks associated with sexually transmitted disease. Some students describe themselves as abstinent or virgins, but participate in sexual activities other than intercourse.

However, others interpret the increasing proportions of abstinent and virgin students as the precursor to a backlash against more permissive attitudes, followed by a cultural shift back to more traditional dating relationships.

Long-Distance Relationships

Another Internet benefit for this generation of college students is its access to tools that make long-distance relationships more bearable and likely to work. Students have access to Skype and other types of video chatting that make it easier to stay in touch with a significant other who doesn't live nearby. This helps college students who are dating a high-school sweetheart attending college elsewhere and those who meet but have to spend time in different locations.

College senior Devon has been in a serious relationship since his sophomore year, and he explains that even though he and his girlfriend live on different coasts, they stay in touch online during school breaks: "We Skype every day for at least an hour, and sometimes we watch movies synchronized with each other so it feels like we're hanging out. She was abroad for a semester last year, and we even Skyped a few times a week while she was in China!" This helps preserve relationships when distance would ordinarily create stress and loneliness.

Because of the Internet, students are also more willing to enter into long-distance relationships. Rather than getting married right out of college and compromising their own plans for that of their spouses, couples are more inclined to part ways to pursue their own plans, staying in touch through video chatting. This is common with traveling abroad after college or going to graduate school in different cities. It also might contribute to a later marriage age among this generation of college students.

The Internet as Therapist and Counselor

While many factors shape young adults' views on relationships and marriage, none has grown so much in students' esteem as the Internet. Some students, too embarrassed to discuss personal issues with friends and family, instead choose to find the answers to their questions over the Internet.

This is especially true of Lesbian Gay Bisexual Transgender (LGBT) teens and young adults, many of whom still fear the repercussions of being outed on campus. Andy (name changed upon request), a Marquette sophomore, says that support websites greatly aided him as he explored the possibility of pursuing a relationship with another man. "I think that the Internet has been an amazing tool for giving the LGBT community a voice...the Internet has also made straight students more understanding of different kinds of relationships." In the months since he began a relationship with a fellow Marquette student, Andy has slowly begun informing friends and family members of his sexual orientation. While he still hesitates to come out in public, Andy acknowledges that people have "so far been overwhelmingly supportive" of his current relationship.

There are all kinds of websites available for LGBT teens, their friends and families. Some sites promote gay rights campaigns, while others provide information about local support groups. In recent years, a number of dating sites have sprung up specifically for the gay community.

Sexuality Beyond College

Attitudes among male and female Internet Pioneers in connection with pornography and human sexuality reflect changing mores. Studies indicate that young peoples' opinions of pornography and sexual behavior are shifting away from the views that their parents hold — toward something more permissive of explicit sexual images and more open sexual behaviors as a kind of normal expression of healthy libido.

Today's media, especially the Internet, allows users to easily access content that interests them — including sexual content — and then to seek out social networks that reinforce the behavioral cues and roles that the content promotes.

A 2011 report entitled "Influence of New Media on Adolescent Sexual Health" suggests that an individual's sexual belief systems are affected by both the online content they access as well as the discussion and exchange of this content on social networks.

Porn and sexual expressions related to it have also jumped from what was once primarily the printed page to the digital realm, and they will stay there and become more available and explicit. Several experts believe that easy access to Internet porn has led to changing attitudes about real-life sex.

According to *USA Today*, the accessible, appealing nature of websites that provide the opportunity for online sexual relations — through the use of avatars and webcams — allow many students to remain abstinent in the real world while having an active, albeit online, sexual life. In addition, porn eliminates any chance of being rejected by a potential partner, a guarantee that real life can't make.

In Search of the Sexual Picture (or, Porn Is Everywhere)

When it comes to sexual content, researchers are finding that Internet users of almost any age can seek out or stumble on an unprecedented variety of material. These days porn isn't tucked away on the top shelf at the neighborhood newsstand. It's no longer something that has to be sheepishly purchased at the public storefront counter. Instead, sexual content awaits consumers within the privacy of their terminals or laptops, on their handheld wireless devices, wherever. No human-to-human transaction is required.

Jason Carroll, one of the authors of a recent *Journal of Adolescent Research* study on porn and college-age consumers, put it this way when talking to *USA Today*: "We're in an age of pocket porn." Pocket porn for almost no pocket change. In the form of short clips, online pornography is almost entirely free, and it has been for most of the lives of Internet Pioneers.

According to the study published in the *Journal of Adolescent Research,* some 69 percent of college-age men at Brigham Young University in Utah reported that they viewed pornography more than once per month. In the same sample group, 10 percent of the surveyed women said they looked at porn with a similar frequency. On the other hand, 31 percent of the young women answering the researchers' questions said that they had looked at porn during the preceding year, compared to 87 percent of the men. Among men, 21 percent said they watched porn every day (compared to only 1 percent of the women).

Consider, for example, Michael, a sophomore at an Ivy League school, who assumes "that I started looking at porn younger than people who didn't grow up with the Internet, but not as young as some of my peers probably did. I began looking at porn when I could get away with it, around sixth grade. I still view porn now, and I certainly get the impression that my peers look at porn."

Michael gets that impression for a reason.

College as a Sexual Laboratory

Technology may be altering the basic DNA of human sexuality among Internet Pioneers and the generations of Internet Natives who will follow them. What we're learning about changing attitudes toward sexuality on the college campus promises to have implications for the world at large.

According to an article from the *Columbia News Service*, in 2005, there were some 50 universities in the United States that offered classes on the subject of pornography. In 2006, a Cornell University professor teaching a course called "Desire", was showing both the porno classic *Deep Throat* and Paris Hilton's 2004 sex video *A Night in Paris*.

Furthermore, studies show that the majority of college-age males are consuming pornography frequently and more openly than ever before. Research also reveals much about college students' *attitudes* toward porn. For instance, female Internet Pioneers appear more accepting of pornography as part of normal sexuality than did the women of the previous generation. Almost 50 percent of the females at Brigham Young said that porn was an acceptable part of human sexual expression. By comparison, earlier studies suggested that on average only 20 percent of their moms were open to the idea of pornography.

Male students confirm the research through their real-life observations. Michael, the Ivy League student, says: "Basically every girl I've dated has been either indifferent or interested in my porn use. They have not demonized it like your stereotypical girlfriend."

The point is that the college women between 17 and 21 who participated in the 2005 study seem to be moving toward a more permissive view. In the same study, nearly 67 percent of young men said pornography was an acceptable way to express sexuality.

Ideology and Sexuality: On and Off Campus

Internet Pioneers' perceptions of sex on the Web are more complicated than simply *more* porn and *less* sensitivity to its presence.

Yes, young women view porn as more normal in their lives, and the current crop of college kids started looking at porn at a young age. But the ubiquity of pornography, as measured through the lens of college students' perceptionsof human sexual behavior, seems to mean much more than that. The very nature of the Internet medium is apparently changing the content.

For one thing, the brand of pornography available online is, according to researchers and users, not the same kind as that found in the typical gentleman's magazine (*Playboy, Penthouse, Hustler*) of the last century. Pornography has become more explicit and extreme. Experts say it's also less universal in aspects such as storytelling, and assumptions of audience characteristics and interests may no longer be accurate.

While "sexting," the messaging of sexually explicit content, has become common among Internet Natives, it has been accompanied by educational programs and outreach initiatives to better inform young people about the long-term implications, dangers, and laws. Facebook's Timeline also reinforces the message that images are online forever, not just available for the moment. A cynical marketing theme for Las Vegas reinforcing this message has become a viral meme: "What happens in Las Vegas, Stays on Facebook!" Las Vegas actually countered this "concern" with its own anti-social media TV ad campaign suggesting people who shared Vegas experiences and photos would be shunned by friends.

Ari Brown is a sophomore at the University of Michigan. He does not call himself a conservative — at least, not on the subject of human sexuality — and he characterizes the collegiate user's Internet perspective on online porn in the following way.

"The vast diversity of porn on the Internet, I believe, has given way to a whole new array of fetishes. Then the Internet does what it does best and arranges them all to be easily available, and then the entire world is finding out that they, too, have strange fetishes. I would liken it to finding out that sexual orientation…is not so clear-cut. Everything is a spectrum."

~ Ari Brown
Sophomore, University of Michigan

"I think that people are a lot more open to things that might have once been seen as perverse," Michael, the Ivy League sophomore, said. "Just because they've seen it and realized it's not that weird. This could even be tied into our increased acceptance of gay relationships. We are a cohort that could easily stumble upon images of gay sex. This just might be connected to its normalization. I certainly think the Internet and even porn was helpful to friends who grew up realizing they were gay, and realizing they weren't alone."

So perhaps what is *hard-core* to one person is a *fetish* to another and normal sexual activity to another. Categories may be assigned differently according to how people self-identify as sexual beings.

What Critics Say: The Hard-Core Truths

Some experts say such easy access to sexual content has an effect beyond Brown's and Michael's suggestions that it simply makes people more tolerant.

Ana J. Bridges, a researcher in the Department of Psychology at the University of Arkansas, writes that pornography can have an unwanted impact on interpersonal relationships. Countries such as England and Australia have banned violent porn, Bridges points out, because pornography, especially when it contains violence toward females, leads to imitative behavior.

Offline Sexual Behavior

Accessing sexual content online can change offline behavior related to gender and sexuality. A 2005 study by Malmuth and Hippen found that males who viewed online material featuring sexually eager women were much more likely to display impersonal, dominant or aggressive attitudes toward sex. The study also found that some men were more likely to espouse negative attitudes toward women — and be more accepting of violence toward women — after watching violent pornographic material online.

When explicit sexual content is reinforced by social networks, teens tend to perceive themselves as sexually mature or even as sexual objects, which can lead to earlier — and riskier — sexual behavior. Exposure to online porn also tends to lead to more permissive attitudes toward sex, dissatisfaction with one's sex life and unreal expectations about others' sexual activities, according to the "Influence of New Media on Adolescent Sexual Health" study.

"I do worry about the normalization of certain things that might lead people to try things they don't really want to do or think they should want to do because they're common in porn...I think those are all things that people can genuinely be interested in, but I don't think they're for everyone or that people should feel compelled to try them."

~ **Michael B.**
Student

Some of the effects are positive. Engaging in cybersex — as eighty to ninety million Internet users did in 2010 — offers a range of benefits. For example, online relationships allow young adults to relate on intellectual and emotional levels rather than just physical appearance. Plus, cybersex allows for sexual interactions that "reduce limitations of gender roles," allowing partners to feel a sense of autonomy.

Melinda Wenner Moyer wrote an article in *Scientific American* in 2011, in which experts challenge the suggestion that viewing sexual aggression leads to imitations or enactments of that aggression. Statistics from parts of the U.S. that have the least access to the Internet show a 53 percent increase in explicitly aggressive sexual behavior between 1983 and 2000. In areas with widespread access to the Internet reports of rape dropped 27 percent in that same period of time.

Other Cultural Factors Affecting Sexual Attitudes

Access to online porn is just one of many factors that affect college students' sexual attitudes and sexual behavior. Studies consistently show that cultural traits such as gender, religion, ethnicity and socio-economic status also wield significant influence on attitudes toward sex.

For instance, a 2011 study of 1,415 college students found that Asian-American and Hispanic students had more conservative attitudes toward issues such as homosexuality, casual and extramarital sex, and gender role traditions than did Euro- or Hispanic-Americans. For females in all groups, sexual conservatism was correlated to strong levels of religiosity or spirituality.

The Future

The use of online platforms and social networking will increase as today's teens grow into tomorrow's college students. As access to ever-expanding online and mobile applications increases, so will online sexual activity.

For researchers, policy makers, educators and others concerned with Internet Pioneers' sexuality the jury is out on what the future holds. Many studies appear to reflect a trend toward casual, spontaneous sex as the new relationship — or more accurately, anti-relationship — norm.

Based on the current behavior of the Millennial generation, it is likely that marriage will continue to be pushed back (if pursued at all), as will childbearing.

Cohabiting will become the official next step toward marriage, whether or not the partnered couple is currently engaged to be married. And as LGBT, interracial and interfaith relationships gain more public acceptance, these non-traditional relationships will likely begin to come out more into the open.

Internet Pioneers are the first generation to engage freely and seemingly without emotional attachment in sexual hook ups. As a society, we need to better prepare children and teens being raised with Internet and mobile technologies to appreciate the value and importance of lasting relationships. Parents, educators, and even online social networks and dating sites will increasingly focus on teaching interpersonal communications, problem-solving and relationship skills. Equipping Internet Natives with the tools needed for building and maintaining successful relationships will support them in their post-hook-up years. When they do want to consider marriage, they will need to know how to turn a relationship into happily ever after.

Chapter 5:
The Third Wave of Women's Rights Activism

The infamous 1968 advertising campaign — "You've come a long way, baby" — may have been launched to convince more women to start smoking, but its catchy tagline still resonates today. From voting to political participation, career trajectories to academic participation, women have broken — or at least cracked — that metaphorical glass ceiling in more than one societal sphere. Women couldn't attend the same colleges as men until 1831. Women's enrollment on college campuses first overtook men's in the 1980s, and the imbalance continues to increase 30 years later.

Women's rights, especially reproductive rights, suddenly were thrust into the spotlight during the 2012 Presidential campaign, as several states considered and passed laws giving the states rights over women's bodies and their role in society. For some politicians and those who vote for them, women may have come too far!

The Nineteenth Amendment floated around the House of Representatives and the Senate from the time of its proposal in 1878 until its ratification in 1920. Almost a hundred years ago, women still couldn't hold political office or even vote.

In contrast, 54 percent of voters were women by the year 2010. Women also held 17 percent of the seats in Congress, 24 percent of state legislature seats, and six of the 50 governorships.

Until 1972, no woman had ever been CEO of a Fortune 500 company. By 2011, 15 women had joined these exclusive ranks. While still a disproportionate figure, it reflects progress, and the percentage will inevitably increase as larger numbers of females gain corporate power and influence. Women's increasing participation in the workforce (projected to grow to 70 percent by 2018), rising representation in politics and high college graduation rates seem to point toward continuing progress toward egalitarianism and gender equality.

Waves of Progress

These societal changes occurred in waves, beginning with the courageous actions of those 19th-century revolutionaries, the suffragettes. The second wave of the women's movement came around the mid-20th century, bringing groundbreaking political, journalistic and academic treatises.

But today, influences that shape young adults' perceptions of issues such as women's rights, gender roles and sexism come from multiple directions, including the pervasiveness of the Internet, the pressures of the media, and the influences of family and peers. Perhaps this is why the views of Internet Pioneers seem to be a curious combination of liberation and ambivalence.

Not so long ago, sexism was institutionalized into almost every facet of life. Women — and the way both men and women perceive their place in society and their rights — have indeed "come a long way, baby." Just how far can best be understood in context of where the journey began.

A Brief Timeline of Sexism

"Home is woman's world, as well as her empire. Man lives more in society. The busy marts of trade, the bustling exchange, the activity of artisan life are his spheres....What is the sphere of women? Home. The social circle. What is her mission? To mould character, to fashion herself and others after the model character of Christ."

~ **Daniel Wise**
The Young Lady's Counsellor (1851)

With this paragraph, Wise neatly relegated women to a life of domesticity. He summarized the feelings of many of his contemporaries: a woman's job involves taking care of the home, safeguarding morality — and staying far, far away from the man's world of business, economics and politics. A woman's life was at home, with a focus on bearing and rearing children. Without reliable sources of contraception, most women had little choice: they were born to be mothers.

Known as the "cult of true womanhood," this paradigm dominated popular thought for generations with its claim on women's inherent:

- Sexual purity

- Religious piety

- Submissive demeanor

- Inferior intellect

- Reproductive imperative

As blatantly sexist and archaic as they seem now for most people, these ideas about the role of women were deeply ingrained in society — in the minds of both men and women. However, a few brave suffragettes in the mid-1800s held revolutionary views.

In 2012, Georgetown law student Sandra Fluke's views toward women's rights should have been considered far from revolutionary. Yet media commentator Rush Limbaugh and others sought to brand her with a "Scarlet Letter" for her views on contraception. Limbaugh, Republican primary presidential candidates, and several governors and state legislators renewed the public discourse on the "cult of true womanhood" and the role of women in American society.

America has served as a role model for leaders of women's rights movements in countries where women are being denied basic rights. Secretary of State Hillary Clinton expressed fear that politically charged debates over these issues could set back not only America's leadership position but also the fundamental rights gained by women throughout the 20th century. Among Internet Pioneers, both male and female, these rights are unquestioned.

Women's Movement: The First Wave

In 1866, Elizabeth Cady Stanton ran for Congress; she received 24 votes out of the twelve thousand votes cast. Two years later, Stanton and Susan B. Anthony began publishing *The Revolution*, a pro-suffrage, pro-union and anti-slavery newspaper. They founded the National Women's Suffrage Foundation the next year and introduced voting rights legislation that would eventually become the Nineteenth Amendment.

The goals of the early women's movement focused on legislation and issues including:

- Voting rights

- Education rights

- Property and property law reform

- Improved conditions for the few women who worked outside the home

- Improved public morality, through offshoots such as the anti-alcohol temperance movement

In the early 1900s, only one-fifth of women worked outside the home, and most left or lost their jobs if they married. However, as the driving forces of the economy migrated away from rural farms and toward urban industrialization, massive societal shifts began to occur. These shifts gradually led to a sea change in attitudes toward women's rights.

Women's Movement: The Second Wave

The publication of two influential books — Simone de Beauvoir's 1949 *The Second Sex* and Betty Friedan's 1963 *The Feminine Mystique* — heralded a major transformation in the women's rights movement.

The goals of feminism's "second wave" shifted from individual rights to broader political aims. Many interpreted the shift as a push toward higher education and increased workforce participation. The percentage of women obtaining college degrees rose from 40 percent in the 1970s to 57 percent in 2006.

With regard to increased workforce participation:

- In 1980, half of all women worked in paid occupations outside the home.

- In 2009, the percentage jumped to 59 percent.

- By early 2012, more than 60 percent of women worked outside the home, and the number continues to grow.

An unexpected outcome is that while participation in higher education and the workforce has increased liberation, it has also increased feelings of ***ambivalence*** about issues of women's rights fed by the belief that activism is no longer required to gain advances. Other factors contributing to this ambivalent attitude include being bombarded with conflicting information about gender roles, women's rights and sexism. These factors are discussed later in the chapter.

Women's Movement: The Third Wave

Most studies since the 1970s show growing public support — from both men and women — for greater gender equality in the home and the workplace. Research also shows decreased belief that women's ideal role is that of wife and mother and increased support for efforts to improve women's rights and status.

However, many studies also show a ***decrease*** in support of feminism. The studies also reflect an increase in both women and men who associate the term "feminism" with negative connotations. Is this simply semantics, or does the issue go deeper?

A 2011 University of Maryland study explored changing ideas about women's rights and roles over four decades. The researchers found that attitudes toward gender roles shifted consistently toward egalitarianism — or becoming more liberal — from 1974 until 1994. At this time, attitudes appeared to stagnate — or even reverse — toward conservatism and traditional gender roles across most demographic groups.

The study listed potential causes for these shifting attitudes, including:

- Backlash against feminism

- Idealization of motherhood

- Media focus on the decline of feminism

A 1997 study showed that while 63 percent of both male and female college students approved of feminist ideological goals, none of the females identified themselves as feminists. Similarly, a 2000 study of 276 college students found that while most agreed with feminist ideals, only 29 percent of the women self-identified as feminist.

The Feminist Paradox

Scholars and activists interpret these results — sometimes known as the "feminist paradox" — differently. Some, like journalist Susan Faludi, feel that this "anti-feminism but pro-women's movement" trend among college students in the early part of the 21st century is a backlash against — and attempt to repudiate — women's victories over the past century. Others see the feminist paradox as a reaction to an unreceptive political and social climate that has weakened and dispersed the ideals of the women's movement.

New York University professor Judith Stacey sees these post-feminist attitudes as "a new form of gender consciousness . . . that includes the incorporation, revision, and de-politicization of many of the central goals of second-wave feminism."

A 2004 study by women's rights researcher Pia Petola explored feminist identity across three generations. The study shows that the college-aged adults of 2004 didn't feel that collective action — or a movement — was needed to decrease sexism and improve women's rights. Most people in this age group agreed with the principles espoused by the women's rights movement, yet they didn't view themselves as activists. These attitudes are similar to the "active but not activists" perspectives of Internet Pioneers.

Internet Pioneers Accept Feminism

College students of 2011-2015 are likely to reject the findings of a 2008 *Sociological Journal* report by Shannon Houvouras and J. Scott Carter on college students' attitudes toward feminism and women's rights. This study found that although most students agreed with the goals of the women's movement — such as gender equality, equal pay and representation in politics — 44 percent of participants described feminists as having negative personal characteristics, e.g., militant, aggressive, whiny, crazy, or man-hating. The use of such derogatory or stereotypical terms indicated hostility toward feminism and, by extension, the women's movement.

Although they are only a couple of years younger than the study sample, Internet Pioneers reject such hostile classifications and tend to be inclusive and accepting in their attitudes. The differences between older Millennials and Internet Natives reflect this shift in core attitudes. Internet Pioneers are more openly accepting than their older cohorts of feminist principles, but they'd probably agree with the study's conclusion that feminism is more about integrating feminist principles into everyday life than activism.

Sexism and Sexualization

Internet Pioneers tend to be sexualized and integrated with members of the other sex at an early age — in large part due to Internet exposure. According to the American Psychological Association, an overdose of media exposure — from the Internet to television — has created a culture of sexualization in which both men and women perceive females as sexual objects.

A 2003 study by Jacqueline Lambiase, journalism professor at Texas Christian University, focused on how celebrity fan sites — often geared toward young women — present female celebrities. Her research showed websites present women in a highly sexualized manner compared with male celebrities. For young women seeking strong, powerful female role models, this barrage of sexualized imagery sent a potent message that *sexualization equals success*.

Internet Pioneers, on the other hand, are more likely to view the opposite sex without bias or inappropriate sexual connotations. Female sexuality is accepted as a norm. In the same context, female Internet Pioneers are more likely to accept male behavior and lifestyles they consider to be immature.

Lady Gaga Hits the Right Sexual Notes

No one embodies this sexual equality quite like Lady Gaga. Ubiquitous on the Internet — a Google search for her name brings up 314 million results — the artist is often upheld by the media — from the *Guardian* to *Ms Magazine* — as an example of "lady power" or a poster child for post-feminism.

However, when the star was asked if she was a feminist, she replied with an unequivocal: "I'm not a feminist — I love men. I celebrate American male culture, and beer, and bars and muscle cars..."

Lady Gaga embraces both the feminist ideal of the empowered female along with the traditional image of the stick-thin, skimpily dressed sexpot. Characterizing the evolving state of gender-related attitudes among today's students, the star strongly defends women's rights and emancipation. At the same time, she presents herself in an unconventionally — and highly — sexualized manner.

The star turns traditional ideas about femininity upside down — while embracing them at the same time. As a 2010 *New York Times* article puts it, "This tension in Gaga's self-presentation, far from being idiosyncratic or self-contradictory, epitomizes the situation of a certain class of comfortably affluent young women today."

Equality Gained — But At What Cost?

Internet Pioneers have grown up in the wake of feminism's second wave. Their feminist grandmothers struggled and achieved greater equality and rights. More women than ever attend college, work in high-paying careers and participate in politics. These opportunities didn't exist a hundred years ago, and they were far less available to women only 50 years ago. Tempering these gains is the increased pressure on women to be physically attractive and participate in the current "hook up" culture, where sexual encounters without relationships seem to be the new norm.

Third Wave of Women's Rights Activism

Young women graduating from college and entering the workforce are better prepared than any previous generation to balance the disconnect between the self-empowerment necessary to succeed and the ongoing trend toward sexual objectification. They are following the Lady Gaga route; i.e., not viewing these trends and behaviors as sexual objectification, but rather embracing them as expressions of self-confidence and personal choice.

Today's college-age women are the third wave of women's rights activism. They live in a post-feminist world, stuck between a rock — feminism's second wave with its focus on equality through careers, education and achievement outside the home — and a hard place — today's pressure to have it all. The goal is to achieve everything: career, modern lifestyle, family life, while still looking and behaving in a way that's seen as traditionally sexy and feminine.

Author Wendy Wasserstein highlighted this irony when she said: "No matter how successful I become as a playwright, my mother would be thrilled to hear me tell her that I'd just lost 20 pounds, gotten married and become a lawyer."

Looking Ahead

Internet Pioneers are bombarded by conflicting information about gender roles, women's rights and sexism from a range of sources. Carolyn Sumner, a former professor at Southern Methodist University believes, "As far as we've come, as a nation and as a sex, we still have so far to go."

Over years, women such as Hillary Clinton, Nancy Pelosi, Nickelodeon's Geraldine Laybourne, Facebook's Sheryl Sandberg and many others have shattered the glass ceiling, but it takes just minutes on the Internet or watching television to see that women are still sexualized and that women's rights are still politicized.

Sumner believes, "The stereotypes that are perpetuated through more subtle avenues such as beer commercials and sports are more powerful weapons than overt sexism. Soft sexism is the new enemy."

A report in the June 2011 *Psychology of Women Quarterly* concluded that men don't realize the effects of such innate sexism; but this is changing as females challenge men when they express inappropriate sexist comments or actions. This is reinforced by the uprising of women against Limbaugh and those who supported his outbursts against Georgetown law student Sandra Fluke.

Although "soft sexism" still exists and women's rights are still debated, Internet Pioneers comprise the first generation that is entering and graduating from college recognizing sexism as inappropriate behavior. The Internet and television have provided much information about sexism and its implications for both men and women. With female college enrollment approaching 60 percent, women are a powerful force for assuring both equal rights and imposing a zero tolerance for sexist behavior. These attitudes will extend into the workforce, into marketing campaigns and into post-graduation relationships.

Chapter 6:
In Spirituality We Trust

Despite their busy lifestyles, Internet Pioneers are more spiritually-minded than earlier generations. Many college students find time to cultivate their spiritual growth.

Dena P., a University of Wisconsin-Milwaukee alumna, learned this firsthand while volunteering at a privately owned New Age library. She was surprised at how many college students used and volunteered at the library. With her college days 15 years behind her, she wasn't sure if she'd have much rapport with these students. Yet she "came to see that these college students who were actively working on their spiritual growth were already quite close to what has been called 'spiritually awakened,' or 'spiritually enlightened.' At a time when they are focused on term papers, preparing for the 'real world' and getting good grades on exams, these young people were balancing their secular studies with meditation, devotional study and reading and learning about the lives of Jesus, Buddha, Mohammed and other teachers and examples of higher states of consciousness."

Study Results: Participation in Organized Religion

My study found that only 27 percent of Internet Pioneers are involved weekly in religious/social organization activities and services while 54 percent rarely or never participate in religious/social organizations. *The World Values Study*, a worldwide survey of religious beliefs, reported that among U.S. youth ages 18 to 24, about 42 percent participated in a religion between 1999 and 2001 — a period in which Internet access expanded into the majority of U.S. homes. By 2008, the *American Religious Identification Survey* found only 22 percent of youths in the United States reported participating in an organized religion.

That drop of nearly 50 percent indicates that Internet Pioneers are less involved in religion than preceding generations, and this drop corresponds exactly with the years in which the Internet became part of their daily life. Factors for the trend are discussed below.

Dogma vs. Information Access

Throughout much of the 20th century, information for young people was limited by where they lived and the adults around them. Youth in large cities had extensive access to information and exposure to greater religious diversity. Youth in rural areas often had little information beyond their community church.

Internet Natives have had an unlimited ability to learn independently — beyond the influences of their religious organizations, schools and parents. News sites report on church scandals like Catholic priest child abuse cover-ups, corrupt religious evangelists and violent Muslim fundamentalism. Social network sites facilitate sharing information and views with peers from other faiths — or those of no faith at all.

As a result, Internet Pioneers are less likely to allow their religion to shape their beliefs, political positions, or education. They are less likely to adhere to dogma or act in ways that are inconsistent with their actual beliefs — or beliefs they recognize as being out-of-step with their contemporaries. Examples include such issues as the widespread support of gay rights and women's choice, regardless of religious affiliation. As a result, Internet Pioneers, in general, are less committed to religious orthodoxy.

Current college students may be willing to listen to parental advice on dating and marriage, but they are not as eager to please religious figures. A number of religious leaders (and elected government officials) advocate abstinence before marriage and avoidance of contraceptives. This is advice that a large majority of Internet Pioneers are not willing to follow. Even most of those who voluntarily have chosen a path of celibacy do not believe it should be a requirement imposed by religious dogma. Gay rights and women's choice are also supported by a large majority of Internet Pioneers, no matter what their religious affiliation.

In fact, some have left their faith altogether because of their qualms with these issues. Nicole Anderson, a student teacher in Minnesota, claimed that Catholic doctrines on birth control convinced her to leave her religious upbringing behind.

"I simply could not be a member of a denomination with such views on marriage and family planning. I think life has gotten a lot better for women since

contraceptives have become available. [Women] now have the option to wait until they are ready to start families. And when they do begin families, women can choose to have one or two kids instead of eight or nine."

~ **Nicole Anderson**
Student Teacher

Some religious leaders have believed access to "dangerous" information in schools represents a threat to religious development in youth. They restricted access by removing books from libraries and banning specific topics in schools. The 1925 Scopes trial and 1999 Kansas exclusion of evolution from state guidelines are two examples. Some states still attempt to control information access with measures that dictate how textbooks report on everything from evolution and climate change to state history.

In the home, popular television has been largely Christian-friendly, with religious characters and real-life religious leaders portrayed as wise and benevolent. Since the late 20th century, however, shows including *South Park*, *Law and Order*, and *Family Guy* have painted a very different picture. From gritty story lines about abuses by religious leaders to biting satire, mainstream television is now as likely to attack religion as to defend it. (Read more on *Family Guy* in Chapter 11.)

New Opportunities for Exploring Religion and Spirituality

Another factor in the shifting trend away from organized religion is the formation of religious groups on the Internet: not only the Internet-based Universal Life Church but Jewish, Christian, Muslim and Buddhist sites, plus hundreds of religious sects.

Discussion boards and web pages devoted to religious education are available to all those who want to explore their faith or network with others from their faith and other faiths. Churches and evangelists who successfully used television and radio to expand their reach now use the Internet to advance and promote their messages. Internet Pioneers are open and receptive to the messages that conform to their own underlying principles of freedom and inclusiveness.

Atheist communities also exist online, in many ways mimicking the structure and tone of religious websites.

Negative attitudes toward religion are balanced, and perhaps even overwhelmed, by the constant expressions of gratitude to God by popular musical talent, Hollywood performers and athletes, along with the emphasis on Christian values by political leaders and candidates.

Toward Spirituality...and Beyond

While active involvement with organized religion may be waning among Internet Natives, a growing percentage of young people are pursuing a spiritual relationship with the divine. They share a belief in life after death and the possibility of communications with those who have passed, rather than a relationship with a faith community or organized structure.

Although the Internet provides access to the gospel of many, an underlying belief in another plane of existence and some form of life after death is spreading among a fast-growing number of Internet Pioneers.

One of the theories being embraced by some Internet Pioneers and being spread through the Internet is the concept advanced by biologist Rupert Sheldrake that all knowledge resides in very real, organized energy fields in the air all around us, or perhaps even in other dimensions that are accessible to us. According to Sheldrake, all knowledge, all ideas and areas of study have their own "morphogenetic field," or "M-field." The more human beings tap into these knowledge energy fields, the stronger these fields become.

According to Sheldrake, there seems to be an energizing effect that runs both ways between human beings and these invisible fields of energy and information. While the energy fields are subtle, they are quite real and have a definite impact. They are reservoirs of data and information and the more people are connected to them, the more they can accelerate current and future learning.

Sheldrake's theory of an energy field that exists in another dimension is, to some, analogous to the Internet: a powerful energy field that connects all beings, is omniscient (has infinite knowledge), is omnipotent (unlimited power), is omnipresent (present everywhere), treats everyone equally and is available to all, and is simple to access and incorporate into your life. Share this same description with theologians and they will believe you are describing God. A logical connection can be made from the Internet to a god-like presence in people's lives.

This connection may seem sacrilegious to many, and I'm even uncomfortable including it in this book. But Internet Pioneers are embracing the concept of existential energy fields that the mind will ultimately be able to connect to and communicate with. This may be an uncomfortable reality, but nonetheless it is a truth that puts the extraordinary influence of the Internet in relevant context.

The Future of Religion

How actively will Internet Pioneers embrace traditional religion in their lives, and what role will religion have?

Factors influencing youth and religion are complex and difficult to measure. Some studies look at youth and religion. Some look at religion and the Internet. Some look at youth and the Internet. To date, no study has combined youth, religion and the Internet. However, comparing data from different studies seems to indicate a handful of trends:

- Active participation in organized religion is waning among young people.

- Changes occurring in religious affiliation appear to be true of the population as a whole — not just youth.

- Among today's religious youth there is a shift toward spirituality and away from organized worship and commitment to the orthodox tenets of one particular faith.

Religious (and other) organizations will actively extend their congregational meetings and services via streaming video and Internet access to religious leaders, from local to global to universal. Group networking will be available through social media; fund-raising will be actively developed online; meetings will convene online; and complaints about everything and anything church-related will spread virally and immediately throughout the congregation and beyond.

Internet Pioneers will lead religion into an era of greater ecumenism, with many church organizations becoming far more proactive in reaching out to their communities and prospective members. Some organizations will probably move in the opposite direction, however, becoming more orthodox, insular and closed.

Internet Pioneers will develop and actively participate in social networks built around spirituality and religious-like beliefs, but not necessarily traditional religions. For Internet Pioneers, the Internet will serve the basic needs for community previously met by actively participating in religious organizations. However, Internet Pioneers will continue to maintain religious affiliation for family and social purposes and to fulfill their needs to attend services.

But for many, the Internet will be the first place they turn to for spiritual connectivity.

In some ways, the Internet has created a social community center traditionally provided by the church. And while the church, temple or mosque is localized, involvement in Internet-based communities has no borders or boundaries and embraces all as equals.

Chapter 7:
The Hidden Messages of Harry Potter

The world of Harry Potter is fictional, but readers would be justified in arguing that Rowling's work has a strong socialist edge and religious overtones.

In the book series, the author uses characters such as Harry's guardian family to depict a middle-class, modern world. Harry's family is weak and mean-spirited; wealthy characters are greedy and villainous. In the movie series, visuals like neighborhoods with hundreds of identical houses reinforce the idea of mindless conformity.

The implication is that this invented world reflects the values of today's real world.

By contrast, however, Harry's life at Hogwarts (a boarding school for young wizards) is a world based on competitive assessment, capitalist values and advancement through merit and hard work. Two beloved Hogwarts characters — Fred and George Weasely — open a successful business together in the sixth book. Central characters like Dumbledore and Potter are wealthy, but they live modestly.

Among the most popular book series ever published, J.K. Rowlings' *Harry Potter* has fans in every age bracket. Internet Pioneers grew up with "Pottermania" and are now in college, with those who first read *Harry Potter and The Philosopher's Stone* at age 11 now graduating and joining the workforce. In short, most Internet Pioneers are intimately familiar with the Harry Potter books and movies, and many have had their psyches and values at least partially influenced by this series.

To date, no major research has been conducted to find out how powerful the effect of these themes has been on the development of the "Harry Potter Generation." Much like the influence of rock music, *Dungeons and Dragons* or ubiquitous television, what research has been conducted is largely inconclusive — it's simply too difficult to eliminate all independent variables from such an event. However, the 60s generation engaged in social activism while reading works such as *Siddhartha*, *Steppenwolf*, *On the Road* and *Lord of the Rings*. This may suggest that certain popular books read during formative years have a strong influence on decisions made by the readers as young adults. So it is with the children who grew up reading Harry Potter. They are beginning to show tendencies that align with the values of the novels — but it remains to be seen whether they have those values because of the series, or if the series owes its popularity to the prevalence of those values.

Progressive Politics and Sexual Attitudes

In a 2005 *Time Magazine* article, Lev Grossman pointed out that the Hogwarts school is a progressive bastion: secular, multicultural, multiracial and gender-integrated. Some students and staff mourn this state of affairs, but they are the villains of the series — or at least the unfortunate products of a bigoted or otherwise backward upbringing.

In a 2005 article, Benjamin Barton of the University of Tennessee points out another potential influence — the author's portrayal of the wizardry governmental authority (the Ministry of Magic) as a rigid, ineffectual bureaucracy incapable of protecting its subjects from any meaningful threat.

One example of the series' progressive stance appears in *Harry Potter and the Goblet of Fire* with the introduction of an enslaved race of "house elves." Heroine Hermione Granger tries to improve the elves' lives through grassroots activism. This activity demonstrates her moral superiority and fairness of mind, rather than portraying her as an adolescent with a knee-jerk reaction to harsh realities. (Among others, John Rose of metrosantacruz.com, has drawn historical parallels between Hermione's mission and that of the American Communist Party.)

Perhaps the most famous — and controversial — progressive stance in the *Harry Potter* universe never appeared in the books. Rather, in a post-release conference for the final installment, Rowling announced that the character of Harry Potter's caring mentor (Albus Dumbledore) was gay. Casting a major heroic character as homosexual might be another subtle influence in Internet Pioneers' generally accepting attitudes toward homosexuality.

From the first book in the series, Harry Potter and his friends consistently break rules and attempt to solve adult problems out of a mistrust of adult capability, intelligence and motivation. Though this behavior may be common in children's literature, the Harry Potter series, especially in later installments, takes youthful rebellion to an arguably anarchistic extreme.

Religious Criticism

Though some Christian organizations have attacked the author for her handling of controversial issues, such as a positive portrayal of witchcraft and homosexuality, other reviewers draw a strong parallel between Harry's story and that of Jesus Christ. In the final volume, *Harry Potter and the Deathly Hallows*, the link is particularly strong. (Harry dies, spends a brief time in the afterlife, and then returns to earth after conquering death itself.) In a 2007 interview, Rowling said that the Christian allegories had always been part of her plan for the series.

However, fans and critics note that Rowling also drew inspiration from non-Christian tradition. The resulting blend is a weave of different influences that strengthens the inclusive nature of the series. Some see the *Harry Potter* series and its overt portrayal of magic and celebration of pagan mythology as a threat to Christian values. This is much like the protests against the *Dungeons and Dragons* game and *Lord of the Rings* in earlier decades.

Some church leaders from mainstream religions (Catholic, Islam, American Protestant) have asked church members to avoid reading the books. These leaders claim that the books actively encourage children to experiment with the occult. In the United States, several schools have banned or challenged the value of the book. In addition, an inside White House source claims that Rowling has never been recognized for enthusing millions of young readers specifically because of the concerns mentioned above.

No legitimate source believes the hysterical fringe reports of sinister, subliminal, or intentionally hidden messages within the *Harry Potter* novels and movies. However — like much fiction — the books communicate an underlying philosophy that has influenced many young readers who came simply for the story. Whether or not that philosophy could be called "sinister" depends on how it is interpreted.

Nevertheless, such attitudes toward the iconic influences of Internet Pioneers lead them to distance themselves from traditional institutions. Instead, Pioneers depend more on their own opinions and role models. As Internet Pioneers form their own religious and political standards, the influences of Harry Potter, Nickelodeon, *Pretty Little Liars* and *Family Guy* will be stronger than the establishment standards of religion, politics or schools. (See Chapter 11 for more on this topic.)

Racism, War and Corruption

Rowling has publicly stated on multiple book tours that she wanted to incorporate many horrors of the real world into the world of Harry Potter. (Rowling formerly worked for Amnesty International, resulting in her awareness of such horrors.) Thus, the characters and — vicariously — the readers are exposed to these darker parts of human nature.

From the start of the series, racism, class discrimination and abuse of power provide a backdrop to Harry's adventures. The death and suffering of war take center stage by volume four of the series. As the power of character Lord Voldemort and his "Death Eaters" escalates, their policies become eerily similar to those of Nazi Germany and other cultures that engaged in ethnic cleansing. The young heroes of the series react with horror and grief as they try to prevent or minimize the effects of such evil. Their confrontations serve as a vehicle for an exploration of morality and rules in an unjust society.

Harry Potter and the "Occupy" Movement

"For the greater good" is a quote right out of Dumbledore's journals about his exploration of dark wizardry — and a quote from the journals of many real life utilitarians. As a powerful and politically influential wizard, Dumbledore's crimes include involuntary manslaughter, assault, high treason, endangering minors, smuggling and blackmail — and those are just the infractions that he admits to.

Harry and his friends behave in a similar vein. In the first book, they use aggressive magic to temporarily paralyze a friend. Rule-breaking becomes law-breaking early in the series. By the sixth book, Harry is using "unforgivable curses" — magic spells so terrible that their use can be punished with execution. Still, Harry and the other heroes are never punished or even asked to account for their choices. Generally, the responsible adults simply wave away their behaviors as understandable given the circumstances.

The contemporary "Occupy" and "Anonymous" movements are strongly in line with themes of social equality, socialist political ideals, a utilitarian definition of just action and a mistrust of authority and institutional structures. They ignore the lines of state and nation, focusing instead on human issues many members consider larger than any individual culture or group. In short, these movements share much of their core values with the values espoused in the *Harry Potter* series. Heroes Hermione, Ron and Harry would fit right in at an "Occupy" encampment. Other characters like Fred and George would proudly hack large corporations to expose their dirty laundry and embrace the WikiLeaks philosophy.

Future Tech Imagined

One way in which the Harry Potter books are almost certain to impact the near future is in the directions taken by technology. The Internet owes some of its existence to the imagination of science fiction writers. Much of our space program is indebted to Jules Verne, Arthur C. Clarke, Isaac Asimov and Ray Bradbury for the inspiration that launched its ongoing success. Steven Spielberg's films *A.I. Artificial Intelligence* and *Minority Report* share visions that are becoming increasingly realistic.

Author and futurist Ray Kurzweil wrote in *The Singularity is Near* that the types of magic seen in the *Harry Potter* series will be everyday sights within the next few decades. He didn't mean actual occult magic, but rather the technological capabilities of a rapidly developing human race. As Kurzweil points out, technology that could simulate magic will be part of daily lives within a few short years — and Internet Pioneers inspired by the Harry Potter series will be the young scientists who bring those technologies forward.

Medical nanotechnology will allow healing that looks and feels like magic both in terms of its capacity and its time frame. As cloning and genetic technologies advance, it's difficult to rule out any possibility. The influence of *Harry Potter* is likely to emerge in every aspect of society.

Although it's hard to quantify exactly how much J.K. Rowling's world-changing series will affect the personalities, politics and morality of young people today, it's almost impossible to argue that it hasn't already. As this cohort grows older and initiates change in the world, the inspiration and influence of these popular novels will continue to be evident.

Chapter 8:
A Socially Conscious Political Force

Internet Pioneers will be a quiet, socially conscious political force to be reckoned with, a bridge between generations that grew up in 20th-century politics controlled by politicians and the news media and 21st-century politics that will be increasingly impacted by wikis, collaborative enterprise and one-to-one online discourse. Internet Pioneers are connected online to the issues about which they're passionate. They're more likely than preceding generations to engage in politics through online organizations and communications than caucuses in high school gymnasiums and door-to-door canvassing.

Election battles are being fought on blog posts, social networking sites, and hundreds of online media outlets. They're updated minute-by-minute and hold politicians accountable for every comment, every inconsistency, every factual inaccuracy, every involuntary facial reaction.

Twitter, Facebook and YouTube are more influential to Internet Pioneers than *The New York Times* and the *Wall Street Journal* combined. When President Obama announced his plans to run for re-election on the 140-character-or-less social media venue Twitter, no one seemed surprised. When he launched his 2012 campaign with a YouTube video, commentators discussed the venue as much as the message — a clear indication that television is gradually taking a backseat to the instant access of the Internet.

Internet Pioneers are well-equipped to sort through and process the multiple strands of communications and propaganda. They have a world of knowledge at their fingertips and they know how to use and exploit it. They have access to the world's finest libraries, opinion writers, philosophers, and media outlets, and they will take all of those voices into account as they make their selections at the polls.

With all this information available, Internet Pioneers are less interested in listening to long speeches and debates. They want concise statements of opinion and they want facts. They want to know whether a candidate is pro-life or pro-choice — not explanations or arguments for or against individual positions. They want politicians to listen to their points of view and acknowledge their right to have them.

Political advisers and campaign managers are struggling to find new and creative ways to engage young adults in political campaigns. According to the Pew Internet American Life Project, the Internet made it possible to better target get-out-the-vote campaigns through personalized communications.

The Howard Dean campaign discovered Meet-ups — in-person meetings arranged within private homes and companies. These turned out to be an effective way to meet young voters within their communities. The Kerry and Bush presidential campaigns set up house parties to make their outreach as personal and effective as possible. Move On uses neighborhood house parties to discuss political issues and organize local outreach initiatives. Campaign tactics used during the early years of the Internet are expanding to embrace more sophisticated social and mobile campaigns.

Internet Pioneers will research the ideology and voting history of the candidates in the 2012 elections and beyond. They will share what they learn with their friends, create their own mini-campaigns, and use a variety of digital and social communications techniques to express their support. They will receive, interpret and share information from a vast network of experts and pundits.

Internet Pioneers will be activists in advancing technologies to enable online registration and voting, with the expectation that online voting is not just practical, it is their right. They will solve the related issues of voter validation and privacy. By the presidential election of 2028 and possibly 2024, online voting will be established, accepted and prominent.

After witnessing years of attacks on the presidency as an institution, Internet Pioneers still express an interest in voting for the next president, and are even more interested in voting in other general elections. Only 7 percent say they do not intend to vote during and after college, with 13 percent not sure. If these numbers hold, Internet Pioneers will prove to be the most politically involved and committed in history, with significant influence over who will win offices for decades ahead. They are a small but potent force.

19th-century philosopher of science Auguste Comte suggested that "social change was determined by generational change and in particular by conflict between successive generations." If that's the case, in the next several years we may experience the most confrontational and societally beneficial "clash of the cultures" that the world has witnessed in a long time.

Chapter 9:
Politics, Social Issues, Occupy and "IDK"

"*IDK. I Don't Know.*" It's a catch-all phrase, but ask an Internet Pioneer a question and his or her response is typically preceded by a disconnected or even semi-perturbed, "I don't know…" followed by a reasonably thoughtful response. Try it. Ask a 17- to 21-year-old questions about politics, issues, their future, their friends and there's a high probability his or her answers will be interspersed with "I don't know." The short-form text version is the popular IDK.

It's not just a verbal habit like "you know". Internet Pioneers are plagued by uncertainty about the validity of their opinions, yet most are very clear about where they stand. Ask them to make a decision and they're as likely to say "whatever" as to offer a choice, even when they have a preference. They prefer to avoid conflict and are wary about how their opinions will be received. They are wary of the polarized hostility they observe in the political climate, so they preface their opinions with a declaratory IDK.

In fact, most have pretty well-informed points of view about a wide-ranging spectrum of issues and reasonably clear perspectives on their future plans. They may disagree with each other, but they are focused, aware, engaged and active. They are also tolerant of their peers with whom they disagree and are willing to listen to and consider opposing opinions. They're confused and offended by those who are unwilling to consider opposing views.

Internet Pioneers' Political Persuasion

Internet Pioneers have been impacted not only by the Internet but by growing up completely within a heavily charged and often negative political environment. They spent most of their early years during the presidency of William Jefferson Clinton and their teen years under President George W. Bush. For them, the presidency carries less gravitas as a result of the barrage of political attacks that marked both presidencies and that has intensified during the term of President Barack Obama. While presidents have always been the target of political dogma and hostility, the extraordinary attacks that now dominate the political landscape have turned off Internet Pioneers. Similarly, they have low tolerance for the polarizing social issues and economic policies that have dominated political debate and discourse throughout their young lives.

Half of the 18- and 19-year-olds in our survey have yet to determine their political persuasion, unable to define themselves as progressive/liberal, moderate, conservative or libertarian. One-third of the older 20- and 21-year-old Internet Pioneers remain unfocused in their political affiliation, but are likely to take a more moderate stance. Among those who declared a political position, 73 percent identify themselves as progressive or moderate, compared to 27 percent who say they are politically conservative. Less than 1 percent of both groups say they are Libertarian, suggesting that the apparent wave of support for Ron and Rand Paul will be short-lived.

A Formidable Voting Bloc

Internet Pioneers intend to participate in the political process. Only 10 percent say they do not plan to vote in the next presidential election, with an additional 16 percent uncertain. Among the Asian Internet Pioneer population, 18 percent say they will not vote and 14 percent of Blacks/African Americans do not intend to vote. Compared to the high percentages of the general population who do not vote and acknowledge they do not plan to vote in the future, Internet Pioneers hold the promise of being the most politically active generation in nearly five decades, yet they are more *unlikely* to aggressively campaign for their candidates or for their positions. For this we have to thank lobbyists, political attack dogs, the 24-hour news cycle that rewards and champions controversy over discourse, liars in the news media and in public office, a politicized court system, and the polarization and partisanship that accompanies discussion of almost every issue that comes before Congress.

The debates and conflicts that have dominated the politics of the past couple of decades have created some confusion and uncertainty among Internet Pioneers, creating a large base of young voters who are still listening to both sides on key issues such as health care without having formed a clear opinion of their own. But on most issues, only a small minority of Internet Pioneers has yet to form an opinion.

Confusion and Uncertainty of Internet Natives:

	% Who Don't Know/Not Sure/No Opinion
Health Care Coverage	41%
Optimism/Pessimism About Future of Generation	37%
Income Taxes	29%
Continued Global Dominance of U.S. Economy	26%
Value of Corporations to Society	24%
Continued U.S. Foreign Military Commitment	23%
Economic Conditions in Next Four Years	20%
I Plan to Vote in the Presidential Election	16%
Future Impact of Generation/Age Group	16%
Plan to Maintain Connections with High School Friends	15%
Legalization of Medical Marijuana	15%
I Plan to Vote in Future Elections	13%
Choice Vs. Right to Life	12%
Second Amendment Right to Bear Arms	12%
Plans After Graduation from College	10%
Environment/Climate Change	9%
Advertising	9%

For most issues, especially social issues that are polarizing society, Internet Pioneers have formed a clear and relatively cohesive voting bloc that will increasingly inform the politics of the nation.

In that context, and understanding that Internet Pioneers tend toward being more progressive and moderate than conservative, it's important to understand their positions on the issues that are likely to dominate the political debate for the next several years and that will define the nation and world in the 21st century.

Political Positions

Overall, Internet Pioneers' training from Nickelodeon [See Chapter 11] and their life-long online immersion are likely to influence them to vote for those who connect most effectively on a one-to-one basis, who are honest and sincere in their opinions, are the least extreme, and who prove open and accepting of those with whom they don't agree.

If Internet Pioneers turn out to be a quiet but cohesive political force, as the statistics suggest they will, and if their influence extends beyond the size of their generation alone, which I believe it will, then they will have significant impact on the future of the nation on several important political fronts.

- There will continue to be polarization on most social and foreign policy issues, but the weight of the population will swing toward more progressive and moderate views.

- 73% of those who take an active position on foreign military intervention say we should get out of our current conflicts soon.

- Only 20% disapprove of same-sex marriage.

- 84% agree that women should have the right to terminate pregnancies in at least some instances, and 53% believe they should have the right in all instances if medically safe.

- Only 24% believe there should be no tax increases of any type.

- 59% believe the government should support health care for all people.

- 64% oppose changes to Medicare regulations that would delay their benefits to an older age.

- 86% believe global climate change is real.

- 60% support the legalization of marijuana in some form.

- Only 44% approve of strict gun control enforcement.

- 49% believe the U.S. economy will worsen in the next four years.

- 52% believe the U.S. position in the global economy will deteriorate.

Internet Pioneers are most likely to support candidates for political office who advocate:

- Smaller government

- A strong but controlled military with a non-interventionist agenda

- Reduction of the dominance of the military-industrial complex

- Individual rights, including abortion, gay marriage, medical marijuana and limited gun control

- Clearly defined economic policies that do not overly advantage the already wealthy

---

Internet Pioneers are not anti-corporation but definitely are wary of government, Wall Street, large institutions, and over-regulation.

They believe in individual rights but are less inclined to support active separation of states along politically-charged issues, believing that the nation is one and undivided, with liberty and justice for all.

Social Issues

Internet Pioneers are progressive on most social issues, actively opposed to military intervention, balanced on gun control issues, and moderate but confused on economic issues. When asked about interracial marriage and same-sex partnerships, Internet Pioneers almost seemed shocked that these topics are still being debated. Penn State senior Allen Vickers referred to comedian Chris Rock's joke that "gay people got a right to be as miserable as everybody else." Ali Nelson, a 19-year-old student in Albuquerque, NM, responded "I don't think the government should even have a say in it."

Internet Pioneers look at LGBT relationships with a new level of respect. Internet Pioneers are overwhelmingly in favor of gay rights issues such as same-sex marriage, adoption and serving in the military. In 2011, overall support of gay marriage in the general population passed 50 percent for the first time. 85 percent of Internet Pioneers say they respect the right of individuals to enter into legally sanctioned same-sex marriages. They are also open to a number of other non-traditional family arrangements. At one time a taboo, interracial marriage now receives overwhelming support from young people. A 2011 *GOOD Magazine* survey found that 85 percent of the Millennial population supported interracial marriages regardless of ethnicity. Support for interfaith marriages is also at an all-time high.

To "Occupy" or Not

We should not confuse the desire of Internet Pioneers to avoid conflict with an unwillingness to take and support a position or to vote in an election. As "Occupy Wall Street" crowds gathered around the country, a common question was, "Where are the college students? Where are the young activists?" The answer is simple. They were focused on their priorities, managing the complexities of their lives, working at their jobs, intent on their lives and responsibilities.

Overall, their politics conform to the underlying issues that brought protesters into the streets, but unlike their counterparts in the Middle East, the Internet Pioneers in the United States are active but not activists, political but not politically involved, engaged in issues but unwilling to actively protest for or against them.

While Internet Pioneers were not taking to the streets and parks, they contributed to the rapid expansion of the "Occupy" movement across the United States and to over 85 nations. College students spread the "Occupy" message on Twitter, Facebook, Tumblr, Foursquare and a variety of other social networking and activist sites. Critics dismiss "Occupy Wall Street" as a disorganized group of disgruntled ruffians. Although there are certainly unorganized elements of "Occupy Wall Street," the movement's virtual platform is the epitome of organization. A variety of social media tools are all linked to occupationalist.org, a one-stop shop where protesters and interested onlookers can learn about the movement's background, core beliefs and upcoming events. A number of other tools are also integrated into the website, including Tumblr pictures, events on Meetup.com, online mapping and all kinds of videos from YouTube and Facebook. Those who focus on the size of crowds in the streets fail to understand the power of crowd sourcing and social media to spread and sustain a message and movement.

"Occupy Wall Street" may have received press attention, but it is certainly not the only social justice movement that's meaningful to Internet Pioneers. Movements started by college students and recent graduates have been sprouting up all over the place. Several of these movements are aimed at changing the ways in which young people purchase and use consumer goods. Activists aim to draw attention to large companies that sell products made in sweatshops. Sweatshop labor has long been frowned on for its low wages and often physically harmful working conditions, but most consumers fail to realize that their purchasing habits are driving the demand for cheap products made in sweatshops and thus sustaining terrible treatment of workers.

Internet Pioneers understand the value of the Internet and the power of communications. Mark Twain said "Never argue with a man who buys ink by the barrel." Internet Pioneers are the first generation to grow up with the availability of online ink by the barrel, and they use it.

Penelope Trunk, founder of Gen Y social networking site Brazen Careerist says that today's college students are anything but apathetic. Generation Z (as Trunk dubs them) "will be so good at processing information that they will open doors we can only knock on today."

Chapter 10:
Education: Every Child Moves Ahead

Some of the doors Internet Pioneers will open are the doors of schools, with a large percentage intending to make education a career.

Internet Pioneers will be leaders in restructuring school systems and education programs, applying technology to take greater advantage of online learning opportunities; increase their resources; enable art, drama and music programs; reinvest in sports teams and physical education; and most importantly, improve communications systems and services. Curricula will expand to prepare students for jobs in an Internet-dependent economy. Growth areas will include gaming development, commerce, video production and content development, marketing and public communications, social media, etc. Other changes will include an increased focus on issues that are vital to moving society forward and about which Internet Pioneers are passionate, such as climate change and political studies.

Internet Pioneers will move into and influence the educational system at all levels: community, state and national. They will advocate and implement online educational programs at the primary and secondary levels.

Internet Pioneers are among the first classes to graduate from high schools that modified their curriculum under "No Child Left Behind," a program that diminished arts programs, physical education, home economics and other classes not focused on math, sciences and basic curriculum. They have witnessed the neglect of basic tools required for a well-rounded education.

In 1987, the American Association for Higher Education Bulletin published "Seven Principles for Good Practice in Undergraduate Education." It called for "best practices" such as the encouragement of greater interaction between teachers and students, prompt teacher feedback to students, active learning, respect for new learning methods, and communicating high expectations. The Internet is finally making these principles a reality. There are challenges: schools must first become technologically wired with Wi-Fi access and charging stations, yet many schools still lack wireless access or even sufficient electrical outlets.

"The web is packed with a vast array of content accessible by teachers and students alike," write David Houle and Jeff Cobb in *ShiftEd: A Call to Action for Transforming K-12 Education.* They point to "the vast library of open educational content published by institutions and individual contributors around the world."

The online Kahn Academy (kahnacademy.org) provides a prime example. The Kahn Academy offers nearly 2,000 (and the number is still growing) teaching videos on YouTube that are known for their comprehensive, user-friendly content. Another example is Open Education Resources (OER), a free resource that operates under the terms of Creative Commons. OER Commons lists an astounding 20,000-plus resources for primary and secondary education.

Future teachers will be curators and facilitators of knowledge tools such as OER and resources such as books stored and available on-demand on the "cloud". Students will be encouraged to find and recommend new resources to introduce into classroom discussions and debates.

The University of Washington has developed online collaborative programs open to all students. The goal is "to promote student cooperation and collaboration," and the programs use tools that allow students to communicate and collaborate about any topic they choose. Such tools include the use of chat rooms as well as "Share Spaces" with simultaneous text and file sharing that enables users to discuss the files together.

Lisa Thumann at Rutgers University points out, "For a generation that has embraced a joystick and a mouse since they were toddlers, these technologies can help them learn how to be creative, how to communicate and how to work together."

Future students will use e-readers (Kindles, Nooks, Apple e-readers). Backpacks loaded with heavy texts will be replaced by the ability to download text, learning tools and support programs into e-readers and tablets. Apple has already introduced iBooks 2 for grades

K–12 and iTunes U for educators. Apple also delivers thousands of college lectures through iTunes U and enables professors to develop complete online courses. According to Walter Isaacson's biography of Steve Jobs, the Apple founder "had his sights set on textbooks as the next business he wanted to transform." The iBookstore will soon feature textbooks from most — if not all — textbook publishers and most have already begun publishing to the Apple platform. Apple also supports the production and publication of e-textbooks. College and K–12 texts will soon be universally available for download to Apple products, Kindles and Nooks.

Home Schooling: Positives and Negatives

In the past few decades, a growing number of parents have sought to limit the education of their children to the home for a variety of reasons, a trend that has been enriched by Internet access.

There are both positive and negative implications of home schooling, and there is continuing debate over its value. Some parents have restricted school access to their children with the objective of limiting their children's exposure to issues with which they disagree. The movement toward home schooling for these reasons may increase in the short-run due to neighborhood peer pressure, but it is doomed to fail. Controlled education would need to be accompanied by an Internet-free lifestyle, and effective home schooling, almost by definition, requires that students have open access to online resources. Home schooling parents will not be able to limit their children's access to information, nor will states, such as Texas and a handful of others that have rewritten textbooks to reflect the political positions of current political leaders.

The Internet is making it virtually impossible to limit access to information and knowledge, and it will ultimately further the erosion of both home schooling and textbooks as viable learning options. Internet Pioneers are too well-informed, too questioning of institutions and authorities — including their parents and teachers — and too resourceful. They have access to too much advanced technology and are being integrated into the mainstream of a global culture. As Internet Pioneers gain control, the institutional efforts to control and manage learning will only serve to advance the move of the classroom to the Internet.

How Will Classrooms Change?

Online forums, message boards, chat rooms and global student interchange will become more accessible to students in and out of the schools. This will enable greater feedback while students are working on their projects rather than after they're completed.

More classrooms are introducing interactive whiteboards and desktops that allow students to ask their classmates questions, interact on a message board while discussing class topics, and communicate in real time with other students and experts from around the world. Both students and teachers can facilitate global discussions and debates with the support of online resources and specially developed textbook "apps." A recent Cisco advertising campaign reinforces this future reality.

The traditional textbook used as the exclusive source of knowledge and answers will become obsolete. In schools that cannot afford teacher specialists, Internet-based tools can facilitate new teaching modules that students can use on their own. Online programs also help teachers stay current both on subject matter and teaching techniques.

Motion and Voice Recognition as Educational Tools

Encyclopedias were once the center of the home library. Parents directed their children to find facts and answers by "looking it up," reading and writing down what they found. However, the Internet has changed and will continue to change dramatically the ways in which we retrieve and interact with information. There are drastic shifts on the near-term horizon in gathering, sharing and curating information through the use of voice recognition and motion detection software.

The Microsoft Xbox Kinect and other motion detection software allow learners to fully immerse themselves by using their bodies rather than mouse, keyboard or controller to interact with the information on the screen. There are infinite implications to the development of this technology. Examples include:

- Incorporating sports training, physical exercise and fitness into classroom curriculum.

- Enabling art and music programs through online learning programs.

- Training physicians/surgeons in complicated surgeries before actual surgery.

- Training in many other occupations.

Voice and motion recognition is truly in its infancy, but MIT and others are developing advanced computer languages that learn and respond to eye movement, brain waves and breath.

Siri, Apple's intelligent software assistant application, allows communication without manual input, enabling students with physical disabilities to control a computer without physical taxation. More than simple voice-to-text dictation software, Siri is an "intelligent personal assistant." Siri works with native applications to handle tasks such as web searching, setting reminders and sending messages. That means students can start research on a topic immediately, set reminders about tests or assignments, even reinforce learning simply by asking Siri to occasionally repeat a set of words, definitions or other information throughout the day.

Siri offers unique benefits to teachers as well. Rather than sifting through reference materials, teachers can quickly ask for the information they want to share with students. Voice recognition software has the potential to improve reading, writing and language skills. For those learning to read, the instant feedback Siri offers on misspelled words can help make a student into a more confident learner. Siri can also assist in aggregating resources for additional learning based on student-specific results. And voice recognition software changes testing capabilities, offering oral examinations tied to applications that instantly evaluate, grade and share results with teachers or administrators from any location.

Remote Learning

Remote — or distance — learning programs will continue to gain popularity and significantly alter the educational landscape. According to the U.S. Department of Education, 4.3 million undergraduate students took at least one online course in 2007–2008. In 2010, 6.1 million college students took at least one online course, an increase of 29.5% in three years. In 2007–2008, online enrollment represented 21.6% of all college enrollment, and in the fall of 2010, online enrollment represented 31.3%. Online enrollment increased by more than 10 percent in 2010 over 2009.

Distance learning programs offer students the opportunity to matriculate from prestigious universities without leaving home. A rural student who wanted to pursue an MBA used to be limited to getting a degree from a local college or moving away from home. Now many universities offer an online MBA, including prestigious schools such as Duke University, the University of North Carolina, Indiana University, Penn State University, the University of

Florida, the Thunderbird School of Global Management, and Arizona State University. The entry requirements are as competitive as the campus-based programs and the degrees have the same level of prestige.

Even prestigious Ivy League schools are offering online educational opportunities. For example, Harvard University offers online courses through the Harvard Extension School, which offers bachelor's degrees and master's degrees in a wide range of areas from the sciences to the liberal arts and offers a wide range of courses online. The Harvard Extension Program is reasonably priced at around $975 per course for undergraduate courses to $1,950 per course for graduate level courses.

The Extension School does have its limitations. Not every course is offered online, most programs require two semesters of residency for the Harvard degree, and there is a six online-course limit for master's degree programs. Still, Harvard is allowing students to pursue a Harvard education without having to spend the entire time on campus.

The College Loan Bubble Explodes

Remote learning also opens up cost-effective opportunities to gain a degree. Students save by eliminating moving expenses, commuting costs, parking, child care, and extra time off work, and there can be significant savings in tuition as well.

With total outstanding college loan debt surpassing credit card debt for the first time in 2011, the looming educational debt crisis could prove as catastrophic as the real estate loan bubble. Students are borrowing more for their college educations, yet declining job opportunities and starting jobs with lower salaries will affect students' abilities to repay these loans.

President Obama has tackled this potential economic crisis by offering incentives to schools and states to keep their educational costs in check. One way to accomplish this is through a less expensive remote learning program. There are several state schools that offer online MBAs at in-state tuition levels, regardless of the state in which the student lives.

- The University of North Dakota charges $363.78 per credit hour for the online MBA, which costs the student a total of $12,378 for an MBA. Compare this to the $35,876 UND charges nonresident students for an on-campus MBA, more than $23,000 more than obtaining the MBA online.

• The University of Nebraska-Lincoln charges $531 per credit hour for its distance MBA program. The degree is a 48-credit-hour degree, so the total tuition for the MBA would be $25,488. If a non-resident attended the University of Nebraska-Lincoln on campus, the student would be charged $916 per credit hour. This would raise the total tuition to $43,968 for the MBA, and this is not including moving expenses, commuting and other expenses.

• The University of Massachusetts-Amherst charges $750 per credit hour for its online MBA. The MBA is a 37-credit-hour program, so the total tuition of the online MBA at the UM-Amherst would be $27,750. A non-Massachusetts resident would be charged $48,178, more than $20,000 higher than the cost of obtaining the degree online.

Remote learning also creates opportunities to study majors that local colleges often do not offer, creating opportunities for graduates of these schools to have wider employment opportunities. For example, an insurance coverage attorney who wants to get an LLM in insurance law has few options. However, the University of Connecticut offers an online option that allows attorneys to pursue their LLM in insurance from anywhere in the world. Such programs greatly expand educational opportunities for all students, as they aren't limited to the offerings of their local colleges and universities. Internet Natives have an expanded array of opportunities to learn, grow, and develop academically, and they have the Internet skills to take advantage of them.

Remote learning programs also open up possibilities for international degrees. Business schools such as IE Business School in Madrid, Spain, the Manchester Business School in Manchester, England, and the Warwick Business School in Coventry, England, are examples of online MBA programs that allow students to explore international educations from home.

Access to Education for All

Numerous studies have shown that individuals enjoy increased health, earnings and longevity with higher levels of education. Increasing the access of illiterate, developmentally challenged and foreign language-speaking students to higher levels of education and training could potentially help close the disparities that exist across socio-economic and ethnic lines. As Lewis and Burd-Sharps point out in a 2010 report, any advancement in human development requires the opportunity for individuals to gain the highest possible standard of physical and mental health. Changing the health and earnings potential of its citizens changes the economic development of the country.

The Future of Education

Pre-Internet industrialized systems will not be easily changed or dismantled. But as Internet Pioneers move into educational careers, they will be powerful advocates for advancing online learning programs and restructuring the educational models to embrace instant global access to learning resources. Internet Natives will receive an education in school that complements and advances the one they gain at home and on their own.

In summary, the integration of motion for kinesthetic learners or as a tool to encourage physicality and fitness; the use of voice to aid impaired or geographically separated students; the integration of fun and flexible learning technology into curricula; and advances into voice-based instant translation applications have educators looking past their current boundaries and into vast possibilities.

Education will progressively move from the organized, highly structured and textbook/teacher-centric classroom to an Internet-centric model using televisions, computers, tablets and mobile devices. From pre-school to post-graduate education, students will depend on the Internet for advancing their education, with the guidance, support and direction of their teachers.

Chapter 11:
Television Explains It All

An awareness of Internet Pioneers' early television experiences can help us better understand their values, attitudes and expectations. Nickelodeon had a strong influence on Internet Pioneers during their formative years, and many of their ideas, perspectives, sensibilities and attitudes can be tracked to these early television viewing experiences.

Nickelodeon programs dominate the list of shows that Internet Pioneers name as their favorites at age 12 or younger.

Internet Pioneers' Favorite Shows from When They Were Age 12 and Younger
Source: Myers Survey of Internet Pioneers, 2011

1. * *Rugrats*

2. * *Spongebob*

3. *Pokemon*

4. * *Hey Arnold*

5. * *Doug*

6. * *All That*

* Nickelodeon programs

Geraldine Laybourne, the educator who led Nickelodeon during its formative years, shares the story of her first visit to the set of Linda Ellerbee's groundbreaking Nickelodeon news program. "Linda had posted a sign that said 'Question Authority.' I told her to take it down… and replace it with a sign that said 'Question Everything.'"

When Nickelodeon was launched in 1990, the network issued a *Declaration of Kids' Rights* that, in many ways, serves as the mantra that Internet Pioneers grew up with and that defines how they perceive their rights and entitlements.

Nickelodeon's *Declaration of Kids' Rights* (June 7, 1990)

In the course of history, it has become pretty clear that all people are born with certain inalienable rights; among them life, liberty and the pursuit of happiness. But these rights haven't always applied to kids.

And that stinks!

Now, 200 years after the creation of America's Bill of Rights, this declaration proclaims to the world that you have rights too:

You have the right to be seen, heard and respected as a citizen of the world.

You have the right to a world that's peaceful and an environment that's not spoiled.

You have the right to be treated with equality; regardless of race, religion, nationality, sex, personality, grades or size.

You have the right to make mistakes without someone making you feel like a jerkhead.

You have the right to be protected from harm, injustice and hatred.

You have the right to an education that prepares you to run the world when it's your turn.

You have the right to your opinions and feelings, even if others don't agree with them.

So there!

"When we first came up with the mission to connect with kids and connect kids with each other through the world of entertainment, we were less a cable TV network and more a philosophy," Gerry Laybourne explains. "We had a wide range of TV including Linda's news programs that covered topics like AIDS and the Gulf War, game shows like *Double Dare,* cartoons like *Doug* and *Rugrats,* live action shows like *Clarissa* and *All That.* We encouraged kids to try new things and supported them when they didn't succeed."

Clarissa Explains It All was the first program with a girl as a central character, an early sign that girls were aware of equality as a central issue in their lives. "She was smart and cool with boys as friends, an attractive central character who all kids would like," says Gerry. "We were trying to create common experiences that could get boys to understand that girls could be cool. In all our programming, a sense of humor was the most important quality we could impart to kids. No matter what challenges our characters were confronting in their lives, with wit and humor they could shrug it off and get through it. We enjoyed making kids laugh."

Gerry acknowledges Nick was "slightly naughty and was not educational per se. We had pies in the face, slime, fun. We were a playful place where there weren't rules about what we could or could not do. We plugged into kids and kids were plugged into us."

"Our pre-school programming was very thoughtful on a developmental basis. What could we teach about cooperation, nurturing, friendships, how to deal with bullies? We did studies to see if our shows were having an effect. We weren't teaching ABCs, but modeling good behavior and getting kids engaged. Blue's Clues *had kids getting off their chairs and interacting with the screen way before the Internet. Our pre-school programming left kids better off than we found them; nicer and better citizens. That honestly was our criteria. We asked a profound question to every producer: 'What does the program do for kids?'"*

~ Geraldine Laybourne
Former Chairman, Nickelodeon

Laybourne developed *The Nick Studio 10 Commandments,* rules and guidelines she gave to producers before they developed any series for the network.

The Nick Studio 10 Commandments

1.   Thou shalt have no network before Nick.

2.   Thou shalt not treat kids like cattle. Each kid is an individual and deserves an individual experience of Nickelodeon.

3.   Thou shalt focus first on kids and not pander to parents…but allow parents to experience the kid joy of Nick first hand.

4.   Thou shalt have kids-only areas.

5.   Thou shalt not covet thy neighbor's theme park. Nick's success comes from being different.

6.   Thou shalt not talk down to kids.

7.   Thou shalt not be predictable — sight, sound, surprise.

8.   Thou shalt give kids a chance to be on Nickelodeon and talk back to Nick.

9.   Thou shalt always strive to be humorous and always change with kids.

10. Thou shalt "bottle" Nickelodeon with wit and humor.

Who are Internet Pioneers today? Nickelodeon captured the imaginations of this group during their most formative years and has, in some ways, helped define their mindset and influence their future.

•   Internet Pioneers value their individualism while recognizing themselves as belonging to many groups.

•   They welcome their parents' involvement in their lives, but they also want areas of their lives to be private and in their own control.

•   They consider themselves to be the intellectual and social equals of — if not superior to — adults and want equality in communications with them.

> - They welcome surprises and both understand and use humor.
>
> - Interactivity is expected; sit and watch them talk back to the TV even when there is no one listening.
>
> - And they like to have fun!

Importance of Television to Internet Pioneers

Television evolved as a natural outgrowth of the development and convergence of cinema, radio and electricity. The nineteenth century was a time of major inventions that led to the Industrial Revolution. In the 20th century, Philo T. Farnsworth patented the television, and RCA developed it commercially. Television evolved by leaps and bounds, and TV programming ultimately influenced generations of people.

Television put the Industrial Age's capitalistic economy on steroids, with new commercials that used sight, sound, motion and emotion to market manufactured goods and services across the nation. Those who are interested in how television evolved will find many histories of the medium, starting with Aaron Sorkin's excellent (albeit somewhat fictionalized) theatrical play *The Farnsworth Invention*. More to the point of this book, television programming and commercials have had enormous impact on the attitudes, beliefs, actions, behaviors and purchasing decisions of Internet Pioneers.

Our survey gave Pioneers ten viewing options and asked which three options they'd eliminate if they were forced to do so.

The results showed that 48 percent would eliminate AOL, Yahoo and MSN. Only 11 percent would eliminate cable networks such as Bravo, MTV, ESPN, Comedy Central, TBS and USA, while 14 percent would remove broadcast networks ABC, CBS, NBC and Fox. (And only 11 percent would eliminate YouTube.)

The survey asked males to name their favorite TV program of all time and *Family Guy* blows away all competition. That program also ranked highly with females, second only to *Pretty Little Liars*. While *Family Guy* and *Pretty Little Liars* are all-time favorite programs, the most influential TV *network* among Internet Pioneers is Nickelodeon and its landmark series *Rugrats*, *Doug* and *Spongebob Squarepants*.

Rugrats, Doug and *Spongebob*

Nickelodeon had huge success with the triumvirate of *Doug*, *Rugrats* and *Spongebob Squarepants*,. The first two were born in August, 1991, and lasted 8 and 15 years respectively. *Spongebob* was born in 1999 and is still running strong. *Doug* followed the story of the Funnie family — mainly, their precociously imaginative son Doug. Internet Pioneers born in 1991 and 1992 named *Doug* as their favorite program of all time.

"What attracted us to these programs is they were invented by people with wild imaginations. There had been (and still is) a school of thought that you only programmed shows with pre-sold characters. Other networks based kids programming on movies or books with merchandising value. We focused on creators with characters living inside them. Doug is Jim Jenkins. Doug's stories are all the stories from Jim's childhood. Everything came from his experiences and imagination. We honestly were not trying to sell product. They were done purely for entertainment."

~ **Geraldine Laybourne**
Former Chairman, Nickelodeon

Gerry Laybourne made the decision, with her team, to put both *Doug* and *Rugrats* on the air. Doug started out as a transplant to Bluffington, and he had to negotiate his newness to town, his middle-school awkwardness, and the painful joy of growing up. It was his inside world — his creative mind — that stole the show. From Quailman to Jack Bandit, from Race Canyon to Smash Adams and Durango Doug, his alter egos had free rein in the course of many episodes.

Rugrats was the vision of Arlene Klaskey, who had kids just as impish as the kids on *Rugrats*, claims Laybourne. The show was developed with their point of view. Bending reality was the penchant of *Rugrats'* creator. From its beginning to the end of its run in June 2004, the program's infant-aged protagonists grappled with a world full of adventure. The gag was that the parents were so consumed by their own creativity or obsessions with perfection that the babies could get out into the world and explore, narrowly escape danger, and communicate everything that they experienced in a kind of madcap malapropism of adult language.

Internet Pioneers were influenced from earliest childhood by what Laybourne describes as "a bold band of programmers who were ferocious in trying to protect kids. We protected them from sexual innuendo and jokes they didn't understand. We spoke to kids about how they can make sense of the world and about what they cared about. We connected the audience with the creative community; we didn't condescend to them and we tried to use connective language to communicate with them. *You Can't Do That on Television* was psychologically the most important show we did, because we did sketches about some of kids' most important issues, like parents who do dreadful things. We dealt with these issues in an honest, relevant way and from the kids' point of view."

What Makes *Doug* and *Rugrats* So Influential?

Nick O'Leary, 19, a Dartmouth College theater major, remembers *Doug* as his favorite show because "it made a certain kind of sense, thematically." Like the transplanted Doug, Nick watched the show during a span that included his own family's move from Connecticut to New Hampshire, just before middle school.

"*Doug* was absolutely my favorite Nicktoon, no question," O'Leary said. "In my mind, *Doug*'s message was that adolescence often seems tough, but it's not that bad. Plenty of episode topics are standard sitcom fare: crushes that don't know you exist, angst about your clothes or your hair, younger kids that want to be 'just like you,' zits, silly fights with your friends. It's possible — make that probable — that it was the first show where I saw most of these topics explored."

"The other thing that I will say about *Doug*'s impact on me as a child is how it encouraged me to develop imagination," he continued. "I know that we typically think of kids zoning out in front of the TV instead of thinking, but…when I saw Doug imagine he was Quail Man, it made me wonder about what superhero I would be."

For Ari Brown, 19, a computer science major at the University of Michigan, the brainy silliness of *Rugrats* made a big impact.

"As a young kid, I could watch it and want to be them," Brown said. "They lived the ideal life. Not because it was perfect, but…friendship, love, adventure, excitement, and danger, all before the age of three. How could you not want to live like that? The dad was an inventor who had his juvenile moments, and he was what I wanted to both have as a father and be." Another *Rugrats* fan, an 18-year-old female college freshman, remembers the dad (Stu Pickles) as a sad character, lost, alone in his basement workshop, and dominated by his wife. The program pushed Brown and other *Rugrats* fans to think about adults in ways that felt more measured than the anti-authoritarian world of *Spongebob*.

Spongebob Squarepants

Viewers don't need memories or reruns to catch onto the ongoing ideas of *Spongebob Squarepants*. New episodes continue to prompt a sophisticated (and at times controversial) audience reaction to its themes of diversity, equality, and sometimes-offbeat fun. A second *Spongebob Squarepants* theatrical film is planned by Nickelodeon for 2014.

The basic premise is the eternally hopeful Spongebob trying to make the best of his somewhat dunderheaded starfish friend Patrick and the grumpy Squidward. The trio frequently seeks to reconcile their desire to have fun with work and deal with the ambitions of Sheldon Plankton (who is married to a computer named Karen), who is out to destroy a competing restaurant owner, Mr. Krabs.

O'Leary and Brown agree that *Spongebob* was — and still is — very funny. "It was purely comedic for me, and its legacy will be in comedy, from naivety and innocence," says Brown.

Years Later: Impacting Internet Pioneers

Regardless of Brown's and O'Leary's final takeaway opinion of *Spongebob*, it helped shape their childhood understanding of adults, contributed to their sense of humor, and perhaps instilled an early anti-authoritarian streak.

"The adults in *Rugrats* weren't mean, they were just misguided," said Brown, comparing the two casts of characters, and then he added: "The adult characters in *Spongebob*, however, were mean.

"Squidward and Mr. Krabs were two main characters who displayed very adult — or rather, non-child characteristics — such as practice, greed, and success," he continued. "Squidward was always practicing his clarinet and chasing success in that field, although he never found it. Mr. Krabs was greedy and successful. These two characters were mean and almost always in opposition to the main characters, Spongebob and Patrick. This sets up conflict and a dichotomy of kids versus adults."

In an article published in *The Atlantic* (August 11, 2011), Spencer Kornhaber expressed a similar opinion. "Shows like *Doug*," he writes, "grappled again and again with the devastating epiphany of adolescence, that there are things about you that you can't change."

Or, as Brown put it: "There is nothing wrong with being your age — hiding and playing pretend in a cardboard box [the *Spongebob Squarepants* episode "Idiot Box"] and not knowing things. For instance, Spongebob failing his driver's test [in the episode "Boating School"]."

Perhaps what Brown is saying is that adulthood, and the journey toward it, is a bargain of compromise — a message that Nicktoons seems to have encouraged.

As an adult, O'Leary recognizes issues of equality that are layered into the shows. To him, *Doug* prompted early thoughts about the subject of equality, especially as it applied to the depiction of Bluffington, the main character's hometown.

"A setting where style might change overnight, so that everyone is wearing green sweater vests and khaki shorts," O'Leary said, or "where the local haunted house was built without a floor, or where everyone is a different color of the rainbow...a not-so-subtle statement about diversity."

For Brown, what might have seemed at the time to be "only entertainment" has also provoked a longer-lasting sensitivity to ways that the adult world — the realm of politics, for example — is not necessarily built of the binaries that news and opinion media often suggest to be the case.

"That type of television — namely *Rugrats* — made me a happier, more adventurous person," Brown said. "And I feel like if I were less adventurous I would be less willing to try new things with respect to politics and group dynamics. For instance, while I identify as a Democrat, once candidates pass a certain threshold, I am very much willing to side with any of them."

Balancing the impulse to divide people and ideologies into neat compartments is also one of O'Leary's takeaways on *Rugrats*, one that seems applicable to politics and issues of community in the adult world.

"It had a perfect villain in Angelica," said O'Leary. "Sweet enough to manipulate grownups but evil enough to really mess with the babies, she is the embodiment of the 'one you love to hate.' But the show did a great job of balancing the impulse to show her getting her comeuppance and reminding us that sometimes the bad guys get away. They also managed to make us feel sorry for her on a regular basis. After all, she's almost as powerless as Tommy, etc., and, unlike them, she doesn't seem to have any friends."

Nicktoons prompted more sophisticated ideas in some young viewers than their parents ever anticipated.

The subtlety of the messages that viewers such as O'Leary and Brown now describe are (partly) the product of what appears to be real thinking on their part — considerations of the characters and scenarios in these three shows, programming that has clearly informed their adult minds — and that apparently continues to resonate.

As Kornhaber said in his article, the trio of cartoons weren't — and aren't — just *good*, they *matter*.

The Philosophy, Psychology and Politics of *Family Guy*

The immensely popular cartoon show *Family Guy* has been with us for more than a decade, having had its debut after the 1999 Super Bowl. Initially canceled after three seasons, FOX brought the show back when faced with a perfect storm of market forces: DVD sales exceeded expectations, reruns on Cartoon Network's Adult Swim block began drawing audiences comparable to those of the *Tonight Show*, and fans circulated a petition that gained thousands of signatures. Clearly, this program resonated with a market segment that actively engaged with the content.

After its brush with an early demise, *Family Guy* went on to become an iconic favorite with the Internet Pioneers who were growing up with it. The show earned an Emmy nomination in 2009, spawned spin-off cartoon shows *American Dad* and *The Cleveland Show*, and retains a cult-like following today.

The program's enduring success begs a few questions, among them: Why is *Family Guy* so resonant with the Internet Pioneers' demographic? And after a decade of exposure to the program's edgy, cynical content, what impact has *Family Guy* had on a generation's philosophy, politics and psychology?

Attempting to neatly describe the program's content isn't easy. Like *Seinfeld*, *Family Guy* is a comedy "about nothing." The plots present a threadbare canvas for a steady stream of bizarre characters, sight gags and wisecracks that invariably skirt (or exceed) the boundaries of good taste and decorum. Writing in *the New York Times*, Dave Itzkoff described it this way: "*Family Guy* is either irreverent or crass, depending on your tolerance for unmannerly humor. Viewers come for its pop-cultural free associations and flatulence gags, not necessarily to debate pressing issues of the day."

"*Family Guy* is anything but a family show. Its humor is about as politically incorrect as television gets," said NPR's TV Critic Andrew Wallenstein. "But what I find most interesting is it doesn't matter what the story in any given episode is about. In fact, there rarely ever is a story. The plot is really just a construct to cram as many one-liners in as possible, one more outrageous than the next. And that's just what [Seth] MacFarlane (the show's creator) intended."

Family Guy as Post-Modern Manifesto

To the extent that *Family Guy* espouses a consistent "philosophy" it would be in its cynical attitude about human affairs, and portrayals of lives led without "meaning." In *Family Guy and Philosophy* (Wiley-Blackmun, 2007) editor Jeremy Wisnewski wrote an essay about the show's "postmodern" outlook. His assessment? "It systematically calls into question our most serious ideas: Truth, Progress, Freedom, Rationality, and the Individual."

Speaking of "serious ideas," one also must add religion to that list. *Family Guy* shines a searing light on all practices it sees as irrational and superstitious. Seth MacFarlane is an outspoken atheist — so *Family Guy*'s parodies of religions of all kinds come as no surprise. ("I think of myself as an equal-opportunity offender," MacFarlane said.)

Cynical Views on Politics and Government

Given the FOX Network's conservative politics, one might expect that a liberal-leaning show would find itself on a tight leash with the expression of political content. Not so, MacFarlane says: "FOX is a company that is schizophrenic in a lot of ways. The news division is very conservative and the entertainment division is very progressive. They really keep their hands out of our business...within reason."

Truth be told, no political viewpoint is off-limits to the show's writers. *Family Guy* exposes and satirizes the political establishment — regardless of which party or politician is in power. Presidents Clinton, Bush and Obama all have felt the sting of the show's satirical treatments. And the Kennedy Clan — America's liberal "Royal Family," got the same "gloves-off" treatment. (MacFarlane admits that his writing team "may have gone too far" with its idea of a PEZ candy dispenser bearing JFK's likeness, issuing its candy pellets through a gaping hole in the president's head!)

In his 1984 book, *Amusing Ourselves to Death*, the brilliant communications theorist Neal Postman expressed concern about the emergence of a "politically ignorant" society, arguing that democracy is undermined by citizens' exposure to media content that is entertaining but not informative. "Americans are the best-entertained and quite likely the least-informed people in the Western world."

Family Guy is hardly a primer in citizenship — but it certainly communicates a point of view about government and politics. The show's consistently cynical portrayal of a local government — the fictional Mayor of Quahog, Rhode Island — provides the best longitudinal indicator of the program's attitude about the "merits" of elected officials. Mayor Adam West (voiced by Adam West of the *Batman* television show) is utterly incompetent and truly bizarre — yet none of his constituents notice or care.

In one episode, voters support a candidate largely because she gratuitously mentions 9/11 numerous times in her campaign speech, thus "wrapping herself in the flag." This episode heightened viewers' awareness of the political pandering that drives so many campaigns. One could argue that this lesson in "political literacy" is a good message to share with viewers who are just recently eligible to vote. The lesson? Quality of government is commensurate with the degree to which it is held accountable by the people.

A Bias for Entertainment

In the end, however, MacFarlane makes it clear that his first priority is producing content that entertains. "People watch the show for laughs...They don't want to hear my personal views on politics." Yet, *Family Guy* remains popular and relevant because MacFarlane tackles the most controversial issues and engages controversial people.

In a case of "real life" intermingling with popular culture, conservative commentator Rush Limbaugh accepted MacFarlane's invitation to participate in an episode featuring the radio personality in its story plot. Although many conservatives viewed this as a "suicide mission" for Limbaugh, the resulting show displayed him more favorably than many mainstream media have.

In a follow-up editorial for the *Washington Times*, Michael Taube (former speechwriter for Canadian Prime Minister Stephen Harper) wrote: "...here's the inescapable — Rush comes off looking like an intelligent, reasonable and likeable conservative. He was portrayed as having strong beliefs and values, a love for his country and a genuine respect for intellectual discourse."

Family Guy's Lasting Impact on a Generation's Psyche

Not everyone sees *Family Guy*'s content as balanced and benign. From the very start, critics actively opposed it with public denouncements, protest letters to FOX and petitions to the Federal Communications Commission.

In 2009 the Parents Television Council (a conservative watchdog group) successfully lobbied for Microsoft to pull its sponsorship of certain *Family Guy* programming. In a speech to Microsoft's board of directors, the PTC's grassroots director (Gavin McKiernan) condemned the show, saying "...[it] consistently presented excessively violent, graphically sexual and profane material." (Given the program's propensity for "pushing the envelope" of current social standards, opponents have easily collected evidence they believe justifies censorship.)

In *Understanding Digital Kids*, author Ian Jukes wrote: "Increasingly, today's children's values are not and will not be inculcated by the family, the church or other institutions in either the present or the future. They are and will continue to be developed by the electronic and visual media that they are exposed to. This is where they will learn many of their social skills as they've become increasingly immersed in the new digital landscape."

"Cultivation Theory" describes a systemic erosion of values fueled by media, a framework first developed in 1978 by professors George Gerbner and Larry Gross at the University of Pennsylvania. Writing in *The Journal of Communications* in 1980, Gerbner and colleagues stated: "Just as an average temperature shift of a few degrees can lead to an ice age or the outcomes of elections can be determined by slight margins, so too can a relatively smaller pervasive influence make a crucial difference. The size of an effect is far less critical than the direction of its steady contribution."

In terms of this direction, television standards of propriety have changed substantially over the past twenty years — leading critics to label this genre as "subversive" comedy shows. First, *The Simpsons* (which debuted in 1989) broke new ground in exploring controversial subjects. Then came *Beavis and Butt-Head* in 1993 and *Daria, King of the Hill,* and *South Park* in 1997 — with each show adding cynical momentum before *Family Guy* made its debut in 1999. For every adherent to Cultivation Theory (or its many variations), there is a critic challenging the validity of its methods and findings. (Many alternative theories focus on the widely differing contexts in which various teenagers watch television. Others stress the predisposition that certain viewers have toward violence or other antisocial behaviors.) Consequently, assessing the lasting influence of this (or any program) rarely yields a consensus.

Looking back on America's political and economic realities during the past decade and the new social media transparency, increased public discontent and cynicism are not surprising, nor are they limited to a few snarky television cartoons. You didn't need to be a *Family Guy* viewer to become concerned about the state of America's politics, economics, and social structures.

Consequently, there are few clear-cut conclusions about the effects of long-term exposure to *Family Guy* — or similar programs. We simply don't have a control group of teenagers who have been sequestered for ten years and isolated from cultural influences. But the fact is, 17- to 21-year-old male Internet Pioneers name *Family Guy* as their *all-time* favorite and, we can conclude, it is among the most influential in guiding their perceptions and behavior.

To be sure, there are anecdotal accounts that these programs have had an impact — from parents, therapists, clergy and social service providers. (Some of this evidence speaks to children's vulnerability, some of it attests to their resilience, and some of it echoes old complaints about "What's the matter with kids today?") Policymakers, academics and psychologists also seek to "read the tea leaves" of national polls and surveys about this generation's attitudes, its political participation and its psychological well-being.

Perhaps the most telling evidence will come as Internet Pioneers themselves become "family guys." What values will they encourage and model for their own children? And later, when they decide what media their kids will see, will the Pioneers' own boundaries make *Family Guy* seem tame?

The Role and Relevance of *Pretty Little Liars*

At first glance, *Pretty Little Liars*, abbreviated as *PLL* by those who love the show, seems like a mere riff on a popular theme: pretty rich girls deal with all of the trials and travails of a privileged life in a perfect town full of rambling houses, luxury sedans, and dirty secrets. The theme departs from the usual as the girls' problems revolve around the mysterious death of their best friend.

Pretty Little Liars draws myriad comparisons to a variety of other popular dramas, from *Lost* to *I Know What You Did Last Summer* to *Veronica Mars*. Briefly, the program is about a group of five girls whose leader, Alison, disappears in the middle of a slumber party. A year later, Alison's clique has fallen apart, only to be re-united by a series of threatening texts from "A," an unidentified bully who threatens to expose their secrets and, occasionally, to cause them bodily harm. At first, the girls suspect "A" is Alison, returned to re-assert control over her friends, who have mixed feelings for her. (Hanna describes Alison as "my best friend…but also my greatest enemy.") But when Alison's body is found, buried in her backyard, it becomes clear that "A" is someone who wants to control the four remaining girls — Hanna, Emily, Spencer, and Aria — for reasons they cannot yet fathom.

Without ever revealing his or her identity, "A" — who could be Alison's murderer or even a spooky ghost from some parallel universe — drives the girls to continue to delve into the cause of Alison's death. In the process, "A" forces the girls to reveal secrets they thought they had planned to take with them to the grave. The uncovered secrets prompt the four remaining girls to work through past traumas, and to form bonds that make the transition from teenage life to adulthood a little easier.

It's kind of *Twin Peaks* for the digital era, say, or *Gossip Girl* with a twist. Within the first 15 minutes of the pilot, it becomes clear that *Pretty Little Liars* is not your classic teen drama. Instead, it's a racy, scandal-driven thrill ride that keys into the fantasies and experiences of a new generation of cultural consumers, the female Internet Pioneers who named it their favorite TV series of all time after less than two seasons.

Internet Pioneers relate to the main characters and their problems. The girls — Aria, Hanna, Spencer, Emily, and their queen bee, Alison (who appears only in flashbacks) — are clearly products of a transformed world. Gossip transmits instantaneously via texting, and children observe adulthood from the moment they first lay eyes on the Internet. Sure, the girls attend school dances — but they also date their teachers, shoplift without consequence, smoke pot, and openly discuss sexual topics with parents and other adults. *Pretty Little Liars* addresses previously taboo topics such as homosexuality, abortion, and adultery, until recently considered too scandalous to even mention in popular teen TV. The girls delve into topics such as running illegitimate businesses, families splitting up, welfare systems and more. They take charge of their lives.

Pretty Little Liars treats its audience like the adults they want to become.

The show, based on author Sara Shepard's popular book series, premiered June 8, 2010, on ABC Family. Program creator Alloy Entertainment (*Gossip Girl, The Vampire Diaries*) successfully pitched the pilot episode as "*Desperate Housewives* for teenagers." (Ironically, the current chair of Alloy is the same Geraldine Laybourne who is responsible for the success of Nickelodeon.) Originally, ABC Family slated *Pretty Little Liars* to run for 12 episodes a year for two years. But after its premiere, which drew 2.47 million viewers (the network's highest rated premiere ever), it became clear that *Pretty Little Liars* was not just another teenage girl drama. It was a cultural phenomenon.

"I thought, 'Oh, how manageable my life will be. I'll get to be home for half the year,'" said series showrunner Marlene King on her original expectations. "And then we were picked up for 22 [episodes] for the first year, and 24 this year." By the end of the first season, *Pretty Little Liars* was the most popular scripted show on basic cable for women between the ages of 18–34, and viewers 12–34. In the middle of its second season, executives renewed for a third season, and King has now committed to five full seasons.

Although the show is driven by cliffhangers and the fact that "A's" identity is never revealed — and won't be, claims King, until the show wraps up in its fifth season — it's clear that something else is attracting the enraptured audience of female viewers to the drama. "People love to tune in, and they're looking for clues and little bits and pieces of that puzzle along with who killed Alison," explains King. "The mystery is only 30 percent of each episode. Seventy percent of it is the world these girls live in and their love stories, their hardships, their hates, and difficulties."

Girls have historically been more attracted to the human narratives of shows like *Pretty Little Liars,* while boys tend to prefer the crude humor of programs like *Family Guy.* The question, however, is really not why the show is popular among teenage girls, but rather why it is more popular than the countless other girl-driven dramas on television.

"It's just a guilty pleasure," said one fan, Leslie Ross, age 19. "I love that it's like my high school, but also that none of the stuff they go through would ever have happened at my high school." The characters in *Pretty Little Liars* are relatable stereotypes — Aria is the outcast who listens to 'Emo' music and wants to be a writer; Spencer is the over-achiever who feels inferior to her perfect older sister; Emily is the sweet-natured jock with conservative parents; and Hanna is the former fat girl turned beauty queen. Viewers can also relate to secondary characters, such as a mother who is experiencing money troubles after a divorce. Almost any girl in America can find herself in one of the girls…but also the self she most aspires to.

Like the early prototype of a strong female character in *Clarissa*, the characters on *Pretty Little Liars* show that despite their flaws and faults, all girls can be their own superheroes. An example of this is when Emily, the star swimmer, bravely admits she is gay and discovers the reward for her bravery is ultimately acceptance. The underlying message of the show is that no matter how dark and deep your secrets are, you don't have to carry them alone. You can get the support you need from friends first, and trusted adults second.

Underlying values give viewers food for thought: one girl falls for her English teacher, but soon realizes it's an unhealthy relationship. Spencer, the goody-two-shoes, rejects the expectations of her career-driven parents, and falls in love with Toby, the moody outsider, who encourages her to be true to herself. And Hanna, the blonde bombshell, finds that being a good-natured, kind person actually grants her more power than if she were to be evil and conniving like the queen bee she replaced, the deceased Alison.

Although the girls turn to their boyfriends for emotional support, they more frequently turn to each other, ditching date nights and exciting opportunities to respond to SOS texts The goal is never to find a male hero to save them — and, in fact, the characters who do so, like Spencer's older sister, are often met with brutal truths about their choices. Instead, the *PLL* message is to show how to gain the confidence to express who you want to be in real life and to know the importance of good friends.

Pretty Little Liars understands that challenges can force kids to react to situations without understanding the implications, and models ways for them to slow down and think about repercussions rather than reacting hastily and dealing with the results later.

Pretty Little Liars enables girls to engage with such scenarios in a fantasy world — while at the same time being thoroughly entertained. "That's become our goal, that during each season we can find one topic where we can contribute and maybe help teens in that area," King explained. And if the ratings for the show are any indication, *Pretty Little Liars* is accomplishing just that, while emerging as a series that will have lasting influence on female Internet Pioneers and, therefore, impact for generations to come.

Do They Still Want Their MTV?

When MTV turned 30, the music video channel that morphed into an entertainment conglomerate gave itself a makeover, implementing new ways to reach the Millennial generation via a multi-pronged approach using social media and activism targeted to college kids. MTV is trying to "keep it as real" as a corporation can.

Millennials — those born from 1980 to 2005 — use the Internet as a platform for self-expression, said Meg James of the *Los Angeles Times*. With its roster of notable (some would say infamous) reality shows, MTV is playing to this audience and to the core segment of Internet Pioneers who sit squarely in the middle of the Millennial generation. With a slogan of "life amplified," MTV has its sights set on authentic stories that explore characters' weaknesses and flaws. Among its gritty reality shows are *Teen Mom, Jersey Shore* and *Awkward* — an irreverent comedy that has shown promise in TV ratings.

But then, MTV has always been pushing the envelope and cultural norms.

When it began airing on MTV in 1992, TV's original reality program *The Real World* featured an openly gay, HIV-infected housemate — something unheard of at the time. But the show helped spur a debate on gay and HIV-infected youth. More recently, Lisa Campbell pointed out on the UK-based website Broadcast that MTV's show *16 and Pregnant* has been a force for change, helping reduce U.S. teen pregnancy rates.

The Reality Situation

Love it or hate it, *Jersey Shore*, in its fifth season in 2012, has been kicking sand in the face of its detractors to become a national pop culture phenomenon reaching across the fashion, health and fitness and entertainment industries. The show resonates with the Millennials and especially the Internet Pioneer audience who name it as their fourth favorite *all-time*

TV series behind *Family Guy, Pretty Little Liars* and *House.* That's ahead of more obvious favorites *The Office, The Simpsons, South Park* and *Glee. Jersey Shore's* party-hearty cast is known for its drinking, fighting, tanning and hooking up — not necessarily in that order.

Just like previous MTV shows that drew the ire of many (think *Beavis and Butt-Head* and *The Osbournes*), *Jersey Shore* has become a global phenomenon, making celebrities out of its cast members. How far has the show pushed into popular culture? In March 2011, Rutgers University paid Nicole "Snooki" Polizzi $32,000 to speak about the reality TV life-style, according to the *Los Angeles Times.* That's $2,000 more than Pulitzer Prize-winning author Toni Morrison got to speak at the university's commencement two months later.

The show drew the ire of New Jersey governor Chris Christie, who vetoed a $420,000 tax break for the series to film in Seaside Heights, New Jersey. In a statement to the *Newark Star-Ledger,* Christie said that he axed the tax break because the show "does nothing more than perpetuate misconceptions about the state and its citizens." But the results of the new Fairleigh Dickinson University Public Mind poll paint a different story, with 41 percent of Americans having a favorable view of New Jersey because of the show. On college campuses, students dress like cast members and club like them too, said Steven Guarino on UPIU.com.

More Than the Shore

MTV's reach on college campuses goes far beyond getting students to imitate *Jersey Shore* antics.

MTV Networks' mtvU is a twenty-four-hour channel with original programming dedicated to college students and broadcast on more than 750 college campuses across the nation, reaching almost nine million students. That channel also runs RateMyProfessors.com, where students can go and rank their instructors.

Taking a stand on issues important to college students, including navigating college admissions and financial aid programs as well as a push to increase awareness of HIV testing, are among the issues MTV supports through its mtvU channel. A Facebook application to help navigate the college financial aid paperwork was the winner of the "Get Schooled College Affordability Challenge" sponsored by MTV, the College Board and the Bill and Melinda Gates Foundation.

Big Business

Far removed from its days as a single cable channel playing nonstop music videos, MTV Networks is a division of media giant Viacom Inc. with more than 150 television channels globally and 400 digital media properties in its stable, (including MTV, VH1, CMT, Comedy Central, Spike and TV Land and, of course, Nickelodeon). *Forbes* estimates that 83 percent of Viacom's value comes from its TV channels, and of those channels, Nickelodeon and MTV are its most valuable. The networks continue to have enormous impact on the psyche of a generation, and the long-term implications for society are significant.

Internet Pioneers reflect the lessons of *Doug, Rugrats* and *Spongebob Squarepants*. While older adults may view *Jersey Shore* contemptuously, Internet Pioneers view it as fun and funny entertainment, and are less inclined to draw conclusions on the state of society, youth or New Jersey. They view reality programs such as MTV's *16 and Pregnant* and *Teen Mom* with sensitivity and a desire to improve the world in which the show's characters live. This attitude derives directly from the implicit teachings of Nickelodeon and a savvy set of principles that guided the programming that defines a generation.

Fascination with Zombies: Why *The Walking Dead* Is So Popular

It's the same "Nickelodeon Slime" principle of fun and lighthearted entertainment that drives the enthusiasm Internet Pioneers have for zombies and vampires. The original guidelines for Nickelodeon program producers point out "Kids have a natural fascination with things that are gross." If you haven't heard, seen, or smelled AMC's *The Walking Dead*, you may want to get checked to see if you're a zombie. The format is similar to that of *Lost*: a bunch of strangers must band together if they want to survive. Instead of a plane crash on some tropical island, *The Walking Dead*'s characters survived some type of zombie apocalypse. They must avoid getting bitten by these mostly slow-moving half-dead creatures (Walkers) to keep from becoming zombies themselves. And it's really popular.

The Walking Dead's second season premiere episode drew an audience of 6.7 million viewers and another 2.1 million viewers for a same-night repeat. Those numbers eclipse the 5.2 million weekly viewers the show attracted in its first season and far eclipsed every other cable television series and most broadcast network drama and comedy programs.

Not Just Watching, Engaged!

The show is not only capturing a lot of eyeballs, it's become a cult favorite, especially among the Internet Pioneer generation of 17- to 21-year-olds. They just can't stop talking about the show. Trendrr, the social media measurement tool, shows that the show consistently averages tens of thousands of mentions every day on Twitter alone.

The show is inspiring events all over the U.S. such as the New Jersey Zombie Walk that attracted 12,500 people this year. What's all the fuss about? Why are Internet Pioneers so excited about zombies and *The Walking Dead?*

Good vs. Evil

One of the ongoing themes of the show is the fight to retain some level of humanity when the game rules completely dissolve. There's no oversight, no police force, no overarching *Big Brother* to modify behavior. What keeps the characters going is the struggle to stay human in a world devoid of humanity.

Lauren Cohan, who plays Maggie on the show, recently said about the show's popularity: "It's not just about the darkness. It goes so very deeply into these characters and how living in this kind of world makes us human or makes us less-than (human)."

It's the Economy, Zombie

Some pundits believe that *The Walking Dead's* success goes hand-in-hand with the struggling economic environment.

"I can't help but believe that this current Era of the Dead draws its power from our economic malaise. If you work in the many white-collar fields that have suffered in this recession, zombies are the perfect representation of the fiscal horror show. The zombie apocalypse is a white-collar nightmare: a world with no need for the skills we have developed. Lawyers, journalists, investment bankers — they are liabilities, not leaders, in the zombie-infested world."

~ **Torie Bosch**
Slate

Seen from this perspective, *The Walking Dead*'s survivors are mostly blue-collar folks — a cop, a hunter, a mechanic — people equipped with the tools, skills, and sheer will to pursue survival when everything they've ever known is gone.

The Only Fear We Have Is...Ourselves

In the *New York Times,* Chuck Klosterman describes the fascination with zombies as a manifestation of our own deepest fears:

> *"This is our collective fear projection: that we will be consumed. Zombies are like the Internet and the media and every conversation we don't want to have. All of it comes at us endlessly (and thoughtlessly), and — if we surrender — we will be overtaken and absorbed. Yet this war is manageable, if not necessarily winnable. As long as we keep deleting whatever's directly in front of us, we survive. We live to eliminate the zombies of tomorrow. We are able to remain human, at least for the time being. Our enemy is relentless and colossal, but also uncreative and stupid."*

Chapter 12:
Rock n' Roll Is Still Here to Stay

Internet Pioneers consider music to be an integral, everyday part of their lives — unlike its role in the lives of Baby Boomers, who may remember watershed moments like Woodstock or other live concert performances. Today's college students view music as the soundtrack to their lives.

Does a particular musician or band rank as "the best" to this Internet Pioneer generation? In one word, no! Our survey asked Internet Pioneers to name two or three favorite musicians or bands, but fewer than 10 percent of respondents could name more than one. Yet many Internet Pioneers say music is "very influential" in their lives. The chart below shows where Pioneers ranked music and other influences as "very influential" and "not at all influential" in their lives.

Influences in Internet Pioneers' Lives
Source: Myers Survey of Internet Pioneers, 2011

	% Saying Very Influential	% Saying Not At All Influential
Parents	57%	5%
Friends	44%	6%
Siblings, Relatives	39%	8%
Schools and Teachers	38%	7%
Music	32%	11%
Internet/Facebbok	24%	12%
Religious Leader/ Organization	22%	31%

	% Saying Very Influential	% Saying Not At All Influential
Books, Newspapers, Magazines	22%	13%
News Reporting on Issues	21%	13%
Camps, Counselors, Coaches	20%	23%
Participation Sports	20%	27%
Charitable Causes	18%	19%
TV/Film Documentaries	18%	17%
Games/Gaming	18%	28%
TV Series (Comedy, Drama, Etc.)	17%	16%
Theater/Dance	14%	36%
Therapist/ Medical Professional	13%	38%

One quick conclusion is that the therapist profession needs to move online quickly to adapt to the needs and lifestyle realities of Internet Pioneers. Another is that parental concerns that television is "destroying the minds" of their children is misplaced and misguided.

Internet Pioneers understand the differences between television reality and the real world, although, as noted in the previous chapter, some television programming is indirectly influential. While there is no group consensus on the most influential musicians, music and the music industry has clearly had a lasting impact.

Internet Pioneers belong to the first generation born with the inherent right to download music for free — or at least it's their opinion that free downloads are a right. Only 15 percent of those surveyed say they always pay for the music they download. Three-quarters rarely or never pay for it. Easy access to music and music sharing, multiple music discovery sites, the music industry's shift to focus on single tracks (instead of albums) have all transformed the way in which people listen to music.

Ali Nelson, a 19-year-old Michigan student, feels music has a constant presence in her life. "I always have music on, all day long. Music has driven my late night study sessions, influencing me to pass my exams." She lists Adele, Beyoncé, The White Stripes, Minus the Bear, Grieves, Eminem, and Kings of Leon among her favorite artists.

Pennsylvania State University senior Allen Vickers may like some "old school" artists like Earth, Wind & Fire or The Temptations, but he prefers to listen to them via iTunes, YouTube, and LastFM. He also likes Jay-Z, Kanye West and newer artists like Pac Div, and Tyler, the Creator.

In a 2010 study published in the *Atlantic Journal of Communication*, researchers at Syracuse University's S. I. Newhouse School of Public Communications found that "social utility was the most important motivation for illegal downloading." In the view of the study, music piracy is a social phenomenon. After conducting both qualitative and quantitative research, the authors concluded that "listening to digital music is an essential part of the college lifestyle."

There are signs of a high level of social acceptance for piracy, with more than 75 percent of Internet Pioneers voluntarily disclosing in our research that they illegally download music. Can a compromise to satisfy the social aspect of listening to music — while still compensating the rights holders — ever be reached? Possible solutions seem to be gaining traction with the (limited) support of Internet Pioneers.

"For artists just starting out…that's their job and everybody gets paid for their job. But it's kind of a right to have music. People should pay for it — that's important — but sometimes the prices are outrageous. I like Pandora because you can listen to the music and the artist is still getting paid. That's better than illegal downloads." Ortiz likes Eminem, Adele, Drake, Beyoncé, Lady Gaga, and loves the Beatles. She values originality in music: "It's important to me in music that people do their own thing."

~ Elena Ortiz
College Student, Albuquerque, New Mexico

Nine percent of male Internet Pioneers name Eminem and Lil Wayne as their favorite all-time musical performers. Linkin Park receives "favorite" votes from 6 percent and the Beatles and Drake receive 5 percent. Males also like Lady Gaga, with 4 percent including her among their favorites. Hundreds of performers and groups are ranked lower, each with just a handful of votes.

Among females, Taylor Swift ranks first, with 9 percent of respondents naming her as a favorite, followed by 7 percent favoring Lady Gaga. Katy Perry, Beyoncé, and Maroon 5 each receive 4 percent of the "favorites" votes. As with the male survey, females divide their attention among hundreds of different performers and groups.

Among Black/African-American respondents, Lil Wayne and Beyoncé stand out with 15 and 11 percent respectively. These musicians are the only performers who receive double-digit support from any respondent group. Asians enjoy Lady Gaga and Eminem, the same performers who captured the highest number of responses from Hispanics.

Popular group Coldplay was named by only 3 percent of respondents. The Black Eyed Peas, Rihanna, Adele, Kanye West, Nicki Minaj, Britney Spears, and Jay Z, among others, were named by 2 percent.

Music for Every Moment of Your Life

Groups and performers are popular for a moment in time and are as good only as their most recent release. Successful performers with a lasting presence are few and far between, with personalities and image often as important as musical talent.

For Internet Pioneers, music is of the moment. They check out new talent, especially independent musicians, and they stay current on dozens of performers. They will find and support new performers, "like" them on Facebook, and even purchase a song or two on iTunes. But it's a rare performer who transcends the most basic level of popularity to capture the attention and money of a large segment of the Internet Generation.

One such performer is Justin Bieber, the personification of a social media rags to riches story. Raised by a single mom, Bieber spent his formative years living just shy of the poverty line. His mother proudly displayed his singing talent to friends and family on YouTube, and Bieber suddenly became an Internet sensation, especially with the post-Internet "tween" audience. A recording contract and hit singles soon followed. Nevertheless, in our survey, Bieber was named as a favorite by only 1 percent of Internet Pioneers, receiving fewer votes than Rise Against and Three Days Grace and just one more vote than Death Cab for Cutie. Even a rare performer like Bieber can still carve out only a small slice of attention.

Social media is changing the criteria for who makes it in the music industry. It's changing the way we connect with our favorites and the way we discover new artists. The Bieber story is an example of the change. In the past, musicians needed radio, MTV and retail exposure, and recording executives limited marketing to the Top 40 performers. Being discovered and discovering new artists outside of the hit charts was never an easy task.

Enter Napster. Although its life span as a free music service was brief, this revolutionary online service completely changed the way in which music was bought and sold. This peer-to-peer online network became prominent between 1999 and 2001, when Internet Pioneers were already Internet savvy and just becoming musically sophisticated. Napster educated this welcoming audience to discover and share music with one another. Legal difficulties brought Napster's free music downloading to an early demise, but the basic premise of sharing music online remained. Napster was quickly followed by similar peer-to-peer file sharing systems, such as Gnutella and Freenet.

The next great music and social media explosion for Internet Pioneers was MySpace. Although MySpace eventually became known more as a means for young people to connect, its original focus was fostering socialization around the music industry and music artist discovery. Performers and bands would create MySpace pages with basic background information, concert dates and pictures. Many artists also allowed users to stream select songs, in hopes that users would like what they heard and would later choose to purchase entire albums.

MySpace launched a number of musicians to the top of the music charts. One notable success story involves Lily Allen, who struggled for years to gain recognition. The artist did manage to sign with record label Regal Recordings but was largely ignored as Regal focused on promoting albums from better-known artists such as Gorillaz and Coldplay. Allen launched a MySpace page that featured the demos she had recorded in 2005. Word-of-mouth attracted over 10,000 MySpace friends to Allen's page, many of them Internet Pioneers who liked searching for new talent. The MySpace attention increased radio station attention. Within a year of setting up her MySpace site, Lily Allen reached the top of the UK Singles Chart.

Internet Pioneers supported the rapid rise of MySpace but also spurred its rapid decline after News Corp (owner of Fox TV, Fox News Network and home of *American Idol*) acquired the site for $560 million. The site hit its peak in 2006 and for a short time beat out Google as the most visited website in the United States. But as students began flocking to Facebook, MySpace was largely left in the dust. Musicians began creating pages on

Facebook and young fans were quick to share those pages with friends and acquaintances. MySpace was acquired in 2011 (for only $35 million plus debt) by Internet newcomer Specific Media and Justin Timberlake.

Today, Facebook and Twitter share the top spot for connecting musicians and fans online. Both networks enable artists to share updates and upload photos and links to music. Facebook apps (such as Ping) allow users to tell friends about their new music discoveries and, in turn, to learn more about the music tastes of friends and acquaintances. Napster's co-founder Sean Parker, who was also the founding president of Facebook, is now focusing on Spotify, a European music streaming service that Parker sees as a way to continue the Napster mission. Spotify users can to stream select artists and albums for free, or they can purchase a membership that provides access to a greater variety of commercial-free music. Although initially independent of social networks, Spotify now has an integration deal with Facebook that allows Spotify users to chat about music and suggest new artists to friends.

The Music Business

As music listening shifts from computers and the classic iPod to smartphones and tablets, the music business is also switching from a focus on downloading tracks to streaming through apps such as Pandora, Vevo, Spotify and Clear Channel's IHeartRadio.

According to TechRadar, in 2011 listeners purchased only 175 million tracks online compared to seven billion streamed tracks.

With relatively low cost and ad-supported subscription services, streaming appeals to students who can discover, share and store a wide variety of music. Streaming is a good fit for those who constantly shift their musical preferences and who like exposure to a steady stream of new performers.

Music has devolved into the equivalent of YouTube viral videos. Find it, share it, enjoy it for the moment, and move on to the next tune that captures your interest. Music is no longer the cultural phenomenon it was in the 20th century, when massively popular performers and groups and waves of musical trends defined generations and eras. Over the years, we had a steady progression of personalities such as Al Jolson, Glenn Miller, Benny Goodman, Tommy Dorsey, Ethel Merman, Frank Sinatra, Judy Garland,

The Everly Brothers, Elvis Presley, Frankie Avalon, Beach Boys, Beatles, Rolling Stones, Bob Dylan, Barbra Streisand, Pink Floyd, The Who, Michael Jackson, and Madonna.

In their eras and at the height of their popularity, large percentages of music lovers would have named these stars as their "favorites." Most of these artists sustained careers well beyond their prime. Even today, they remain among the favorites of X-Gens and seniors. The Classic Rock genre remains among the most listened to by all generations and The Beatles remain a top seller on iTunes.

In contrast, Adele, 2011's Billboard Artist of the Year and a multiple Grammy Award winner in 2012, is named as "favorite" by only 1 percent of male Internet Pioneers and 3 percent of females. And despite the most successful concert tours of 2011, U2 and Bon Jovi are named as favorites by fewer than 1 percent of Internet Pioneers.

Future of the Music Industry

Music personifies, more than anything else, the dangers associated with a reluctance or refusal to shed the baggage of the pre-Internet world. After a slow start, the music industry continues its transformation as it finds ways to meet new and demanding requirements for easy access and complete consumer control. Rather than anticipating and proactively responding to new technologies and their impact, the music industry wasted time by clinging to business models and talent relationships that were quickly becoming outdated and irrelevant.

The old traditions revolved around executives identifying, developing, promoting, selling and profiting from musicians. That world has unraveled. While the industry scrambles to recover and rebuild, the fans are in charge — and Internet Pioneers have led the charge. Their tastes are eclectic, diverse and constantly changing. Musicians themselves have easy direct access to their fans and often have an active dialogue with them through fan pages, blogs and videos. While Vevo has become a popular industry-owned site for music videos, YouTube and other music sites offer discovery engines and distribution tools that consumers and artists themselves can control.

After Hurricane Katrina in 2005, Micah Nickerson and Damain Randle wrote a protest rap song, inspired by a quote from rapper Kanye West. They put the song, "George Bush Doesn't Care About Black People," online, where Marquise Lee, a video producer found it. Lee then created a video for the song, which was posted online.

The song writers and the video producer intentionally designed the work to give users free access under Creative Commons licenses. More of these collaborations are likely to occur, as the pathways for putting work online expand. Social networking sites such as Facebook will close gaps and degrees of separation between musicians, producers, collaborators and fans. Internet Pioneers, who grew up with social networking and are adept at it, will lead the charge.

Music's role in the lives of Internet Pioneers reflects their unique power and the power the Internet has granted them. They will demand more musical choices than past generations and more channels through which to consume their music. They will continue to listen to new artists and the classics, as illustrated by iTunes' re-release of the 27-track *1* album of the Beatles greatest hits. Although the album originally debuted in 2000, the iTunes release rocketed to the top of the charts — ahead of Adele's hit album *21* and Lil Wayne's *Tha Carter IV*.

Chapter 13:
Celebutantes, Cewebrities and the Celebrity Cult

The Internet has introduced a new brand of celebrity — the celebutante — known more for outlandish behavior than traditional talent. Internet Pioneers are the first generation to grow up with these celebutantes, elevating and then demoting them. The Pioneers also relate to more traditional celebrities with a perspective radically different from older generations.

Britney Spears, perhaps the first of the celebutantes, began her career before the development of the Internet. At that time, recording and television studios were very demanding, but Britney was a precocious child with genuine musical talent. She combined her talent with an edgy stage presence to develop a persona that captivated a worldwide fan base. Public interest was sustained by behavior that grew more outrageous: multiple public breakdowns, short-lived affairs and marriages, drug abuse and viral distribution of shocking photos. Her fame peaked between 2005 and 2008, when Yahoo reported people searched "Britney Spears" more than any other person on the Internet. Ultimately her disintegration generated more interest than her success as a precocious singer and dancer.

Celebrity in the 20th century was controlled by media distribution. Film companies, record labels, radio stations and television networks provided the most reliable routes to fame. The Internet has slowly eroded that monopoly on star-making. The Internet's democratic distribution is logistically and economically available to anyone with a web connection, empowering anyone who wants to display a talent (or lack thereof) to do so.

Success for those self-promoted ideas and personalities is far from guaranteed, but it no longer depends on a third party.

The Internet's lower barrier for entry has changed the nature of *who* can become a celebrity and *how* a star is born. It may also be changing the relationship between consumers and the celebrities themselves. Internet Pioneers have grown up with an unprecedented amount of their "mental real estate" devoted to celebrities. Modern celebrities have more — and closer — access to today's young adults. The celebrity news business uses sources across all media to provide young adults with information about their favorite celebrities. As a result, Internet Pioneers are less likely to take statements at face value. Only a small fraction of Internet Pioneers consider celebrity endorsements when considering donations to a charity cause. They are more motivated by friends' recommendations, social networks and information they gather through Internet research.

Even as the Internet was developing, television was undergoing its own metamorphosis. Cable television spawned hundreds of channels desperate for cheap content. From this need came a new type of entertainment — the reality show — that advanced and institutionalized the role of the celebutante. These shows made stars of 'Snooki' Polizzi of MTV's *Jersey Shore* and Kim Kardashian, whose E! reality series *Keeping Up With the Kardashians* gained enormous popularity as fans flocked to watch a family whose only talent appeared to be spending large amounts of cash. Ozzy Osbourne, with the support of his family, developed a new fan base with his MTV series *The Osbournes*. Nick Lachey and Jessica Simpson sustained popularity with MTV's *Newlyweds: Nick & Jessica*.

Perhaps the best known celebutante is Paris Hilton, an attractive heiress whose fame was marginal and talent undefined until the viral Internet release of an explicit sex video, *A Night in Paris*. Her Internet-based fame led to a reality show, *The Simple Life*, which was short-lived but had a cult-like following.

Paris, now in her thirties, may have more staying power than many of her more talented contemporaries. More than ever, stardom depends on image marketing and Hilton is no empty-headed bimbo. She is a granddaughter of hotel executive Conrad Hilton, and she has demonstrated her canny business sense and ability to turn celebutante notoriety into economic opportunity. Her release from a short prison term assured her extensive coverage across multiple TV channels in the United States and around the world. Paris has produced a variety of reality shows for several cable channels and has branched out with successful beauty and clothing lines. Paris may prove to be the first of many Internet-dependent celebrities who are able to sustain lifelong popularity through personal marketing.

Despite the prison and sex scandals, Hilton describes herself as a role model for children and young adults, claiming to teach them self-esteem. Some consumers disagree, criticizing her children's clothing line as "party clothes for young sluts." Internet Pioneers are more ambivalent, perhaps remembering how they emulated the Spears and Hilton look by wearing similar revealing clothes in their early teens.

However, today's Internet Pioneers are also less likely to reward self-absorbed instant celebutantes who depend more on sensation and controversy than talent.

Brittany Saale, a 21-year-old college psychology major, explains: "This type of celebrity worship doesn't influence me. I may copy a hairstyle I like, but that's about all."

Internet Pioneers have outgrown their early teen-age interest in celebutante behavior. Today they're judging and emulating their favorite celebrities based on positive social values, and this will continue in the future. Saale reflects this trend. "I like Pink because she's for women's rights and represents a strong female generation…the message is what's important." Saale (who dresses in jeans and T-shirts) dismisses the appearance of her scantily-clad, multiple-pierced idol.

The Dawn of Cewebrities

A "cewebrity" (ceWEBrity) is an individual who achieves fame among the Internet Generation solely through a presence on the Internet. The Urban Dictionary describes a cewebrity as an "online celebrity, rarely ever actually famous, but often wildly popular on sites like YouTube or Twitter."

Jessica Lee Rose used YouTube to become the first Internet cewebrity, making and posting videos under the user name LonelyGirl15. The videos showed a young, home-schooled teen as she sat on her bed, pouring out her private thoughts and fears. Fans 'connected' with LonelyGirl15 and her experiences. Viewer numbers rose to astronomical heights. LonelyGirl15 responded by slowly revealing more intimate details of her life.

The sensation ended when LonelyGirl15 was outed as an actor, 19-year-old Jessica Lee Rose. Rose was under contract to EQAL, a small entrepreneurial Hollywood studio. When the LonelyGirl15 saga ended, the studio went on to make branded entertainment videos for Philadelphia Cream Cheese. Its original goal of producing viral online video brands and then attracting sponsors didn't work out, and EQAL is now creating content for established studios and marketers. Jessica Lee has built on her YouTube popularity to gain more acting roles.

Fourteen-year-old Rebecca Black became a cewebrity by showcasing a reasonable amount of talent on a less adequate song and video. Results were mixed: Rebecca became the number one most downloaded YouTube artist in 2011 with her low-budget "Friday" video, but she also had the dubious honor of winning the most "I dislike this" votes.

User-Generated One-Hit Wonders

Viral videos are the Internet's version of the "one-hit wonder." An Internet piece goes viral when the first people to find it share it with their friends, who share it with their friends, who share it with theirs. The result is an exponential growth in the popularity of a specific piece — sometimes resulting in millions of views per day.

Rebecca Black and many other "webstars" (Freddie W, Nice Peter, Ray William Johnson, Toby Turner, Wil Wheaton, Pop17, gaming guru Monte Cook, the Annoying Orange and TheHill88) represent a new kind of role model. They demonstrate that anyone can achieve some fame — and even income — with limited talent and without traditional industry support. Those who are handy with a video camera can generate huge YouTube audiences with "warm fuzzy" videos such as twin babies talking to each other or somebody tickling a kitten. Such videos often get more than 50 million page views on YouTube.

Disconnect Between Celebrities and Cewebrities

Forbes publishes a popular list of their Top 25 Internet Celebrities. Unfortunately, the list demonstrates a lack of understanding of the true zeitgeist of the Internet.

The *Forbes* list focuses on talented individuals who have used the Internet *and* corporate support to launch careers in more traditional media. These celebrities are, on average, 38 years old, with several in their 50s. *Forbes'* focus — understandably — is on bloggers who write on tech, entertainment and politics (Matt Drudge, Michael Arrington, Amanda Congdon, Jeff Jarvis), marketing (Seth Godin, Chris Brogan), and celebrities (Perez Hilton).

The Top Internet Celebrities on the *Forbes* list would be unfamiliar to Internet Pioneers or Internet Natives (with the possible — but outdated — exception of Jessica Lee Rose). On the other hand, Internet cewebrities are well known to Internet Pioneers. Yet the legacy media continue to overlook these personalities despite the fact that ***many cewebrities generate millions more YouTube views than all 25 on the Forbes list combined!***

The Internet has become a true launching pad for a wide range of talented people. For example, Twitter phenomenon Justin Halpern got a book deal and a network television show based on his feed *$#*! My Dad Says*. Author Larry Correia leveraged self-published fiction into a multi-book science fiction contract.

Celebrity as Career Goal

While the goal is typically to leverage online fame into corporate deals, more and more Internet Pioneers are content making a name — and a living — for themselves solely via an Internet presence. Creators of YouTube videos, blogs, podcasts and newsletters can generate revenue through advertising or by selling upgrades, books and services.

Many people can easily use their cell phones for video recording, editing and distributing content. The quality is high and the cost is dramatically low. This enables anyone with even marginal interest to take a shot at becoming a YouTube cewebrity. The sheer number of potential viewers and readers makes a living wage possible for those willing and able to create and post content…a process requiring only a smartphone video camera and Internet connection.

The process is still evolving. To date, cewebrities who gain financial success are the exceptions; the majority gain only fleeting fame with little financial reward. But Internet Natives are more likely than past generations to view "celebrity" as a viable career option. A 2010 poll of children age 7 to 13 revealed that eight out of ten believe they have a chance of becoming famous.

This belief shows how the online cewebrity culture will change ideas about fame. As fame becomes easier to achieve, it'll become less valuable in the eyes of Internet Pioneers, a commodity unworthy of their time, attention and money.

Internet Presence as Career Requirement

On the other hand, people in traditional celebrity professions are finding an Internet presence is essential to maintaining their own careers. The Internet will be, if it's not already, the major influence for establishing celebrity. Those people who understand how to use the Internet effectively to market themselves and socially engage their fans are most likely to establish *and* sustain their careers. Examples are the consistently popular celebrity Twitter feeds and websites that focus on news and announcements that keep traditional celebrities in the public mind.

Stars will always rise to receive attention and income disproportionate to their actual contribution to society. However, as more people derive their income from careers that rely on public exposure, the cachet and economic appeal of simply being a celebrity will decrease.

Changing Concept of Celebrity

A 2011 report in the *Journal of Cultural Studies* indicates that the role of celebrity reporting is changing as celebrity becomes accessible to more people. In fact, the very concept of celebrity is changing. Anyone with a cell phone can tweet and post photos of the comings and goings of even the most marginal celebrity. The ubiquity of celebrity social networking and cultural visibility is making celebrity status less relevant, interesting and economically valuable. In turn, traditional media will have less incentive to cover celebrity news, further diminishing its appeal and value.

> *"We spend a lot of time (and editorial space) idolizing these celebrities. We're green-eyed about their wealth, beauty and success. But whoa — when they crash, they really crash. We might not be as thin or as rich, but things also don't seem to implode as spectacularly."*
>
> **~ Dorothy Robinson**
> **Columnist, *NY Metro***

Writing about Demi Moore, Robinson's comment reflects the cultural shift away from celebrities as role models. Interest in celebrities will continue in the short term, but for all intents and purposes, the cult of the celebutante is over.

Chapter 14:
Is It All Just a Game?

Online games are an awesome phenomenon. From *Farmville* to *World of Warcraft*, virtual gaming is an unqualified hit with the Internet Pioneer audience. Only 17 percent do not participate in online or console games. Console games like Xbox and Wii are growing in popularity among Internet Pioneers. Sixty-eight percent play console games, with half of this group spending more than an hour playing *every day*. In contrast, virtual gamers spend an average 75 minutes daily playing and console gamers play an average 80 minutes daily. How do we even begin to comprehend the long-term implications?

Ever since Pac Man and Pong, a debate has raged over how such games affect young people. Stakeholders include parents, educators, health professionals and other experts, plus of course the gamers themselves. The answer can never be black and white because the impact depends on many factors, including player age, number of hours spent playing, and the type of game.

Depending on their structure, games can enhance social relationships or they can isolate the player from his or her peers. There's a big difference between a 17-year-old boy who spends 20 hours a week alone playing *Call of Duty*, an 18-year-old girl who spends a few minutes daily tending her crops in *Farmville*, and a 20-year-old who occasionally plays *Madden Football* with his friends.

In 2009, an Iowa State University study reported that one of ten video-gamers demonstrated addictive behaviors, finding that gaming affected school work, social development and family relationships. The study further identified *pathological players* as those who played around 24 hours a week. (Players in this group also had a much higher rate of ADD and ADHD diagnosis when compared with casual gamer groups.)

"What we mean by pathological use is that something someone is doing — in this case, playing video games — is damaging to their functioning. It's not simply doing it a lot. It has to harm functioning in multiple ways."

~ Douglas Gentile
Science Daily

Do Violent Games Beget Violence?

One of the biggest concerns about video games is that some games, particularly realistic warfare games, increase violent behavior. A 2000 study by the American Psychological Association found that violent video games increase aggressive thoughts, feelings and behavior. The study found that the impact of video games on aggression was much higher than the impact of watching violent television and movies because the video games allow the player to interact and become part of the violence.

According to psychologist Wendy Walsh, co-host of the syndicated TV show *The Doctors,* "[the issue stays in the] public awareness and debate because we keep having new, more violent, more interactive versions of violent video games coming into the marketplace. And the research is pretty conclusive that [violent games] are very dangerous for children and teenagers."

Walsh says some studies show a direct link between violent interactive games and increased aggressive behavior, thought and affect (acting in an intimidating way). Such games also act as a stimulant, increasing physiological arousal. They have also been correlated to a decrease in pro-social behavior, such as empathy and awareness of others' needs.

Assigning Blame for Violence

Other experts caution against blaming video games for violent acts.

"When some tragic event happens or something surprising or important happens, our society's initial reaction is always to find a cause to pin whatever it was that happened on something else. I would say that recently, video games have been a particularly handy punching bag for a lot of that. You could just as easily say, 'Hey this person did the shooting, and he read books, as well'."

~ Jose Zagal
DePaul University College of Computing and Digital Media

Zagal also says it's possible that people who are predisposed to violent behavior seek out violent video games. "If there's someone who's really into gory movies, and happens to also be a psychopathic criminal, the question is whether that person is drawn to gory movies because they are a psychopathic criminal, or are those violent movies somehow strengthening his psychopathy?"

In short, it's important to consider the context in which even violent games are played, and to remember that the spectrum of games ranges from *Dora the Explorer* to *Mortal Kombat.* As such, it's impossible to make a blanket statement that all video games increase violence.

Social Impact of Gaming

When people think of kids and video games, they often picture an adolescent boy sitting by himself and playing for hours. Dean Lorraine Branham of the S.I. Newhouse School at Syracuse University expands that negative image to include interconnected gamers: "active gamers may be connected but disenfranchised. There's something anti-social in the way some of them consume gaming media and the messaging they get from games that espouse violence, misogyny and other anti-social behaviors. I find it troubling."

Social Benefits of Gaming

However, those concerns are becoming less troubling for others. Thanks to skyrocketing popularity, public awareness, and technology, today's game creators offer many opportunities for socialization. Many experts point out that the positive social impact of video gaming should not be ignored.

"People who play a lot of games tend to play them in a social context. They might be playing with friends in the same place, or they're playing alone for an hour or two, and then going to school and talking to their friends about what happened, how to solve a certain problem. Games are a form of culture, and they encourage sharing and communication."

~ Jose Zagal
DePaul University College of Computing and Digital Media

In his PBS article "Reality Bytes: Eight Myths About Video Games Debunked," MIT Professor Henry Jenkins writes that 60 percent of gamers play with friends and 33 percent play with siblings. Because today's game creators design many games for multiple players online, the opportunities for socialization have increased. Additionally, Jenkins writes that even when people take turns as single players within larger groups, the time spent cheering each other on and talking about the game is socially enhancing.

The popularity of Zynga games, such as *Words with Friends*, *Farmville* and *Mafia Wars*, has added another dimension to the social aspect of playing video games, because the focus is interacting with other people virtually through the game.

For example, in *Words with Friends* (estimated downloads: ten million plus) players increase their vocabularies while competing with friends through Facebook, tablets, computers and smart phones. One unexpected benefit of Zynga games and *Angry Birds* is that they appeal to all ages, from teens to seniors. Many parents and children enjoy playing the games together.

Games for Fun and Exercise

Another concern about video gaming is that children and teens may not get enough physical exercise because of the time they spend online. A June 2004 study published in *Obesity Research* showed a strong link between use of electronic games and obesity. According to a *WebMD* article about the study, every hour spent gaming doubled the risk of obesity for children.

Other people argue that the advent of active games, such as the Xbox and Nintendo Wii, decreases the risk of obesity associated with video gaming. When playing active Wii and Xbox games such as bowling and golf, players move their bodies as they would if they were playing the actual game. Other games, such as the Wii Fit system, are specifically for exercising. Occupational therapists use Wii for patients of all ages. And like some other games, the Wii and similar active games can help improve eye-hand coordination.

Realistically, however, the fitness benefits aren't equal to playing basketball all afternoon or running around a soccer field or a tennis court. There is still valid concern about video games taking the place of outdoor activities.

Brain Drain or Brain Booster?

Early video games may have been "brain drains," but today's market includes many educational games such as *Who Wants to Be a Millionaire, Big Brain Academy* and *Are You Smarter Than a Fifth Grader?*

An interesting study published in *Computers and Human Behavior* (2011) found that playing video games increased children's creativity — even when the games weren't specifically marketed as educational. Other studies tout the benefits of games that teach perseverance and problem solving.

Where Does the Time Go?

As mentioned earlier, a key concern is the amount of time children spend playing games and how it affects their time for other activities. In 2008, The American Academy of Pediatrics (AAP) released guidelines stating that children should have no more than two hours total of screen time per day, i.e., total combined time spent on video games, computers and television.

A recent AAP press release states that screen time — including television and child games — has no benefits whatsoever for infants and toddlers.

This seems doubtful.

Any parent with an iPad or iPhone and a toddler can tell you how quickly the child learns to navigate a television screen or even an app or two. Trying to eliminate or restrict access to screens seems pointless and perhaps even likely to hamper a child's development and ability to adapt to the Internet Age.

The argument that any screen time does children no good at all is not only moot, but absurd. Computers, online games, social media and television are advancing children's learning and creativity in unprecedented ways.

Conclusion: Gaming at a Crossroads

Despite the many studies and opinions on the impact of video games on young people, there are too many variables to make a definitive statement about whether the impact of video games is good or bad. Internet Pioneers and Internet Natives are likely to spend more and more time engaged with gaming media. As interactive television takes off, with two and even three linked screens, interest in interactive games will increase.

Virtual gaming activities will also become a norm for Internet Natives. Forty-three percent of Internet Pioneer gamers purchase game-related virtual goods using virtual currencies. In 2011 the global virtual gaming goods and currencies business was valued at 13 billion dollars. Facebook is discovering that one of its primary growth businesses is running a virtual gaming economy: controlling, managing (and hopefully not manipulating) the value of multiple virtual currencies.

Currently males are far more likely to purchase virtual goods, but females are catching up quickly. An interesting side-note: among those Internet Pioneer gamers who do *not* currently purchase virtual goods, 80 percent say they would do so if it were possible to earn virtual currencies by watching commercials during online games.

Educators and psychologists can and will debate the merits and problems related to gaming, but it's more valuable to focus on the reality. Gaming is already part of young people's lifestyles. Censorship and aggressive content controls, whether they be parental or governmental, will be a misdirected effort.

To put this in perspective, many arguments against gaming could be applied to any activity that becomes addictive for a small segment of the population. A passionate stamp collector who spends hours with a magnifying glass, stamp books and searching on eBay could be described as anti-social.

Growing pains are inevitable as Internet Generations integrate their native games into their culture. Internet Pioneers *are* active gamers. They are also the most socialized and possibly the most well-adjusted generation in history. They are the best educated and, according to several studies, the least violent in history. They are prepared for the challenges and opportunities that lie ahead.

Chapter 15:
Children of 9/11

Is it any wonder Internet Pioneers are immersing themselves in television programs, videos, music and games? They are not only the first generation to grow up with the Internet, but they are also the first generation to have been emotionally defined by 9/11. The single most significant event in defining the hopes, fears, behaviors and attitudes of Internet Pioneers happened on September 11, 2001.

Eighty-three percent of 17- to 21-year-olds have personal memories of that fateful day, according to the Myers Study of Internet Pioneers.

9/11 and the decade of war and divisiveness that have followed were incredibly life-altering for Internet Pioneers. The differences between those who recall and do not recall 9/11 proved far more significant and relevant than the more typical differences based on age, region, ethnic heritage or personal beliefs.

Every analysis of our study proved conclusively that 9/11 has had a meaningful effect on the beliefs, media consumption, opinions, plans and attitudes of a generation. 9/11 was a traumatic day for Internet Pioneers — one that has resonated throughout their lives and remains the psychological foundation of many of their attitudes.

It's logical to assume that the differences in attitudes among those who recall and do not recall 9/11 are caused by conditions other than their recollection of the tragic day... conditions such as ethnic heritage, economic circumstances, geographic location, politics or even gender. But a thorough review of the data proves that, while there are examples where these other factors also play a role, the recollection of 9/11 stands alone as a defining day in Internet Pioneers' lives that has and will continue to have lasting influence in almost every sphere of their existence.

The long-term effect of 9/11 on society, politics, business and relationships truly cannot be measured in a survey, but we can conclude that the role and influence of 9/11 on this generation — and therefore on the long-term future of our country — are meaningful in ways that cannot be easily measured or defined.

More Politically Engaged, Progressive and Global

Internet Pioneers are far more likely to be politically engaged and progressive when they recall the events of 9/11. Forty-three percent of those who recall 9/11 define themselves as liberal/progressive/moderate compared to only 28 percent of those who do not recall the events. Conservatives capture 19 and 13 percent, respectively. Twenty-five percent of those who recall 9/11 claim no political persuasion versus 45 percent of those who do not recall it.

Seventy-eight percent of those who recall 9/11 definitely plan on voting in the 2012 Presidential election, with an additional 12 percent possibly voting. Among those who do *not* recall 9/11, only 51 percent plan to vote.

Forty-two percent of "recallers" believe it's important that the United States continue its current overseas commitments but get out soon, compared to 30 percent of those who do not recall 9/11. Fifteen percent vs. 9 percent favor maintaining a military presence indefinitely, suggesting that the continuing war commitment may have a greater importance to the 2012 elections and beyond than assumed, at least among Internet Pioneers.

Fifty percent of those who recall 9/11 have traveled multiple times outside the United States, compared to only 26 percent of those who do not have personal memories of 9/11.

More Social and Connected

Internet Pioneers who recall 9/11 are more social and connected. Sixty-four percent of the 17- to 21-year-olds who recall 9/11 have more than two hundred Facebook "friends," compared to 53 percent of those who do not recall it. Those who personally recall 9/11 are 15 percent more likely to use check-in apps and to post videos to YouTube. Forty-seven percent versus 34 percent of them are Twitter users.

Chapter 16:
Around the World with Internet Pioneers

Internet Pioneers are more globally oriented, with a spirit of solidarity toward cultures that previously may have been perceived as too far away or too different. The Internet Generation does not embrace a partitioned world, reflecting the open nature of the Internet. Sixty-eight percent of Internet Pioneers say they want to travel internationally for a significant amount of time, and many of them will fulfill that wish, making global friends and associations that will last a lifetime thanks to Facebook, LinkedIn and other social media.

Most colleges and universities encourage their students to spend a semester abroad; high school travel programs are available through myriad youth groups, religious organizations, and private tour programs. A growing percentage of Internet Pioneers have capitalized on these opportunities, the first generation to be truly global in their understanding and relationships.

Ali Nelson, a self-described frequent flyer and college student, is not exactly sure what she wants to do with her life but when asked about her goals she was sure of one thing. "I know for sure that I want to travel around the world and live in various countries for a while. My goal is to be as cultured as possible and to use that in daily life."

Rasa Levickaitė, of Vilnius Gediminas Technical University in Lithuania, argues that Digital Natives, due to the proliferation of social networking, perceive their world as one without time and space limitations. "They are growing up faster. They are in education earlier. They are being exposed to marketing younger. This Internet-savvy, technologically literate generation has been shaped to multi-task. They move quickly from one task to another, placing more value on speed than accuracy. They have only known this wireless, hyperlinked, user-generated world where they are always only a few clicks from any piece of knowledge." Levickaitė observes that Internet Natives utilize the Internet and social networking to forge global connections more than their older counterparts do.

Keith Dugdale, director of global recruitment at KPMG, agrees that Digital Natives may be more attuned to global social issues than they are commonly given credit for. "Having grown up with a raft of anti-discrimination and pro-family legislation, it is to be hoped that [they will] be more diversity-aware."

Internet Pioneers are more likely to have friends from other cultures and countries than previous generations, many of them having grown up in integrated and ethnically balanced school environments and viewing fully integrated television programs. Although there is not much hard data available, it seems safe to infer that this early multicultural exposure has influenced their views on various social issues. They are likely to take a progressive point of view on immigration, less likely to agree with protectionist policies and more likely to favor policies that assure normalized and healthy relationships and open trade with nations around the globe.

Allen Vickers, a Penn State senior studying Broadcast Journalism, had this to say about America's ongoing immigration debate. "I don't think it's as bad as a lot of people say it is, but I think there are definitely problems. I have no problem you know, because America started off on immigrants. Legal immigration is fine. I don't mind anybody coming here that wants to make America a better place or make a better life for themselves." Ali Nelson simply believes "it has to be fair."

This desire for a fairer world isn't confined to immigration. Internet Pioneers are more at ease with other cultures than preceding generations. Their peer groups and social circles are more multicultural. This is the first generation since the 1950s that will have the opportunity to travel openly to Cuba, and South America will become a more important travel and business destination for them. They relate to China as a major economic force and political conundrum rather than a feared Communist enemy, and they have grown up with Asians of all cultures being an integrated part of American society.

When asked about their friends, all of the young people interviewed for this book stated that they had diverse groups of friends, and that race and ethnicity were not factors when choosing friends. Many Internet Pioneers speak languages other than English, many fluently, and they enjoy speaking to others on and offline in their native languages. Internet Pioneers pride themselves in the fact that they surround themselves with people who are culturally different. Some have dated members of other cultures in the past and do not view that as an especially significant fact.

Surprisingly, or perhaps not so, many Internet Pioneers are not well-informed on the Iraq and Afghanistan conflicts that have been raging for most, if not all of their lives. It's hard to determine if this is because the longstanding military conflicts are viewed as 'non-events' since they've been present throughout their lives, or if this is due to other factors. Ali Nelson feels the wars that have spanned her lifetime "should be a semester-long required college class to educate everyone."

Vickers supports the American troops but questions the longevity of the military conflict and the American presence on foreign soil. "Maybe we stayed over there too long. The kids over there grew up with an American presence and now we're leaving and they have to figure it out for themselves. I hope for the best for them. I really want the soldiers out of Afghanistan. It's like…okay…we should be leaving now. We're not helping them anymore by staying."

One possible reason for the dearth of knowledge some Internet Pioneers have when it comes to foreign affairs and war is their distrust of mainstream media. Nelson was blunt in her assessment of traditional media sources. "I don't trust it because it's all propaganda. When I do watch/listen/read it, I understand it's only been created this way to sell as much of it as possible. I don't take it seriously." Vickers, who credits Twitter as his primary news source (he follows journalists he respects from various news outlets) is similarly distrustful. "You can't just sit there and watch what Rush Limbaugh says or Wolf Blitzer. If you want to know anything about the complete story you have to research it yourself. You can get your news from anywhere but most news media have their own agenda. To me that was kind of made clear with the whole Penn State [athletic sex scandal] thing. They're reporting like it's the end of the world at Penn State and it wasn't. I was there the whole time and it wasn't. They all have their own agenda."

The Internet, a constant presence throughout their lives, will continue to be a powerful influence on Internet Pioneers. We can assume that their ease with other cultures, expanded social networks, and ingrained wanderlust will produce adults who move to wherever the jobs and opportunities are. They are a global generation that views diversity and equality as the norm, not an ideal to be fought for (and against) as it has been by previous generations.

Chapter 17:
Culture Jamming and Internet Memes

Culture jamming describes a tactic used by many anti-consumerist social movements to disrupt or subvert corporations and cultural institutions. Culture jams are intended to challenge the idea of "what's cool" and expose commercial culture by re-figuring logos, fashion statements, and product images. Culture jamming sometimes entails transforming mass media and advertising to produce ironic or satirical commentary.

Cultural jamming is also made successful by its ability to "resonate culturally across socio-economic and age groups as well as borders," reports Michele Micheletti and Dietlind Stolle in a *Cultural Studies* article, "Fashioning Social Justice through Political Consumerism, Capitalism, and the Internet."

Culture jamming's main tool is the Internet meme. Lance Bennett of the Center for Communication and Civic Engagement defines Internet memes as "condensed images that stimulate visual, verbal, musical, or behavioral associations that people can easily imitate and transmit to others." Beth Bulik of *Advertising Age* defines the meme as "any cultural information transmitted from one mind to another...something — an idea, art, person, joke, even advertising — goes from unknown to extremely popular very quickly."

The Internet meme is a force to be reckoned with. Whether it takes the form of a dancing cat or a college protest, the Internet meme is capable of changing the world. Until now, the meme has largely been derided as a procrastination tool for slacker college kids, but those very college students are working hard to challenge such unfounded stereotypes.

Internet memes can take the form of videos, pictures, hashtags, or even simple words and phrases. Memes have been a part of society for a long time, but their influence has only increased with the rise of the Internet. Social networking sites such as Facebook, Twitter and Tumblr allow users to share all kinds of content. Sometimes, a video or a picture will catch on with a small group of young Internet users. These users, often enrolled in college, recommend the content to others. Once in a while, this will spiral out of control, at which point the content officially reaches meme status.

Memes range from silly to spectacular, but all share one thing in common: a remarkable impact on the culture of students in high school and college. The attitudes and behaviors of many students have been shaped by prominent Internet memes. Memes are typically humorous or satirical but there are many examples of more serious Internet memes.

OWS: Occupy Wall Street

For example, the majority of Internet Pioneers understand the far-reaching impact of the meme #OWS, also known as the Twitter hashtag for the "Occupy Wall Street" movement. An Internet user needs only to type #OWS into a search engine to find a wealth of resources pertaining to "Occupy Wall Street" and associated protests in other locales. The "Occupy Wall Street" movement arguably would not have been a force to contend with had the movement not harnessed the power of social networking. No matter what their political leanings might be, most Internet users now know that #OWS signifies both the official "Occupy Wall Street" movement and the greater effort for social justice.

FWP: First World Problem

One of the more popular memes among Internet Pioneers is "First World Problem" (often referred to as FWP), which refers to "problems" experienced in Western society that seem trivial when compared to the prevalent issues in developing nations. The meme has been criticized for making light of a few real problems that really are worthy of attention (such as eating disorders), but it also demonstrates that today's young adults are aware of their privileged status and is an acknowledgement that the problems and issues confronting many in this generation pale by comparison to the problems faced by their counterparts in third world countries. The meme personifies the unique perspectives of Internet Pioneers who struggle with many of the same problems of older generations. But thanks to their global connectivity they are very aware that their challenges are insignificant compared to those in less fortunate circumstances.

Here are a few more memes that have been especially popular among Internet Pioneers:

Humorous/Cynical Cultural Memes

• **_Demotivational Posters:_** Most people have seen motivational posters with inspiring passages and pictures of people accomplishing amazing things. Demotivational Posters turn this concept on its head, instead depicting ridiculous pictures with even more ridiculous captions. For example, one popular demotivational poster shows an escalator leading up to the entrance of a fitness store. The caption? "Exercise: Welcome to America."

Although they are intended primarily for comic relief, the satirical element of demotivational posters also reveals what many college students view as the futility of the positive thinking industry. Ten years ago, young people were devoted to positive psychology. Today they feel that positive thinking is not the answer to all of life's problems.

• **_Tebowing:_** Every football season, there is some athlete who captures the attention of millions of fans and causes a media frenzy. For the 2011 football season, this player was Tim Tebow, the starting quarterback of the Denver Broncos (and now of the New York Jets). Tebow's unorthodox performance may have hit headlines, but the quarterback gained notoriety for displaying frequent expressions of his deep Christian faith. His habit of kneeling on one knee and praying during football games spurred an Internet meme known as "Tebowing." In this meme, students post pictures of themselves kneeling to pray in unusual locations, such as in the middle of a busy intersection or, in the case of several celebrities, on the red carpet. The intent of most students may be to poke fun at Tebow, but plenty of others express admiration at Tebow's unapologetic demonstration of faith.

• **_People of Walmart:_** Viewed as unbelievably offensive in some circles, the _People of Walmart_ meme involves goofy and sometimes disgusting pictures of the many people who shop at Walmart. A few highlights from the site include: a mug shot of a woman caught making meth in a Walmart, dozens of men and women sporting mullets, shoppers dressed in nothing but underwear and a minivan stacked with dead raccoons. Some college students view the _People of Walmart_ meme as an updated form of the redneck joke, while others point to it as a prominent display of long-standing stereotypes surrounding working-class people.

Serious Cultural Memes

- ***Lt. John Pike Pepper Spray Video:*** The "Occupy Wall Street" movement brought about a storm of reactions in the world of social networking. One video went viral almost immediately. The clip showed a policeman spraying students at close range during a UC Davis protest rally. What was especially significant about this video was the fact that the students were all lined up peacefully in a row. College students quickly got hold of photos of the policeman and photoshopped them to form satirical pictures. Examples include Lt. Pike pepper-spraying a baby seal, a kitten and even Obi-Wan Kenobi. In one interesting mix of memes, a student photoshopped Pike pepper-spraying a kneeling Tim Tebow.

- ***Weinergate:*** In another stunning mix of politics and viral Internet sensations, Congressman Anthony Weiner created a bitter legacy with a single lewd photo. Weiner intended to send the photo in a private message to a college student but it was subsequently Tweeted out for the world to see. Twitter users marked the resulting controversy with the hashtag #Weinergate. The term soon made it into the mainstream media and is now the chief means by which Americans refer to the scandal.

Marketing Meme

- ***Old Spice Commercial:*** Occasionally, a successful meme translates into commercial success for large companies. This was certainly the case in 2010, when Old Spice released a series of commercials starring Isaiah Mustafa. The campaign proved wildly successful, reviving Old Spice's place in the much sought-after eighteen to thirty demographic. According to KnowYourmeme.com, "In August 2011, Old Spice Guy was highlighted as part of G4's month-long popularity contest called MEMEFIGHT, featuring 32 Internet memes reviewed and selected by a special panel of Internet culture experts. Following a series of user-voting contests, Old Spice Guy took the victory in the final round against Demotivational Posters, once again reaffirming the impact of the marketing campaign."

Political Meme

- ***Obamagirl:*** As Barack Obama's presidential campaign started to gain momentum in 2007, a YouTube actress drew on the candidate's celebrity status among college students by starring in the music video "I've Got a Crush On Obama." In this video, the woman dances seductively in front of photos of then-Senator Obama, singing lyrics such as "Baby, you're the best candidate." The video was just one of many expressions of "Obama-mania" that took place on college campuses during the 2008 election campaign.

Nike Sweatshop and American Apparel Memes

Whether used as comic relief or a tool of social upheaval, Internet memes are capable of making some real changes in the world. The current generation of college students and recent graduates understands the significance of Internet memes and is prepared to harness that power for future endeavors.

In one of the most successful culture jamming memes to date, activist Jonah Perreti engaged in a series of email exchanges with a custom Nike website. Perreti wanted to customize a pair of Nike shoes to include the word "sweatshop" in hopes of calling attention to Nike's notorious use of sweatshop labor in third world countries. Nike's immediate refusal should come as no great surprise. What is surprising is the reaction spawned by Nike's response to Perreti's request. Perreti condensed all the email exchanges into one email, which he sent out to everyone in his email address book. Almost overnight, one simple email transformed into a huge viral email campaign, which then turned "quickly into mass media news and culture content, carrying with it questions about the limits of consumer freedom and the discomforts of making a fashion statement with expensive shoes made by child sweatshop labor."

Perreti was able to spread a compelling message over the Internet back in 2001, before Facebook and Twitter even existed. If he could alert the world to the injustices of sweatshop labor with a simple email, there's no saying what the current generation of college students can and will continue to accomplish with the help of social networking.

Recent examples of meme-infused culture jamming abound. In the summer of 2011, 24-year-old Nancy Upton made headlines with a series of photos that rose to stardom in American Apparel's plus-sized modeling contest. Dubbed the "Next Big Thing," the contest's supposed intent was to find "fresh faces" to star in a "bootylicious photo shoot."

Upton had no problem with the idea of plus-sized models in American Apparel's advertisements, but she did take issue with the patronizing attitude displayed in the clothing retailer's contest promotions. She retaliated with a series of racy pictures that showed her scantily clad while pigging out on ice cream, chocolate syrup, chicken wings, and cherry pie. Young women almost immediately launched the photos into viral status, sharing them with friends on Facebook and visiting American Apparel's website in droves.

Upton won the most votes hands down, but her victory was not recognized by American Apparel. This rejection only added fuel to the fire, as social network users continued to post the photos while voicing their opinions on the place of plus-sized models in today's society. The news media caught on and American Apparel found itself defending the controversial decision in front of legions of journalists and broadcasters.

The clothing retailer eventually gave in, later inviting Upton to company headquarters for a tour and a discussion about marketing to plus-sized women. Eager to make a positive change, Upton went on the trip, took the tour and talked with the executives. Upon her return, Upton still didn't feel that American Apparel was taking her (and other plus-sized women) seriously. She did, however, appreciate the fact that her activism provoked a national discussion that, arguably, would not have been possible without the help of millions of socially networked teens and young adults.

Chapter 18:
Internet Pioneers' SMS Language

It's called texting or SMSing (for Short Message Service), and chances are you're already using it. LOL, IDK, FML and WTF (Laughing Out Loud, I Don't Know, F*** My Life, and What the F***) are possibly the four top text messaging shorthand "words" to emerge into the American lexicon. Text messaging is, in essence, a language of its own. It requires learning and practice, like any other language, in order to communicate effectively and be understood. Many text abbreviations and 'words' share a common meaning and interpretation. Others continue to be added to the language by users. The most common texts described above may soon be overtaken by SMH (meaning Shaking My Head or Sex May Help); TBH (To Be Honest), and HMU (Hit Me Up).

It's not uncommon for groups of teenagers or college friends to develop their own text abbreviations as part of a secret code, decipherable only by members of their exclusive group. This enables them to send secret messages between each other without others being privy to what they are saying.

NetLingo and Urban Dictionary explain other popular text shorthand and remain the go-to-places for an answer to the latest WDTM (What Does That Mean) shorthand. The chart on the following page includes some favorite terms in current use.

Texting Dictionary — Favorite Terms

- ACORN — REALLY NUTTY PERSON

- ASL — AGE SEX LOCATION

- BABY — BEING ANNOYED BY YOU

- BHOF — BALD HEADED OLD FART

- BFF — BEST FRIENDS FOREVER

- BUMG — BARFING UP MY GUTS

- COO — COOL

- GAL — GET A LIFE

- GSOH — GOOD SALARY OWN HOME GOOD SENSE OF HUMOR

- HMU — HIT ME UP

- IDK — I DON'T KNOW

- IRL — IN REAL LIFE

- LOL — LAUGH OUT LOUD/LOTS OF LOVE

- NBD — NO BIG DEAL

- OMG — OH MY GOD

- PRW — PARENTS ARE WATCHING

- ROFL — ROLLING ON THE FLOOR LAUGHING

- SMH — SHAKING MY HEAD or SEX MAY HELP

- 10Q — THANK YOU

- TISNF — THAT IS SO NOT FAIR

- TMI — TOO MUCH INFORMATION

- TBH — TO BE HONEST

- WRU — WHERE ARE YOU

- s^ — WHAT'S UP

- ^5 — High five

- *$ — STARBUCKS

- ,!!!! — TALK TO THE HAND

Texting Habits of a Generation

Eighteen- to 24-year-olds spend more time texting — sending and receiving an average of 100 plus messages daily — than they spend on almost any other activity. That's just shy of 40,000 texts per person, per year, a number that is more than double the comparable figure for 25- to 34-year-olds, and 23 times the figure for text messaging users who are 65 or older.

Just over one in ten 18- to 24-year-olds say that they send or receive more than 200 messages on an average day — that equals 6,000 or more messages per month or a whopping 72,000 in a year.

Less Talking, More Texting

According to the 2011 *Pew Research Study on Americans and Text Messaging*, active text messengers are much more likely to prefer texting to calling.

Along with the increased use of texting, Internet Pioneers have become phone adverse. Making a simple phone call to request information, place an order, deal with a conflict or even speak to a friend or parent can be an exercise in futility. The trend extends beyond U.S. borders and includes places like Japan and Hong Kong, where mobile technology has been more advanced and texting became the norm for young people several years ago. According to the Pew Research study, text messaging and taking photos are the most common non-voice applications Americans use on their mobile phones. However, the use of texting is surpassing the use of voice calls among the Internet Native generation, and the trend appears to be growing among other age groups.

Texting: Not So New

Text messaging has been in common use for decades. The use of abbreviated texts is common in hundreds of disciplines, including medicine, science, business and the military. The first "FYI" probably adorned a business memo more than a century ago. Some of these common terms have become so embedded in our day-to-day language that their actual meaning has been lost, but everyone knows their intended meaning. Examples include RSVP for "Répondez S'il Vous Plaît" and SOS for "Save Our Souls."

The Study of Texting

The study of texting has existed longer than you might think. In fact, this field is already 20 years old, with volumes of research in various linguistic sub-fields. Computer Mediated Communication (CMC) is a new offshoot of the field. Noted linguist Susan C. Herring (Indiana University), defines CMC as "Text-based interactive communication via the Internet, websites and other multimodal formats, including mobile communication." Currently, most scholastic research doesn't consider CMC (computer-mediated communication) as "writing." However, as texting becomes a more prominent form of communication (and as voice-assisted writing gains accuracy), researchers may need to redefine traditional views of "writing."

Study Results: Gender Differences

In terms of gender differences in texting, research was done in a number of countries including Norway, where teenage girls and young adults text most frequently. Their messages were both greater in number, longer and more syntactically complex. Fifty-two percent of Norwegian girls' text messages contained complex sentence structures compared to 15 percent of the boys' text messages. A similar German study indicated these broad differences between girls and boys are common. Girls are more likely to place emphasis on emotional exchanges, contemplate reasons behind interpersonal incidents and discuss, through text language, how incidents have affected them. Boys, however, typically place greater emphasis on speed; their messages tend to be brief, informative and practical.

Texting: A Negative Influence?

Outspoken opponents of text messaging include Steve Pain of the *Birmingham Post* and BBC Radio journalist John Humphrys. They believe texting language has devastating effects on grammar, sentence structure, spelling and vocabulary. In his comments on SMSing, Humphrys demeans "textese" as promoting lazy and sloppy English language habits that hinder students from learning proper punctuation and grammar.

Many educators tend to agree with these findings, believing that the text language system contributes to a decrease in interpersonal skills among teenagers and young college students.

The new text language also raises some concerns about writing skills. On the college level, writing requires the use of correct grammar, punctuation and spelling, all nonessential in the world of texting. Some educators worry that text messaging hinders the development of important skills including creative writing, essay writing, the ability to express personal viewpoints, and many others.

In some schools, the criticism of text language began when text slang began to appear in assignments and exams. This was a natural byproduct of texting as an integral part of students' lives, indicating a need for students to learn the appropriate times and places for using this language.

Texting: Positive Aspects

In contrast to the criticism, some studies show positive aspects of the new text language.

Francis Katamba, professor of Linguistics at Lancaster University, expressed his belief that texting is a means of enriching modern-day communications by stimulating the thought processes. Professional linguist and author David Crystal expressed positive findings in his research report *Txtng: the Gr8 Db8*. Crystal concluded that SMS language did not promote a lower literacy rate nor did it cause bad spelling among those who used it. On the contrary, he pointed out that text messaging could actually improve young people's literacy rates due to providing greater opportunity to practice their reading and writing skills.

Crispin Thurlow and Michael Poff of the University of Washington. point out that "…most empirical studies maintain that texting does not pose a threat to standard English teaching and learning….Although there may be some diffusion of texting style into 'formal' writing (e.g. school work), texters almost always recognize that language is context specific."

Young people are inherently aware of key pragmatic considerations such as context, relationship and communicative intent in their writing, finding creative ways to be even more expressive through text language than they are able to be with traditional words and sentence structure. Research also suggests that the creativity of texting poses little threat to spelling. Tools such as automated spell checks have already decreased concerns about spelling literacy in real-world writing activities, and this trend is likely to continue.

Beyond Texting

New voice-aided Artificial Intelligence (AI) technologies, such as Apple's Siri and Google's Chrome platform, will need to adapt to texting and understand requests made using the shortened language.

Of course, texting may find itself usurped with a life cut short, or at best, sidelined, much as radio was overshadowed by television. Texting language may ultimately prove to be a communications skill unique to the first generations to grow up in an Internet world.

Future generations will continue to develop communications technology designed to optimize voice recognition. But even future voice recognition with its AI boost reaching very high accuracy levels has a flaw — lack of privacy — so a combination of texting for interpersonal communications and enhanced voice messaging for search queries is likely to evolve.

Farfetched as it may seem, future generations will be empowered with cognitive input and may merely have to think to generate messages on a holographic display. There is always new technology waiting in the wings to advance the state of communications.

Into the Future

Beyond the academic, what can we make of our emerging text language and the current crop of college age (and younger) practitioners? Are they gaining efficiency of communication at the expense of sentence structure, knowledge of grammar and basic writing skills? And more importantly, will this new communication style impact how this generation thinks, writes and communicates beyond texting?

Chapter 19:
Impact of Wikis, Wikipedia and WikiLeaks

User-generated content is all around us, from Wikipedia to WikiLeaks, from comments on Yelp to the Huffington Post and your average, everyday blogger. It's the world we live in, the air we breathe, the culture that surrounds us. The ability to instantaneously self-publish writing, photos and videos has become commonplace — both in the U.S. and throughout the world.

The result has been a boon for free speech, education and communication, even as it has raised issues regarding security, privacy and verifiability.

A Brief History of the Wiki and Wikipedia

Wikis are named after "wiki wiki," the Hawaiian word for "quick," and they officially date back to 1995. Ward Cunningham, a Smalltalk developer, created the first wiki, *The Portland Pattern Repository*, as part of his company's website. The wiki improved communication between software developers discussing programs and identifying software patterns.

That first wiki is still active, and includes over thirty thousand pages. As with all wikis since, it had the hallmark feature of pages that could be edited within a browser. The concept was simple yet revolutionary: allow multiple users to edit or add to a site, and enable them to see what others added.

Wikis are used for a variety of projects and purposes: companies can create collaborative wikis to enable managers around the world to work together on programs, proposals and initiatives; teachers use wikis so students can collaborate on projects; and co-authors use wikis to write books together.

Wikis and Wiki-Like Sites

In fact, wikis and wiki-like sites have become ubiquitous in our daily lives. Even social networking sites such as Facebook and LinkedIn have a wiki-ish quality. On these sites, people can contribute to the content of their friends' walls and collaborate to create what social media experts call an "ambient awareness" of each other's doings, as discussed in a 2008 article by Clive Thompson in *The New York Times,* "Brave New World of Digital Intimacy." The comment function common in blogs, news articles and social media is modeled on the wiki world as well, since "comments" enable users to participate in the processing and delivery of content.

In 2001, Wikipedia, the online encyclopedia of everything, was launched, and since then it has garnered much acclaim and become one of the most-visited sites on the web. In 2011, Wikipedia raised twenty million dollars in funding support directly from the site's users, testifying to the value it offers to a large and passionately connected user-base. Due in part to Wikipedia's success, today there are thousands of public — and private — wiki sites.

Wiki Tools

There are a variety of tools available for people wanting to start their own wikis. Some, like PBworks, are geared toward corporations wanting to facilitate communication between employees. Others, such as Wikispaces and Google Docs, offer free individual wiki hosting for small groups. Even blog hosting companies, such as Wordpress.com, provide blog options that allow for multiple users and editable websites.

This use of wikis is mirrored in the corporate world, where private wikis are used to facilitate projects that may have players in many different parts of the world. For that matter, Google Docs allows editing by multiple parties and gives all of them instant access to the edits and changes of others. Wikis are ideal for recording conversations, debates and arguments among collaborators. Wikis are living documents, and they allow for a living, breathing discussion among participants while recording that discussion as part of the creating, editing and revising process.

WikiLeaks: Too Much Sharing?

There are downsides to wikis, however. For one thing, not everyone wants everything instantaneously shared.

Take WikiLeaks, for example. This site, founded in 2007, is devoted to publishing and sharing government and corporate secrets. It has come under fire for releasing documents and information that compromise military security. Numerous documents related to U.S. military actions and secrets have been published on the site, drawing the criticism of many who would like to see the site shut down or censored.

For its part, WikiLeaks defends its practices, saying on its site that its "goal is to bring important news and information to the public. We provide an innovative, secure and anonymous way for sources to leak information to our journalists (our electronic drop box). One of our most important activities is to publish original source material alongside our news stories, so readers and historians alike can see evidence of the truth."

This argument — that WikiLeaks is providing the truth — is a powerful one. In fact, the reason WikiLeaks has made commentators, government officials and corporate leaders so uneasy is that it *is* revealing the truth. And the truth can, potentially, endanger others: diplomats, the military, and national security.

WikiLeaks allows people to post information without providing any context or explanation, making it difficult for readers to interpret and understand it. Open access to information is appealing and, in many ways, is a hallmark of an open, democratic society. There are legitimate arguments to be made, however, for protecting national security.

In the court case against Army Pfc. Bradley Manning, accused of posting secret documents on WikiLeaks, defense attorneys argued that the fact that these documents were available revealed lax security measures on the part of the military. WikiLeaks raises questions about who has access to what, and how it should be publicized. Wikileaks illustrates how informational wikis have changed more quickly than the laws that might regulate them.

Within these limited parameters, however, the possibilities and promise of wikis are almost endless.

Wikis and Education

Security breaches and political battles aside, wikis are dramatically transforming education. They provide an ideal platform for sharing and collaboration. Teachers are using them to facilitate learning in and outside of the classroom. Wikis will help a new generation of students learn how to work together and increase their productivity.

Educational wikis differ from sites like Wikipedia in that participation is limited to a private group or community. The group then uses the wiki for a pre-determined purpose or project. Only group members can edit and share the information on the wiki.

Wikis and Citizen Journalism

Journalism has experienced the greatest impact from user-generated content and the wiki revolution. The availability and accessibility of wiki-like platforms for reporting the news has transformed how journalism is practiced, who practices it, and why.

News organizations realize that everyone who carries a cell phone can, in some way, report unfolding news. As a result, many organizations have designed platforms specifically for capturing this content.

CNN, for instance, has iReport, which allows users to upload their videos, pictures and stories about ongoing or breaking news events. CNN describes this service as follows: "iReport is an invitation for you to be a part of CNN's coverage of the stories you care about and an opportunity to be a part of a global community of men and women who are as passionate about the news as you are."

Other news organizations have followed suit, calling for news tips, stories, photos, audio files, blogs and other content from users.

The Yahoo! Contributor Network (Y!CN) is a growing platform that publishes content from users including freelance journalists, business owners, wine experts and many more. The Y!CN model, unlike CNN's iReport, also pays users for their content.

Curating and Controlling Wiki-Content

Nevertheless, legitimate news organizations cannot simply publish or broadcast anything that comes along. If a news organization is going to stamp its brand on content, the content needs to be verified and curated. Curating involves controlling, filtering, shaping and distributing content. Curation of user-generated content has become key to using and distributing this content responsibly.

Wikipedia is an example of how curating has grown out of an early wiki model: many people have specific Wikipedia entries they watch, ready to fix or edit anything that is erroneously changed in those entries.

New models of journalism will need more stringent gatekeepers, professionals who will sort through the content, decide what gets published, what gets featured and what gets removed. After all, contributors aren't necessarily equipped with the skills to report or package news or other content. CNN's iReport staff curates when it decides what videos to endorse, highlight and feature on its site.

News content also needs to be put into context — blurry cell phone videos of riots and audio recordings of meetings are often meaningless on their own.

There is a fine line between curating and censorship, but that has always been the case in publishing.

Wikis and Marketing

Businesses are publishing and distributing user-generated content as their primary content. Sites like Yelp rely almost entirely on the reviews submitted by users. Other sites, like Kaboodle, combine social networking with user-generated content. The site encourages users to post information about their entertainment choices and purchases, find and compare merchandise, and network with other shoppers.

In fact, all social networking sites, from Facebook to Flickr, rely on content created by and shared between users. Though users generally can't change each other's content, as they can in a true wiki model, the contributors do influence other users with the content they post and distribute.

Just as Internet Pioneers expect their friends, relatives and colleagues to be engaged proactively on social networks and in interactive wikis, they also expect the opportunity to be engaged with business colleagues, marketers, retailers and governmental agencies.

Wikis and Business

As Internet Pioneers enter the workforce, they will bring with them an understanding of social engagement and wikis and will begin integrating them more and more into the day-to-day processes and operations of their employers.

Wikis will emerge not only as a tool for communicating with customers, but will become a required component of the human resources management of companies large and small. Employee and executive wikis will enable active communications among teams and whole workforces. Auto assembly plants will have their own quality control wikis and auto companies will have a wiki for all employees. Wikis of auto dealers will enable best practices to be shared and consumer complaints to be addressed quickly. Wikis for owners of specific auto models will allow owners to voice complaints easily and will assure that auto companies cannot hide these complaints as they have done in the past.

Whistle-blowing remains an offense in most corporate and governmental cultures today, with whistle-blowers often being discredited and fired from their jobs. In the case of WikiLeaks' founder Julian Assange, whistle-blowers can become internationally wanted criminals. But in the evolving wiki-centric culture, whistle-blowing will be a day-to-day reality that enables individuals to openly voice their concerns within a community. Individuals will be safe from retribution when their concerns are supported (or voted down) by the community. Involved parties will have an opportunity to respond quickly. Organizations need to establish wikis and social connections among their employees and teams or have the networks forced upon them by employees who develop them. There are no restrictions or costs to prevent anyone from establishing a wiki and socializing it to small and large groups.

In the 20th century, society shifted from an unconnected series of small communities in which everyone knew everyone else's business to a disconnected world in which societies and organizations could control the flow of information to and from their members. Wikis are a powerful force for returning communities to an interconnected web of shared knowledge and common interests.

Wikification of the World

New applications for wiki-like applications will further enable sharing, editing, curating, commenting and socializing. Internet Pioneers and Internet Natives will quickly adopt these applications into their work and personal lives. Applications including user-created and curated content will be a normal part of decision-making as Internet Pioneers depend increasingly on recommendation engines, curated user-generated content, and socialized content for their news, information, shopping, entertainment and day-to-day decision-making.

Internet Pioneers will be leaders in developing and implementing wikis and social networks within companies, non-profits, governmental agencies, global societies, religious congregations, schools and classrooms, fan clubs and associations. Wikis will become ubiquitous as a basic communication resource for building links among people with common interests and enabling them to share their perspectives and points of view, while at the same time enabling immediate feedback from others within their wiki community.

To Internet Pioneers, wikis are more than another source of information and knowledge. The great challenge will be to introduce these tools to older generations who have grown up in a world in which privacy of information — whether personal, corporate or governmental — has been a right.

Of all the applications that have emerged from the Internet, wikis may prove to be the most important and influential in impacting almost every aspect of society — from the individual and family unit to governments and global relationships. The ability to freely gather and communicate information is an awe-inspiring freedom that we have only begun to understand, deal with and integrate into our lives.

Chapter 20:
Jobs and Careers

Internet Pioneers have grown up with the expectation — both theirs and their parents — that they will readily find jobs and earn good salaries when they graduate from college. They've come to expect instant gratification, instant access to information and instant feedback from friends, teachers, parents and employers. They are now confronted with a new reality — a job market that is not offering the universal acceptance and instant gratification they have come to expect.

According to a 2011 *New York Times* article, employment rates for recent college grads fell in 2009 and 2010. They fell again in 2011, along with starting salaries for those able to find jobs. Less than half of the jobs these graduates find require a college degree — leaving these workers with student loans to pay off on low wages previously paid to high school graduates.

High school graduates are finding it even more difficult. And, as military veterans return from Iraq and Afghanistan, government and private programs will support and assist them, creating an even more challenging job market for college graduates for several years.

What's the Future?

In November 2011, at Bob Jones University campus in Greenville, South Carolina, a group of Internet Pioneers discussed their views about the Internet and the impact that the current financial climate and economic outlook will have on their job searches when they graduate.

"I don't know exactly what I'm going to end up doing, but it won't have anything to do with my major," said Mary Coleman, a 21-year-old Journalism and Mass Communication major from Spartanburg, SC. Mary studied communications and professional writing and graduated a semester early with honors. But her prospects upon graduation weren't great, so she began the paperwork required to attend Officer Candidate School and is now working toward becoming an officer in the Navy. "My internships and coursework during college were great, but I still don't have the experience most companies want," Mary said. "At least I know there's a future in the military." English major Elizabeth Rogers agreed. "I'm graduating. To what? Can't be sure. I guess I'll need to figure out what's next."

The resounding cry from Internet Pioneers is *What will I do next?* They are accustomed to a lifestyle they can't finance with the kind of entry-level jobs available to those right out of college or even a few years beyond college.

"A degree isn't enough," said Karissa Kincaid, a junior majoring in professional writing. "You can't just be good…you have to have a shining resume, a load of talent, and all the right connections to get a good job out of college. The rest of us…well, I know I'm going to have to take what I can get out of college and work towards my long-term goals."

Doubling Up on Work and Study

More than 60 percent of current college students are already working at jobs to pay college costs. Slightly more than 50 percent intend to get a job immediately after graduation, while 30 percent intend to go to graduate school. Only 7 percent intend to "take time off," and 10 percent have no plan for their future. Students recognize that their graduation will coincide with a challenging employment market and limited job availability. Sixty percent of current college students believe it will be more difficult to get a job in the future than it is now. Only 14 percent believe it will be easier.

When it comes to their future, 40 percent of Internet Pioneers say they are optimistic about the future of their age group. Twenty-three percent say they are pessimistic. Looking forward to when they and their classmates are 30- to 35-years-old, only 23 percent say they expect their generation will be having a meaningful and important impact on political, business and social issues, while 40 percent say they will be having some impact. On the pessimistic side, 21 percent believe they and their classmates will have little meaningful impact.

Rather than complaining or protesting, students are doubling up on their academic efforts, participating in internships and building networks.

When asked to describe their ideal jobs or to define their vision of a successful life, not one of the interviewed students mentioned money. Several experts believe that high salaries will be less relevant as mortgages, bank loans and even car ownership lose their value as a way to maintain status among friends. This may be true, but it's also possible that salary won't motivate Internet Pioneers regardless of their economic future.

"…for many people, [the inability to secure mortgages] may be as empowering as Generation X thought home ownership was. As long as there is a plentiful supply of rental accommodation, it's possible that the expectation of vast salaries, as well as the intense pressure to perform, may give way to a less frantic and more fulfilling type of working life."

~ Richard Doherty
Sales Director, Jobpartners Talent Consultancy

In fact, several Internet Pioneers interviewed for this book had similar answers when asked what constitutes success. Their responses mentioned helping other people, making a lasting difference, and solving problems — not hefty paychecks and astronomical bonuses. Despite his worry of sounding clichéd, journalism major Allen Vickers agrees.

"[Success is] being able to realize that what you've done in your life has touched a lot of people. Romeo Brown hosts a blog titled, 'You measure success by how many people you bless.' And that always stuck with me. When I get older I want my messages to reach people. It's not about money as much as knowing that I've helped somebody become a more positive person. I mean money would be awesome — don't get me wrong — but that's not the measuring stick."

~ Allen Vickers
Student

The key to understanding Internet Pioneers' attitudes toward big business and employment is to understand this generation's definition of success. For Internet Pioneers, the definition of success is not simply accumulating wealth. In fact, some are actively hostile toward this definition. Many Internet Pioneers aren't motivated by the same things as earlier generations were. Accumulating money isn't enough to keep them focused on repetitive or non-challenging tasks or in jobs they find unfulfilling or ethically unrewarding.

So what motivates this generation? They seek variety in responsibility, social engagement and collaboration, relevance, and a knowledge that they are contributing to something larger than themselves or the business they work for. *The Reflexive Generation,* a report by the London Business School's Centre for Women in Business, notes that a misunderstanding about attitudes toward wealth could be key to the perception that Millennials have little work ethic.

Cautious Corporate Relationships

Baby Boomers gained a detailed and visually graphic knowledge of the Vietnam War by watching television. Internet Pioneers, on the other hand, have had continual exposure to the economic collapse of the United States and the global economic crisis. They've witnessed corporate and government dishonesty and mismanagement — from "Too Big to Fail" to auto industry bailouts, Congressional battles over tax cuts, and 99 percent vs. the 1 percent. They have watched the "Occupy Wall Street" movement grow. They've witnessed the trend of outsourcing jobs to third-world countries with cheap labor, partnered with attacks on U.S. labor unions and their longstanding role and value for American workers.

Internet Pioneers have viewed the "perp-walks" of high-profile executives who mismanaged or cheated stockholders out of billions of dollars. They've been exposed throughout their lives to highly publicized economic scams, from Enron to Bernie Madoff. Pioneers are well aware of the gap between the middle class and the most wealthy business owners and stockholders, and they see the political battles between change and status quo.

Is it any wonder that Internet Pioneers are wary of big business?

Yet the wariness runs both ways. Corporations are also cautious. Some business experts expect a crisis of human resource management when Internet Pioneers enter the workplace. Consulting firms like Kelly Staffing and Red Tree offer training modules that assume the Millennial applicant is an outspoken, bold thinker who is highly proficient technologically, but who also has an inflated sense of self-worth and lacks manners and social skills.

Millennials, according to Jordan Kaplan, professor in Managerial Science at the Long Island University Business School, are unlikely to respond well to the almost military, top-down command structure of most big businesses. Internet Natives have grown up questioning authority and with a sense of their own competence, empowerment and responsibility. Reasons for this include years of watching Nickelodeon with its model of "questioning everything," and parenting styles that favored treating children more like peers than children.

The empowerment and sense of self that is evident in the actions of Internet Pioneers is a double-edged sword in the corporate world and often misperceived by many old-school managers. On the down side, older co-workers and managers perceive this age group as demanding, entitled, and unwilling to abide by the traditional structure of rank and authority within a business. Corporations may feel they have to nudge Internet Pioneers to be productive and to operate within the organization's guidelines. Other barriers include the Internet Pioneer mistrust of big business and lack of corporate loyalty.

However, their sense of empowerment gives Internet Pioneers two advantages when working with and within big business.

Advantage of the Front-Row Seat

Growing up with constant Internet access has given Internet Pioneers a "front-row" view of people with no extraordinary connections achieving real and important success and communicating it effectively. Whether they're looking at the rise of a simple Internet meme, or watching hours of TEDTalks, this age group understands and has internalized human potential in a way previous generations couldn't. Furthermore, they've freely commented in response to professional news gathering organizations, corporate blogs, and op-ed columnists. They are equals online and expect their voices and opinions to be acknowledged and heard in corporate boardrooms as well.

This sense of empowerment extends to the arts, education, medicine and other areas where decision-making has been closed and hierarchical.

This has also affected the jobs of reviewers and critics of the arts, travel, restaurants, etc., as anyone with an Internet connection can comment on his or her own experience and offer recommendations. Today's consumers are relying more on these critiques than on the advice of professionals.

Social sites such as Pinterest offer a new form of response and criticism. Users "pin" images that appeal to them, and other users have the option of re-pinning or commenting on those pins. Facebook and Twitter empower opinions on just about any subject. This interactive form of criticism and response will continue to grow as Internet Pioneers, who perceive this as a normal part of the critical process, gain prominence in the arts and business.

The Advantage of Open Minds

The second advantage of empowerment applies primarily to minorities among Internet Natives. Web anonymity means previously defining characteristics such as race, gender, sexual orientation, appearance, age, etc. are not known. As a result, individuals are judged on the quality of their ideas and their willingness to put them out there, and little else. For example, the lack of preconceived ideas about their age has helped Internet Pioneers to achieve success in web publishing and starting Internet-based movements or enterprises. A corollary to this second advantage is a noted lack of prejudice among this age cohort. Growing up in an environment where such things are of secondary — if any — importance has given Internet Pioneers open minds. This acceptance can only improve their performance in the workplace, enhance diversity and improve corporate capabilities for embracing the growing multicultural consumer population.

Traditional organizational models in the corporate world are breaking down in the socially interconnected Internet-based environment — and Internet Pioneers are very comfortable ignoring these structures and the hierarchical barriers that distance senior management from their newest colleagues. If you want to connect with a customer's CEO, your youngest employee may prove more competent at getting access than an experienced middle — or even senior — manager. The challenge is making sure he or she is prepared with the right message when the CEO reads and responds to his or her LinkedIn or Facebook message.

More and more, experienced executives trained in traditional corporate models will need to fast-track Internet Pioneers into responsible corporate roles. Older executives will find value in partnerships with Internet Pioneers who are tech-savvy at a level previous generations don't begin to approach.

By combining their social networking sophistication and their ability to telecommute and access information globally, Internet Pioneers will lead a movement toward corporate collaboration at an unprecedented level.

Expertise at Multitasking and Social Media

Courteous body language and respect for social mores relating to communication with senior colleagues are skills easily addressed through training. Internet Pioneers bring a different kind of social skill to the table. These young adults have grown up accessing chat rooms and social networks where they routinely communicate with peers from all over the world. They are experts at multitasking complex conversations through multiple modes of media. Examples include the ease with which they upload videos to YouTube, create podcasts and maintain multiple text conversations while doing homework.

Internet Pioneers reflect a paradigm shift in the way people and organizations will collaborate and communicate in the future. Internet Pioneers are experts at communicating in their particular idiom. Put in charge of projects where this idiom is an asset, as most projects will be into the foreseeable future, they can outperform older colleagues despite any perceived shortcomings in other communication arenas.

It's true Internet Pioneers will enter the corporate world and accept jobs in health, education, energy and other fields with a perspective and attitude different from that of previous generations. They bring to the workplace a set of fundamental beliefs about human rights, equality, diversity, fair pay, globalization and work/life balance.

In addition, Internet Pioneers have little confidence in the loyalty of employers toward them — and thus see no reason to give employers their undivided loyalty. This generation will follow multiple career paths, often engaging in entrepreneurial ventures while working in traditional jobs.

Fewer Internet Pioneers are majoring in traditional fields, with only 33 percent of males and 18 percent of females following the traditional math/science/engineering path. Psychology and premed majors account for 8 percent of male and 18 percent of female students. Communications, English, humanities and languages are attracting 17 percent of college students. Students in majors focusing on political science, history, pre-law, or international affairs account for 9 percent, with many students having double majors.

Majors that are attracting a growing percentage of Internet Pioneers include education, health-related fields, social sciences, computer science, information technology and digital media, fine arts and criminal justice. Many of today's college students are in majors that will ultimately prove unrelated to their career goals. While this was often also the case for previous generations of college students, the key difference is that Internet Pioneers already know and admit it. College is, for them, as much a life experience as an education, with internships, study abroad and work-study programs proving more relevant to their eventual career path.

Steffani Russell, a senior majoring in English/Professional Writing, shares a common perspective on the job hunt. Many of Steffani's friends, frustrated with the difficult job market and companies seeking employees with more experience, aren't sure if they'll end up in a career that's related to their chosen field of study. "… [Some students] are just here to get a degree," Steffani said. "They have specific career plans, they know how to get there, and they see a degree — not an education — as the key to reaching their long-term goals.

"I'm at the point where I really enjoy being in school. If I don't have any strong prospects for a job related to English education or writing after I graduate, I'll just go on to grad school." Steffani said she plans to take a combination mission trip/course-for-credit this summer in Africa, and then return to school for her master's degree in English. Her plans are to have "faith that God will provide" an avenue to utilize her education and her skills when the time comes for her to enter the business world full-time.

The common thread among these students is the need to make themselves visible and available to potential employers with an online presence. "If someone wants to see samples of my writing, I can give them links to published articles, online versions of print stories I've gotten published, and my personal blog," Steffani said. "If they want a resume, I can email them the one I want them to see in a heartbeat."

Grad School as an Option

Many students are choosing the grad school option. Graduate school is appealing to grads who can't find their niche in the job market. In the meantime, it provides students with more education and experience in their chosen fields.

However, the trend seems to be that graduates are less likely to take the MBA route and are more likely to look for programs modeled around apprentice-like training.

Connecting Grad School and Business

An emerging trend in post-graduate education is to enroll MBA students in dual-degree programs linking an MBA with non-business disciplines such as art and design. The Johns Hopkins University's Carey School of Business has launched a joint MBA/MA in Design Leadership through a partnership with the Maryland Institute College of Art, as well as art schools in Canada and Europe.

This generation recognizes the need to understand business, whether they're heading into corporate careers or launching a personal website. They're more inclined to enter programs that will lead to defined professions and jobs instead of open-ended educational programs that provide little value for real-world application. And, as the Internet Pioneers begin their careers, they will come with experience and an intuitive knowledge base that will qualify them for positions well above typical entry-level training jobs.

Despite this, many will be forced to accept jobs at salaries too low to repay their college loans.

Putting a Meaningful Life Ahead of Money

The Internet has created new job opportunities that are just beginning to be understood and exploited, and these will become increasingly relevant. For example, visual artists have opportunities to distribute and market their work in ways that were unavailable to previous generations of artists. Instead of pursuing the gallery circuit, a young artist can set up a website and social networking page to promote and sell art directly. Online marketplaces such as Etsy and Saatchi Online allow artists to reach potential customers. Visual artists have access to online collectives that put them in touch with artists across the globe. Collectives such as SlashThree.com allow digital artists to showcase their work and connect with others working in the same medium.

Different Perspectives on Work Ethics

Internet Pioneers are likely to have a more positive attitude and work ethic than older members of their digital generation. Although Pioneer attitudes toward big business, work-life balance and their place in the world are similar to the sense of entitlement of their older age cohort group, they differ in key ways. Internet Pioneers express a sense of empowerment that seems to come directly from their perceived ability to make real change happen on a local, national and global scale. They understand the need for hard work, fulfill their commitments, and are sufficiently aware of life's complexities and the need to moderate their expectations and to have realistic goals.

In contrast to the pessimism of consulting firms such as Kelly Staffing, Internet Pioneers are *unlikely* to protest or act out any mistrust through poor job performance. They are *more likely* to focus on reasonable career goals, applying their technological savvy and gaining the experience they will need to make changes. They will actively apply a deep understanding of social communication to their work, sometimes eliciting results impressive for people so young.

Lifestyles of the Non-Upwardly Mobile

The life model for Generation X and Tom Brokaw's "Greatest Generation" was to commit totally to a job and job security. For the Greatest Generation, this meant mothers in unpaid work at home and fathers who were rarely home.

For Generation X, it meant both parents working long hours outside the home with children in the care of daycare centers, nannies, babysitters, relatives and a string of after-school enrichment activities. More men in this generation have taken an active role in child-rearing, and this pattern will accelerate among Internet Pioneers and Natives, who will be more likely to put families ahead of careers, even changing jobs and careers to adjust to changing family requirements.

According to the Bookends Generation study conducted by New York City's Center for Work Life Policy, 89 percent of current college students report valuing flexibility in their work life as among the most important aspects of a happy work environment.

For Baby Boomers, flexibility meant leaving work early to catch their children's ball games or dance recitals. For Internet Pioneers, flexibility includes the ability to work from home — or anywhere — as an acceptable option. Tim Ferriss' *The Four Hour Work Week* even suggests putting in a full week's worth of work from a tropical island. As long as the island has wireless connectivity, this scenario is entirely possible for the next wave of Internet-bred corporate managers (assuming they can pay off their student loans and afford to travel).

This focus on outside-of-work success may lead to a very different work landscape than before, with greater flexibility in how jobs are performed so long as benchmarks are met, and with the need for *corporations to demonstrate social responsibility far beyond the degree to which they contribute today*. Internet Pioneers will be less tolerant of corporate malfeasance and will be aggressively intolerant of a Profit at Any Cost approach to corporate strategy.

Because the generation overall considers global impact as important as financial gain, today's college students may be able to alter the direction of businesses as a whole — first by altering employment policies and later through their influence within the management chain.

Again, the Internet Pioneer generation of college graduates doesn't feel bound to follow the implied contract of job loyalty that served their parents and grandparents. For earlier generations, a college diploma meant a middle-class job and upward mobility. However, a combination of economic recession and overabundance of college-educated candidates means this is no longer true.

The Next Great Generation

Red Tree Leadership, a management training consultancy, describes today's college students as potentially being the "next great generation."

How big businesses choose to deal with this incoming cohort of new team members over the next few years will have a powerful influence on the future of each company. Corporations that underestimate Internet Pioneers and Internet Natives do so at their own peril. Internet Pioneers have the potential to change, streamline and improve business ethics and communications from the ground up.

Internet Pioneers may need guidance from senior colleagues about the politics and social mores within corporations, but senior managers will, in many ways, have far more to learn from their younger colleagues. Internet Pioneers have grown up with the ability to multitask, to access information at any hour, and to conduct work from any place with an Internet connection. Many will be willing to work for less money, and even for more hours, if given the flexibility to work on their own schedules with liberal telecommuting opportunities.

Even with the challenging reality of a tough job market for Internet Pioneers, they have the values, work ethic and self-esteem to face these challenges with determination and vision. They may initially step back and wait for more appropriate timing — meanwhile accepting roles they perceive as jobs rather than careers. But they will inevitably gain a foothold in small businesses, large corporations, education, government, non-profits, the arts and organizations. Once they gain that foothold, their unique perspectives and skills will enable them to mature quickly in their roles, bring new insights, and move up the career ladder into positions of increased responsibility and authority.

Employers who recognize these individuals and seek their counsel, contributions and ideas will be well rewarded. On the other hand, employers who fail to empower Internet Pioneers will find themselves rapidly becoming irrelevant.

Finding Their Way

Internet Pioneers prefer to avoid conflict, are uncertain of how their opinions will be received and are, therefore, often reluctant to voice them forcefully. They may, however, begin to find that voice as they move through their college years, gain more confidence, emerge into graduate schools and the workforce, and realize how advantaged they are and how uniquely qualified they will be to manage organizations and direct strategies. Internet Pioneers are likely to achieve success following the volatile economic and social climate of the next two decades, more so than the X-Gens who are finding themselves less relevant in a business world that is increasingly digital.

As the nation and world emerge from the period of upheaval caused by the technological inventions of the past two decades, we will move faster and further into the application period of the Internet Transformation. As change accelerates, the need for economic, political, societal and organizational stability will increase.

From our current perspective of economic uncertainty and political dissension, the future may seem hazy. Internet Pioneers are just a few years away from imprinting their values on the nation and world.

Their priorities and challenges will be many: to advance logic, honesty and human rights into the corporate mainstream, and to assure that we return to policies that are of, by and for the majority of the American people and the people of the world.

In the coming decades, Internet Pioneers and subsequent generations of Internet Natives will dominate the workforce. Those organizations that empower them will be best positioned for success.

Chapter 21:
Facebook, Google, Trust, Piracy and Privacy

While a majority (74 percent) of Internet Pioneers who take a position on the value of corporations agree that they make important contributions to society, only 20 percent believe they make *many valuable* contributions, while 26 percent say corporations are *destructive* to society. Of those who believe corporations in general are destructive, most judge Internet companies Google, Facebook, Apple, Amazon and Twitter by a different standard. Three-quarters of those with negative attitudes toward corporations believe these large Internet companies should NOT be judged by the same standards as other corporations, and they do not subject them to the same negative pre-judgments.

This was evident in the online uprising against the Stop Online Piracy Act (SOPA) and Preventing Real Online Threats to Economic Creativity and Theft of Intellectual Property Act (PIPA) in early 2012. Congressional efforts to enact laws that would curtail online piracy and copyright infringement were supported by most leading entertainment companies and had broad bipartisan support in Congress.

That support collapsed when Google, Facebook, Reddit, Wikipedia and other sites protested and activated their user bases to speak out against the laws. Google alone generated seven million petition signatures in one day, and Wikipedia went black for a day of protest.

Internet Natives love interacting with one another over social platforms, and they are determined to do whatever it takes to ensure that their favorite sites remain open. Each day, millions of students take advantage of free online sites but are aware of the legal consequences of piracy. Andy Jensen, a senior at California State University, considered taking his YouTube videos down if one or both of the bills passed. "I heard that you could get in trouble just for using the wrong background music or even having a TV show playing in the background of your YouTube video. I'm a poor college student and really can't afford to pay whatever exorbitant fine they choose to slap on me." To help with the cause, Andy signed an anti-SOPA petition and then posted the link to the petition on his Facebook wall so that friends could sign it as well.

Like Andy, thousands of college students alerted their friends to SOPA and PIPA, either by linking to petitions or blacking out portions of their Facebook pages. Although there's little clarity about the actual legal consequences that concern Andy, a number of students took the protest effort a step further by asking their college administrators to black out official university websites. Colleges such as Syracuse University and the Massachusetts Institute of Technology (MIT) listened to concerned students and obliged their website black-out requests. University officials at MIT claimed that the passing of SOPA and PIPA would result in large sections of the university's official website being shut down. They were especially concerned about online students who access most of their lectures and assignments over the MIT website. The concern was that much of this content would be liable under SOPA.

Within a week, the acts had gone from almost certain passage to a very public and ignominious defeat. When it came to established corporate and political forces against leading digital sites, the Internet proved a far more trusted and powerful force. Senate Majority Leader Harry Reid responded to the protests with an indefinite suspension of the SOPA-PIPA vote. Support for these bills remains strong in both the Senate and the House, but representatives have demonstrated a willingness to step back and consider changes. This development represents a major success for college students and other protesters who have worked so hard to safeguard the online freedom of expression they currently enjoy.

The anti-SOPA protests provide tangible proof of the importance of social networking to today's college students. Most students view social media as highly enriching and are willing to fight to ensure that it remains available in the future. They enjoy the many opportunities provided by Facebook, Twitter, YouTube, Tumblr and dozens of other social networking sites. And if the millions of Tweets, Facebook status updates and YouTube videos concerning social justice movements such as "Occupy Wall Street" and "Stop American Censorship" are any indication, students are making full use of social media tools.

As far as college students are concerned, social media and social justice are both here to stay, and the powerful influence of the leading Internet-based companies in defining and advancing social causes is a direct result of the trust Internet Pioneers have in them.

Consumer Trust

Consumer trust is a huge asset and advantage for companies as they plan their marketing and strategic business decisions. It's a dual-edged sword, though. Trust can be quickly eroded when corporate decisions are made that run counter to the standards and expectations of these same consumers. For example, Yahoo's distinctive position with young people is eroding as the site struggles internally and externally with its identity, focus, purpose and core marketing message.

Achieving and maintaining trust among Internet Pioneers will yield not only financial rewards but enormous competitive advantage, political clout and social influence.

Privacy is one of the key ways this advantage may be manifested. Because Facebook has continued to serve its core college-age audience even as it has expanded across all demographics and to a global user base, this audience will continue to serve Facebook and support the company's somewhat confrontational approach to privacy issues. Facebook alone is positioned to defend society against almost certain restrictive governmental privacy controls. Internet Pioneers are likely to be the most active voices against these controls, but if not for their trust in Facebook, they might be advocates of greater privacy regulation.

"Privacy is very complicated and one of the hardest design problems. Giving people a large page full of controls seems like the best solution, but in practice it is not because people need to make decisions about their privacy in context with what is going on around them. For example who they are talking to, what they are talking about, and the benefit they receive from sharing personal information with other people. There is also a tension between the volume of data and accessing that data."

~ Paul Adams
Facebook

It seems inevitable that some politicians will identify personal privacy as an opportune political hot potato and again launch a campaign to impose greater Internet privacy controls. If sites are heavily regulated with privacy controls, a great opportunity to bring people together with other people and businesses based on their expressed interests, needs and desires could be missed. Political opportunism could, in the short term, derail many of the most promising emerging opportunities of the Internet.

The current controls, all self-imposed, are reasonably extensive, but Adams is "worried that every single action will require opt-in authorization. The web could become unusable if there is a pop-up every time you click with terms and conditions you have to approve."

Under the current self-regulations, users provide a one-time authorization and can rescind that approval. Facebook users are very sophisticated in their under- standing of privacy issues and their rights. According to our study, 93 percent of Internet Pioneers ex- press concern about how much personal information they share online, and are sufficiently sophisticated to protect themselves. "If you look at all the latest research on young people, they do care about privacy and consequences," confirms Adams.

> *"When you look at recent research on young people, from researchers like danah boyd and institutions like Pew, it's clear that many young people have made time to understand privacy controls on the web. Many of them better understand the value derived from being more open with privacy controls than many older people do. They experience the benefits of sharing openly, in terms of the positive social feedback they get. Many know how to post to specific friends, or how to exclude specific individuals from seeing certain content."*
>
> **~ Paul Adams**
> **Facebook**

Evan Schweitzer, a college freshman from New York City, remembers "in the beginning of Facebook, I bought into being friends with everybody. Back then it was cool to have 5,000 friends. Now it's not so cool. It's huge, but it is invading and I like having my privacy."

Facebook Communities

Older Internet users are, according to several studies, actually less concerned about pri- vacy than Internet Pioneers, and they are also less competent to manage the privacy settings that sites like Facebook and Google provide. "A lot of good can come from people opening up and sharing," Adams believes.

There have been privacy fears and backlash dating back to the introduction of the printing press and even the alphabet and the written word, if we can go back that far. It is reasonable to believe that people were concerned about maintaining the privacy of their stories when the first scribe began writing those stories down. If something could be written down, it could be held against you. With the advent of the printing press, the printed word distrib- uted to many was a clear invasion of a person's right to control to whom, how and when he delivered his message.

Privacy concerns are not new, but Adams believes we are returning to a time not unlike when people lived in villages and communities of 150 to 200 people and everyone knew each other's business. "It was in each other's best interests to share and be open because it made life easier," he points out. Social networks are enabling people to identify and communicate with small groups that they identify and control.

Internet Pioneers' Relationship with Facebook

The average Facebook user, according to Facebook research, has an average of six groups with 10 to 15 members each — family, friends from activities, school, past jobs and schools, their community, etc. Internet Pioneers tend to have more than six discreet groups and more people in each of those groups. More than 90 percent of Internet Pioneers today are on Facebook, with an average 415 "friends" each, compared to the average 150 friends among the total Facebook user base. More than 20 percent of Internet Pioneers have 500-plus friends and only 4 percent have fewer than 50 friends.

The most active Internet Pioneer Facebook users with 500-plus friends are more con- centrated among females and Black/African Americans; they are less concentrated in California but otherwise evenly dispersed throughout the rest of the country. Seventy-one percent of Internet Pioneer Facebook users say they personally know at least 90 percent of their Facebook friends, and only 5 percent personally know less than one-third of their friends. This runs counter to data on average social network users. Research from anthropologist Robin Dunbar and others suggests that the average person can manage only about 150 friends. "Our brain has physiological limits. Most people can only remember about 500 people, and can only remember the relationships between about 150-200, in other words remember who knows who," says Adams.

Internet Pioneers, with an average of more than 400 friends, fall into a group that will be early adapters of the tools being developed for curating and managing large circles of friends.

Product development at Facebook, Google Plus and other social networks is focusing on helping their users manage and organize communications with independent groups of friends. Circles and communities will become much more important as people separate out groups of friends who don't know each other and may have different interests. People want to communicate differently with friends, work colleagues and families. It doesn't work to combine these disparate groups in a single blended online world.

As Facebook members age, it's inevitable that the size of their networks will grow as they maintain connections with people who become less involved in their day-to-day lives. It's not human nature to "unfriend" those with whom they have had a previous relationship, as Facebook becomes the only resource available to maintain all those contacts. Social networks will therefore grow over time beyond the 150 average, and Internet Pioneers' social networks will quickly exceed five hundred and more. They will have a network of people that is too big to remember and deal with, so a priority for them will be curation tools and database management resources. They will seek out better ways to direct their communications to smaller discrete groups and to manage different messages for different groups of friends.

A strategic priority for Facebook is to maintain a balance between user demands for greater use of personal information and advocacy groups' demands for greater privacy controls that restrict use of this information.

Facebook began its extraordinary sprint to the top echelons of digital native companies by targeting college students, and it continues to achieve its greatest success with this group, many of whom now consider Facebook to be the single most important resource for their communications needs.

> *"I totally understand the arguments against Facebook but I have friends all over the world from theater camp. If not for Facebook how would I stay in touch with them? It's a pretty big deal. It's easy to find out what people are doing. I don't have to put a lot of effort into knowing what's going on with my friends because it pops up."*
>
> **~ Laura Schwartz**
> **18-year-old student, Manhattan**

As the now popular lore goes, Facebook was created in a college dormitory. While the movie *The Social Network* dramatized the story of Mark Zuckerberg and *thefacebook*, Facebook is still appealing to college students for many of the reasons that Zuckerberg originally imagined. It is the best social network because Facebook resembles *real life*, if for no other reason than because so many people are on it. Students communicate on it as if they were in a cafeteria. They share pictures and exist in a sort of dual universe in which it sometimes seems that if something doesn't happen on Facebook, it's not real. Even those students who may not prefer it to other social networks or who may not be active on any social network are on Facebook simply because everyone else is. It is self-perpetuating. And *everyone* is on it.

Facebook remains a place for students to gather and socialize and share, and it remains an integral part of college life. Facebook's utility and universality has allowed it to evolve into a tool for information gathering and sharing. Colleges are even using Facebook to recruit students. To stay relevant, Facebook is constantly looking to add features and functionality to improve the user experience. Facebook has expanded far beyond its college roots, but the DNA of the company as a social network bringing students closer together remains. Facebook is constantly updating its user interface and has expanded it to incorporate a Timeline feature that retains every update, photo, shared experience and all other activities users include in their Facebook profiles. And Facebook has adapted to an increasingly mobile generation.

"These days, it's about reaching students where they are — which is mostly (but not always) on their cell phones or laptops," wrote Bruce Horovitz in *USA Today*. Facebook is still in college dormitories, but it has evolved to travel with the student as part of every-day life. The company works hard to remain useful and universal in an ever-changing and hyper-competitive world. So far, it's working.

Google and the Privacy Conundrum

Google is used every day by even more people than Facebook, and Google is an embedded part of the basic daily language of people around the world. Google, through its multiple technology platforms, has access to and stores an extraordinary wealth of information and insight into the daily lives of its users.

In March 2012, Google consolidated its privacy policies for sixty Google products and services into one. On the surface, this appears to be a consumer-friendly act intended to simplify the cumbersome process of downloading and reading privacy policies. The full Google Privacy Policy is published in the addendum for your own easy reference (and as a capsule for comparison as it changes over time). Google is trusted by its users to protect them and protect their interests.

But technology guru and blogger Shelly Palmer expressed serious concern about the consolidated privacy policy.

"On March 1, 2012, Google consolidated the privacy policies for 60 of its products creating the singularly most significant database of the Information Age. The aggregation of these data will empower Google to correlate and contextualize our thoughts, aspirations, actions, physical locations and the timelines for the basic processes of life."

"I don't think any single thought about the aggregation of data or the use of technology has ever made me as uncomfortable as this announcement. On its best day, with every ounce of technology the U.S. government could muster, it could not know a fraction as much about any of us as Google does now. But now is not what I'm worried about. I'm not even worried about this decade. Just imagine a database that could automatically determine what you are most likely going to have for dinner after your bowling league Tuesday night, where you are going to have it, who it will be with, whether you are feeling good or have a cold, if you and your wife are fighting, how your day was at work, what you are thinking about buying, who is helping you with your decisions about it, what chronic illnesses you are dealing with, what meds you are on, etc, etc, etc. And this isn't even the scary stuff."

~ **Shelly Palmer**
MediaBizBloggers.com

What scares Palmer is the "existence of yet-uninvented ways to manipulate data for good and, inadvertently, for bad. I'm worried about the good intentions that pave the road to hell," he exclaims.

The debates over privacy protection reflect a conundrum — how can data best be protected when more and more information that has always been personal and private is voluntarily shared on platforms that are fundamentally public? How can consumers best understand the implications of sharing their data and clicking "I Agree" when they haven't even read the privacy policies to which they are agreeing? Will companies like Facebook and Google use and misuse the trust that Internet Pioneers have placed in them, and will that trust erode as a result? If trust is misused and privacy rights are reinforced and regulated, will the value of these platforms and others be diminished?

Few issues are more critical for the future of the Internet than privacy. Facebook and Google will be the dominant forces in advancing the case for access to consumer information and limited consumer control over that information. We now know, from SOPA and PIPA, that the forces of government and other large corporations are helpless by comparison. Whether Google and Facebook respect and honor the trust their users have placed in them will determine whether Palmer's fear is well-placed or overstated.

Chapter 22:
Apple Closes the Loop

Apple may be the largest public company, but it also is judged by a different standard, one defined by Apple and based on the company's ability to identify with Internet Pioneers. This standard also enables Pioneers to identify with Apple.

Apple has mastered the concept of being the company with must-have products on college campuses and maintaining an incredibly high user-satisfaction score. Apple's core strength is its ability to create and then meet a need. Anastasia Goodstein at *Bloomberg Business Week* noted that Apple's silhouette ads feature people of all ages, but added "Most brands will never be able to fully replicate Apple's zeitgeist moment with the iPod and its continued success with teens and young adults."

Who knew they needed an iPhone or an iPad? The brilliance of Apple is how its innovation has created new ways for people to enjoy their lives. And what is most fascinating is while the products are not designed for teenagers, they appeal to teens as well as everyone else. Whether you're 6, 16 or well past 60, the odds are good that you own an iPod, iPhone and/or iPad. The Apple brand is ubiquitous. More Apple products are being sold each month than new babies are born!

According to a small survey of college campuses by Hudson Square Research's Daniel Ernst, the percentage of students who owned Apple *computers* rose from 33 percent in 2009 to 51 percent in 2010. Apple's reach into the mobile world of iPods, iPhones and iPads with cutting-edge designs and an almost-cultish following brings a company word-of-mouth marketing that is hard to match. As a result, according to *CNN Money*, "Apple's share of student spending increased materially."

The Apple Store's experience-based marketing that allows potential customers to actually use the products is a key differentiator for the company. According to Jim Nichols at Forbes.com, "People who experience a brand through a store or other interactive program were more likely to positively identify with that brand." There is something universal and fun about Apple's approach to consumers that appeals to the young and the young at heart. But it is deeper than a faddish brand. Apple has loyal customers, and the base has grown larger and more loyal over time, while its designs have become hipper and more sophisticated.

"A computer absolutely can be sexy. The focus on design clearly appeals to those on college campuses. Apple aggressively markets on college campuses and uses campus reps to host workshops, throw events, and build relationships with students, faculty, and parents."

~ Jonathan Ive
Head of Design, Apple

Apple's college reps collaborate with the Apple team to run marketing programs on campuses, from sales promotions to increasing awareness of Apple products. Getting students and parents at a moment when a computer purchase is on their minds is just part of Apple's approach. Combining the eye-catching and even, according to *Wired*, "classroom-inspiring design," Apple is clearly tops on most Internet Pioneers' want lists.

Apple is also at the forefront of a mobile revolution, and Internet Pioneers by their nature are early adapters. According to Brooke Crothers at *CNET* news, "Apple has become a mobile device juggernaut...so, if it's more or less a zero-sum game, Apple's post-PC devices will continue to take share away from the diminishing PC juggernaut by bringing young buyers into the more profitable (for Apple) MacBook Air fold."

Conflict Between Open and Closed Systems

Apple and co-founder Steve Jobs were at the forefront of what Jobs's biographer Walter Isaacson calls "the most fundamental divide in the digital world: open versus closed." This divide continues to pit Apple's closed strategy against the open-source strategies of Microsoft and Google.

"The hacker ethos handed down from the Homebrew Computer Club favored the open approach, in which there was little centralized control and people were free to modify hardware and software, share code, write to open standards, shun proprietary systems, and have content and apps that were compatible with a variety of

devices and operating systems. With the Macintosh, Jobs became the founding fa-
ther of the other camp. The Macintosh would be like an appliance, with the hard-
ware and software tightly woven together and closed to modifications. The hacker
ethos would be sacrificed in order to create a seamless and simple user experience."

~ **Walter Isaacson**
Steve Jobs

Internet Pioneers are confronted in much of their lives by the fundamental conflict between open and closed.

- They share their lives like an open book on Facebook, Twitter and Foursquare, yet they value their privacy and are reluctant to share their opinions and beliefs.

- They value the Apple promise of simplicity in both design and functionality, yet they are eager to 'pimp out' their iPhones with an endless variety of customized cases, covers and stickers.

- At college, they tend to stay within their own closed campus environment with college friends, yet eagerly leave for months for a semester abroad, opening themselves to the world.

- They seek summer jobs and internships to learn skills that can train and prepare them for a career, yet favor course curriculum with as much diversity and open-ended requirements as possible.

- They jealously guard and value their closest friendships, yet open themselves to a wide social network and eagerly move back and forth among multiple circles of friends.

Internet Pioneers, in many ways, personify the fundamental Microsoft/Google vs. Apple conflict between open and closed within their own lives. Looking toward the future, it's likely they will want to marry the two, find common ground in the conflict and allow both camps to thrive. For them — and for all future generations — the key issue is whether Apple, or any company, can achieve the exceptional blending of technology and artistry that Jobs inspired at Apple. That is the ultimate reward of the closed loop.

In Isaacson's excellent biography of Jobs, Jobs suggests, "The reason Apple resonates with people is that there's a deep current of humanity in our innovation. I think great artists and great engineers are similar, in that they both have a desire to express themselves. In fact some of the best people working on the original Mac were poets and musicians on the side. In the seventies, computers became a way for people to express their creativity."

Internet Pioneers share a desire to express themselves, through their music, fashion, use of social media and almost all aspects of their lives. Yet, they also choose to avoid conflict. Perhaps it comes from the lessons taught them by Nickelodeon, which encouraged and empowered them to express themselves but also taught cooperation and equality. No company has captured the zeitgeist of Internet Pioneers as effectively as Apple. Internet Pioneers grew up with Apple, as they did with Nickelodeon, as an embedded part of their lives and especially their online experiences. They are the key consumers of Jobs's innovations and the generation that will both reflect and carry on his transformative energy and vision.

Jobs, as co-founder and CEO of Apple and CEO of Pixar, was responsible for Apple computers and products including the Macintosh; iPod, iPhone and iPad; iTunes; Apple Stores and the App Store; iCloud; plus *Toy Story* and other Pixar mega-hits.

As pointed out by Isaacson, "Steve Jobs thus became the greatest business executive of our era, the one most certain to be remembered a century from now. History will place him in the pantheon right next to Edison and Ford. More than anyone else of his time, he made products that were completely innovative, combining the power of poetry and processors. With a ferocity that could make working with him as unsettling as it was inspiring, he also built the world's most creative company. And he was able to infuse into its DNA the design sensibilities, perfectionism, and imagination that make it likely to be, even decades from now, the company that thrives best at the intersection of artistry and technology."

This description of Jobs also provides a broad overview of what defines Internet Pioneers and sets them apart. They are creatively inspired. They reward innovation and uniquely embrace the intersection of artistry and technology. Yet, unlike Jobs, they are sensitive toward the realities and needs of others and sensible about the realities of the issues they confront and the pressures they face.

Like Jobs, they are likely to be remembered and written about for many years.

Chapter 23:
Marketing and Internet Pioneers

Advertising is shifting its focus from mass media to the individual; it is interactive and needs to be engaging; it connects consumers directly to additional information and purchase; it is being tracked on a micro-second by micro-second basis with patterns of behavior and marketing results far better understood and utilized; it is mobile, social and online; it is global and hyper-local.

Rather than sending coupons en masse to millions of consumers through Sunday newspaper inserts or mailed coupon packets, marketers will integrate special offers into on-line consumer conversations that are relevant to the product being marketed. In addition to inserting commercials intrusively into mass-distributed television programs, marketers will shift budgets into curated content that relates to their product category and that engages consumers in an interactive relationship.

The shifts away from traditional advertising and marketing will be profound. Most marketers are struggling to adjust to these radical and challenging shifts, but to Internet Pioneers, they are obvious realities.

New Perspectives on Digital Marketing

The Internet and connected mobile devices will be the most important marketing tools for communicating with Internet Pioneers and the generations of Internet Natives that follow them.

As Internet speeds accelerate exponentially over the next few years, online and mobile video viewing will become the norm, although traditional television network programming will continue to dominate the viewing experience. All media will require applications and interactive two-way options for social interaction, commerce, and content enhancements.

Second-screen content synchronized with television and videos is tailor-made for an already active online audience that's primed to jump in if the content is worthwhile, and the technology is simple. This technology already exists, and every leading television network is producing for multi-screen interplay. As all content is becoming more social, mobile and interactive, the underlying principles that have guided media for the past five to six decades are being restructured.

Back in the 1950s, the introduction of the credit card dramatically changed marketing and retailing. New technologies are making it even easier: for example, credit card-linked deals that let consumers embed coupons and special offers directly on their credit cards to be applied at the point of purchase. Discounts are automatically applied when the consumer buys the specified product or service.

The credit card will disappear, displaced by mobile devices with embedded RFID chips and visual scanning. These radio frequency chips will have the capacity to connect directly with responsive chips attached to products, billboards, kiosks, and products. Discounts will be offered and accepted on mobile devices. WiFi technology will link consumers' mobile and other devices directly to television, radio and online commercials. Looking further ahead, similar chips might be embedded in the body for communication or other applications — similar to embedded identification chips already in use. As chips and mobile devices become the primary distribution vehicle for coupons and special offers, print media will become increasingly moot except as specialized upscale vehicles for enhanced content presentation and as parts of memorabilia collections.

New Strategies for Marketers

Marketers will require strategists, creative teams and media experts who are truly immersed in the digital world and who understand the challenges of digital marketing. Marketers will retain experts in traditional marketing as they transform their operations to emphasize digital strategies, but the two distinct practices of legacy and digital marketing will be progressively intertwined and interdependent.

In the United States, digital marketing communications investments will increase from $52 billion (9 percent of marketers' total communications budgets) in 2011 to a projected $170 billion in 2020 (30 percent of total budgets).

By 2030, when Internet Pioneers and Internet Natives are dominating the corporate world, digital marketing will capture 60 to 70 percent of all spending. That does not mean traditional media companies or agencies will disappear, although many will. Companies that thrive will be those that embrace digital media and hire Internet Pioneers. Legacy media companies that make a quick and intelligent transition to socializing their content will thrive.

Yet for the most part, the advertising business remains entrenched in models and practices that are unchanged since television was introduced in the 1950s. The industry still relies on systems that have been in place since the beginning of the newspaper business in the 19th century. The industry is responding to digital expansion, but not quickly enough.

An *Adweek* study of marketers finds that 77 percent believe the days of traditional media channels are numbered; 68 percent say they need to shift their reliance on broad-based media to more of a one-to-one focus; and 73 percent believe the days of strategic consistency are over and that future marketing campaigns will need to emphasize inspiration and engagement. Nevertheless, their actual spending patterns are just beginning to reflect this strategic shift.

Venture Capital Has Built the Marketing Infrastructure

Companies like Apple, Google, Amazon and Facebook have a decided advantage in marketing their products and services because of their brand equity, which will continue to serve them well for years unless they suffer a colossal failure.

Investments in building the infrastructure required for digital capabilities and marketing today also are distinctly different from the digital investments required even a decade ago. Billions of dollars have been invested by venture capitalists in building out the infrastructure required for digital conversion. Unlike any technological revolution that has come before, the Internet Revolution is being funded through venture capital and is focused on supporting — not dismantling — traditional corporations and their assets.

Established companies, rather than needing to take the risk of building digital assets from scratch, now have access to thousands of small companies that are ready, willing and able to make infrastructure investments for them. Digital bridges, tunnels, and roads are built. Advanced digital tools and capabilities have been imagined, created and developed, mostly through venture investment, and are available for low-cost installation and implementation. It's now an issue of whether corporate organizations can manage their own legacy hierarchies and the natural resistance of an inbred corporate culture, and if they will act to embrace and adopt digital conversion and upgrades.

There are thousands of VC-funded companies that have fully developed Internet-based capabilities and tools available to traditional companies for the asking.

Marketing to Internet Pioneers

Companies that market products geared toward young adults have always understood the importance of looking beyond traditional print and broadcast media campaigns to reach young consumers. According to promotions firm Re:Fuel, college students spent about $36 billion on items like clothing, computers, cell phones and food in the 2010–2011 school year. But gaining share of this market is the tip of the iceberg for marketers who establish and build brand loyalty that may last for decades. According to a *USA Today* article, companies target young adult consumers because of their disposable income and the hopes of establishing them as lifelong customers whose income will grow over time.

Over the past few years, marketers have ramped up their efforts, but they may not realize just how different Internet Pioneers are from earlier generations, or how important understanding Internet Pioneers will be to their future. While many companies are using digital media and shifting their creative marketing focus to target an Internet-savvy audience, their strategies are often Internet-enhanced 20th century campaigns that remain rooted in traditional advertising models.

Why They Love Brands and Advertising

Internet Pioneers are the most brand-aware consumers in history — advertising is a distinctive form of content that's always been a part of their lives.

Advertising has had an enormous influence on Internet Pioneers. They grew up watching commercials on Nickelodeon and accept commercials as content. They're accustomed to cable television and websites dedicated to their interests and ads specifically targeted to them. Nevertheless, they pay little active attention to advertising messages and tend to fast-forward through commercials or occupy the time by texting friends. A minority claims to like advertising, while others regard it as a necessary evil that pays for free content.

A non-stop wave of new products and aggressive advertising has left Pioneers somewhat immune to their impact and relevance. It's estimated that more than three thousand brand message exposures bombard the average college student *every day*. Most ads simply disappear into the whitewash of irrelevant content.

Unlike past generations whose brand loyalty started with the family's product choices, Internet Pioneers are more open to trying something new. They have their own set of brand loyalties, biases and perceptions. Their brand preferences are transient; but once committed, they're quick to become not only brand loyalists but ***brand activists***.

Fashion Hauls

Brand activists will actively "like" a brand on Facebook, evangelize a brand through blogs, and share comments on consumer websites. Many brand activists make YouTube videos of themselves testing and seamlessly promoting new products (usually without payment). Fans follow and watch for the latest video. One of the biggest trends in the worlds of fashion, social media and advertising is *fashion hauling*, a practice referred to by NPR commentator Viet Le as "PG porn" for the young fashionista crowd. In this game of show-and-tell 2.0, shoppers set up web cams in their bedrooms in order to proudly display their purchases for the masses. Drawing items from their shopping bags one by one, they offer commentary on their favorite details of the clothes and accessories, along with their plans for wearing these pieces. Some fashion haulers are big into designer outfits, but many others do their shopping at discount stores such as Forever 21, J. C. Penney, Target, American Eagle and Urban Outfitters. When displaying hauls from these stores, the goal is to teach viewers how to look fashionable on a budget. Fashion Hauls are at the foundation of a new trend that differs from traditional advertising models by directly connecting brands, brand evangelists and consumers through YouTube video blogs (although YouTube is not itself monetizing these videos).

Although fashion hauls began popping up as soon as YouTube was released, they burst more prominently on the scene in late 2008. Of course, the economic recession also came into full force at the same time. One common explanation for the explosion of haul videos is that, unable to go on big shopping trips themselves, users were able to live vicariously through their favorite fashion 'vloggers'. Time magazine went so far as to say that "millions of girls were watching the videos the same way that they watched Justin Bieber videos." Even more importantly, retailers have seen sales increase when a product is highlighted in a haul video. A Forbes article reported that a Guess watch that was featured in a haul video sold out in record time.

J. C. Penney has used haul videos as a cornerstone promotion for teen back-to-school shopping the past two years. In 2011, the retailer encouraged customers to create their own haul videos of the store's products by hosting an online vote for the best video with prizes such as a trip to New York and an iPad. "We're inspired by the confidence and influence of today's teens. They are true evangelists, sharing their individual style and encouraging others to take the latest trends and make them their own," Bill Gentner, interim chief marketing officer of J. C. Penney said. The retailer's "Haul Nation" campaign has been a leader in the use of haul videos and sparked many individuals to create their own on YouTube.

High school and college students were the first to jump on the fashion hauling trend. Sisters Elle and Blair Fowler led the way with their YouTube channels, both of which attracted millions of views from fashion-forward teens. Self-professed as ordinary girls with a love for fashion, the two began sharing tips on finding the trendiest looks without breaking the bank. As their videos grew in popularity, the girls began receiving free products from a wide range of beauty and fashion companies, all with the simple request of having their items appear on Elle and Blair's channels. While the two girls' lives have changed, they continue making affordable fashion a priority. Blair has over 959,000 subscribers to her YouTube Channel while Elle has more than 714,000 followers. A recent video of Blair's, in which she described her favorite television shows and shampoo in painstaking detail, generated over 692,000 views in a few weeks.

Similar "unboxing videos" share the process of opening, configuring, and activating high-tech gadgets.

Making Emotional Connections

More than any other generation, Internet Pioneers understand the value of their advocacy, and they are very sophisticated in the understanding and knowledge of the nuances of product marketing.

Internet Pioneers *do* take notice of effective advertising, but they're highly selective in their choices. They value and reward advertising that connects emotionally, shares valuable insights and that informs them about new products and services targeted to their interests. But they're just as likely to respond in a deeply negative way to advertising that strikes the wrong chord.

Marketers and agencies are trying to strike the right chord by using non-traditional marketing strategies to gain market share. Unfortunately, marketers and agencies are not yet up to the task. But they *are* trying.

The New Challenges for College Marketers

Hundreds of companies are battling it out with non-traditional marketing strategies to gain market share and 'mind share' with Internet Pioneers. To reach Internet Pioneers on college campuses and beyond, companies must be innovative in finding new ways to integrate their products into the Internet Pioneer lifestyle and culture. Among other things, offline experiential and event programs, smartphone apps, online videos, interactive and two-screen television will be increasingly important marketing tools.

"Traditional marketing techniques — like national advertising campaigns on MTV or in Rolling Stone — don't resonate with college students the way they used to. Nowadays, companies need student ambassadors to create marketing events, like mural painting or video contests that are relevant to their particular schools... Students who participate tend to promulgate brand messages."

~ Matt Britton
Chief Executive, Mr. Youth Marketing Agency

According to a *New York Times* article, marketers are hiring an estimated ten thousand American college students to represent them on campus. Red Bull, Hewlett-Packard PCs, Nike, Microsoft, Ford, American Eagle, Target, Pepsi, Coca-Cola and Ben & Jerry's all have sophisticated on-campus marketing efforts. Apple has dedicated stores on large campuses and has space in many college bookstores.

A *Wall Street Journal* article (April 4, 2012) headlined "Big Marketers on Campus" reported that tech start-ups are enlisting college students to engage their social networks and campus relationships on behalf of the brands. "For start-ups," writes reporter

Katherine Rosman, "college students are marketing gold. They love web products and tell friends, real and virtual, about everything they do, see and buy. They will work, free, at a time when even non-paying internships are harder to land."

Vending machines remain ubiquitous on campus, but fast food chains are acquiring rights to open within student centers. As the *Times'* Natasha Singer commented, "Corporations have been pitching college students for decades on products from cars to credit cards. But what is happening on campuses today is without rival, in terms of commercializing everyday college life."

Redefining Creative Success

Soon, ad agency creative teams will wake up to the shift of commercials from intrusive forced-feeding of messages. Instead of simply creating awareness and retention, commercials will motivate consumers to opt in, both to viewing and to take some form of action. Every commercial will have a Facebook "like" and "dislike" icon, and creative success will be defined by viral distribution and consumer feedback. Traditional 30-second intrusive commercials with little viral interest will fade into oblivion. Independent and documentary filmmakers whose messages resonate with consumers will be funded by corporations that want to be associated with those messages, and who will benefit as viewers pass along those videos with their feedback.

GE's *FocusForwardFilms* (focusforwardfilms.com) initiative is funding 30 well-known documentary filmmakers to tell three-minute stories of innovation and invention about which the filmmakers are passionate. GE provides distribution and promotional support for the films and is also underwriting international competitions, inviting professional and amateur filmmakers to submit their films. A disproportionate number of entries are from Internet Pioneers.

Case Study: Unilever Dove for Women Campaign

Unilever has been at the forefront of the digital marketing trend, bringing its message to the college market through provocative YouTube videos, product placement in video games and Apple's iAd marketing platform. The company integrates product promotions with college sports and other events of interest to Internet Pioneers.

Unilever's Dove brand, both the men's and women's product lines, has enjoyed particular marketing success with Internet Pioneers.

Unilever's most successful campaign ever, the Dove "Real Beauty" campaign, was launched in 2004. Unilever describes the campaign as "promoting the idea that beauty comes in all shapes, sizes and ages." In addition to promoting the brand and products, the campaign made a positive impact on the public by offering alternative ways of thinking about beauty and helping parents to discuss ideas about beauty with their daughters. The campaign included a 75-second online video (*Evolution*) that demonstrates how professional stylists and computer photo-editing are used to transform ordinary-looking women into fashion models.

The video cost the company almost nothing to produce, but the payoff was huge. The video gained tremendous online exposure. The result was over 3.5 million YouTube views and prominent play on mainstream television news shows including the *The View* and *CNN*.

Marketing Vox estimated that the company's initial exposure in the weeks after the video was triple that of a Super Bowl ad for the same product line. Unilever followed up on the success of *Evolution* by releasing additional online videos, *Onslaught* and *Amy*.

According to Unilever research, the Dove campaign was among the most successful in history — affecting not only brand perception but also affecting consumers' perceptions of themselves (and their friends).

Why did the campaign succeed? When the campaign was introduced, Internet Pioneers were in their early to mid-teens, the most formative years for bodily self-perception. In a culture that had positioned inhumanly thin models as the pinnacle of beauty, the Dove message may have been the most influential in the lives of these young women.

While models remain tall and thin and television series like *America's Next Top Model* glamorize traditional symbols of beauty, Internet Pioneers are more likely than previous generations to embrace beauty in all shapes and sizes. It's a lesson they learned while watching Nickelodeon.

"Kids in Nick shows like All That were not skinny Hannah Montana look-alikes; they were all shapes, sizes and looks and not so gorgeous."

~ Geraldine Laybourne
Former Nickelodeon Chairman

Internet Pioneers form a small generation whose members, while fashion-savvy and into make-up, are less likely to fall into unhealthy eating habits, emotional disorders, and anti-social behavior patterns based on their own appearance or the appearance of others.

While Nickelodeon and Dove's "Real Beauty" campaign cannot claim all of the credit, they played an important part in communicating a message to young women that can influence their long-term health.

Case Study: Dove for Men Campaign

The Dove for Men product line has also developed several innovative marketing campaigns.

During the March 2011 NCAA Division I Men's Basketball Championship, Unilever launched an iAD campaign for the Dove for Men line with advertising delivered through iPad. By integrating the campaign with a sporting event important to college students with the innovative technology of the iPad, Unilever was able to deliver its message successfully to the audience.

In 2011, Unilever combined a high-profile sports event with innovative technology to launch the Dove for Men line. In a variation of the "Real Beauty" message, the campaign focused on supporting young men as they establish their identity and gain self-esteem. Or, in Dove's words: helping young men to be "comfortable in their own skin."

The Dove video series presents former football player and ESPN commentator Kirk Herbstreit, known as "Herbie" to fans, sharing personal experiences that have helped him become comfortable in his own skin. The Dove Men+Care "Journey to Comfort" uses the online video series to share stories from respected men whom young men can "relate to on their journey to becoming comfortable with themselves." The stories were shown throughout the college football season, including the Bowl Championship Series (BCS), ESPN's "Year of the Quarterback", and at dovemencare.com as part of a season-long Unilever sponsorship.

Unilever's Axe product line has also successfully pushed the envelope in creating intriguing campaigns that have helped to create the top-selling male personal care product line. A *Business Insider* article describes how Unilever decided to target a specific type of male and designed ads that would send the message to the "Insecure Novice" that Axe products would help him attract the attention of attractive women.

Axe Body Spray used this strategy in a highly successful campaign aimed at teens and college males. Introduced in 2007, the campaign was primarily web and video based. It featured the Bom Chicka Wah Wahs, a fictional female rock band. Andrew Adam Newman (*New York Times*, Oct 2007) described the appeal: girls in lingerie and stilettos singing the promise "If you have that aroma on, you can have our whole band." The campaign was a success with its emphasis on sexuality and appeal to the male desire to be more attractive to women. The campaign helped to establish brand identity and drove up the sales of the product.

In summary, Unilever's marketing toward college students has been successful in both profit and exposure. By using media that's already integrated into the daily lives of students and keeping the content provocative, Unilever has tapped into the buying power and probable product loyalty of Internet Pioneers. And by staying on the cutting edge of delivery and content, Unilever has set a benchmark for other marketers.

Case Study: Coke vs. Pepsi

The longest war ever waged hasn't been fought on battlefields. Rather, it's been conducted between Coca Cola and Pepsi, two iconic brands with a similar anchor product; cola, the beverage that has defined America since the beginning of the 20th century. Established respectively in 1886 and 1903, Coke and Pepsi have historically competed for consumers and shelf space. Today, they have almost equal shares of the beverage market.

In the first half of 2011, Coca Cola garnered 35 percent of beverage consumers, a slightly larger share than Pepsi's 32.9 percent. This was largely the result of aggressive marketing campaigns, many of them aimed at young consumers who have yet to establish brand loyalty.

These consumers include the 21.2 million Internet Pioneers and the 15 million college students who have especially high demand for the high-energy caffeine beverages that are the forte of both Coca Cola and Pepsi.

The idea that Pepsi and Coke are brands with different appeal has roots in the Pepsi Generation, a themed advertising campaign that began in 1963. Rather than claiming that Pepsi was just as good as Coke, the campaign set out to convince consumers that Pepsi drinkers were different — and more forward-thinking — than the older, more traditional folks who bought Coke. For a long time, the image of Pepsi drinkers being younger at heart prevailed in the media, from the revitalization of the "Pepsi Generation" campaign in the 1980s, to the commercials starring Michael Jackson and Madonna in the 1990s. In the mid-2000s, Britney Spears resuscitated the phrase "For Those Who Think Young" in her retro commercials for Pepsi.

Both Coca Cola and Pepsi have significantly altered their marketing strategies to target young consumers, focusing on creating inexpensive content to be disseminated via social media rather than on traditional advertising campaigns. In many ways, these campaigns provide marketing lessons for the future — successful tactics that will be copied and unsuccessful strategies that marketers will avoid.

Coca Cola's digital strategies for college students aim toward a global market while remaining locally relevant. Pepsi's campaigns have shifted heavily toward celebrity endorsements and music campaigns. In the last four years, Coke has amassed nearly three times as many media mentions as Pepsi.

Coke's success in the digital realm is due in large part to "The Happiness Machine," a viral video initiative. Coca Cola representatives travel to college campuses around the world and install Coke vending machines that are far more than beverage dispensers. Rather than ejecting the expected — a single Coke bottle — these machines dispense multiple sodas, pizzas, and in some cases, 20-foot subs. (Hidden compartments are custom-built into the machine.)

Recipients react with shock and amazement, giggling and calling out to friends as hands appear in the slot, bearing unlikely (and magical) gifts. A hidden camera records their reactions which are then used in creating videos. The first video (recorded at St. John's University, New York City) was released on YouTube on January 1, 2010. It went wildly viral, getting over 700 thousand hits in the next five days. Within a week, it had one million views, taking it to the top of the viral video chart. Several more videos have been distributed, and their success has contributed to the corporation's ability to cut back on marketing expenditures by almost $45 million.

The success of Coca Cola's "Happiness" campaign among Internet Pioneers lies in the simplicity of its core concept. Rather than being about consumerism, the videos are simple, feel-good productions that echo Coke's traditionally wholesome, Norman-Rockwell-like ads of jolly Santas, nuclear families, polar bears and dewy-faced youths. They associate the brand not with fame or unobtainable goals, but rather with an emotion that anyone — despite his or her religious affiliation, language capabilities, ethnicity, or belief system — can relate to on a visceral level.

"What Coke really gave away was a sense of happiness that created an emotional connection with the brand," explained Paul Iannacchino, the creative director of Definition 6, the agency that conceived of the "Happiness Machine" campaign. "Students involved in this video were caught up in their everyday lives, and this little moment touched them. We used free stuff to surprise people, but what we gave away was happiness and a smile. The key is engagement, whether you were there or just watching; free stuff was just the catalyst."

Coke also engages in more traditional forms of marketing to Internet Pioneers, signaling the importance of the generation to the brand, including Coca Cola Music, which promotes *emerging* artists by recording them singing Coke's advertising jingle, "Can You Feel It." In 2010, the brand launched Expedition 206, a program that sponsored three 20-something adventurers' travels around the world, reporting on Coke and its effect on people in 206 countries. The company also resorts to less tasteful forms of sponsorship, which include the "Coca Cola Beach," a party spot for Spring Break on South Padre Island in Texas. Free trips to the event are given away through a college campus "Text-To-Win" campaign, which offers other prizes such as gift cards from Target and Visa.

Pepsi and Social Responsibility

While Coke has actively targeted college students, Pepsi has staged campaigns that target a socially engaged audience in general. These campaigns included "Pepsi Refresh", the company's main marketing initiative introduced in 2010. The campaign invites people to submit ideas that they think will change the world. These include fundraising campaigns to buy uniforms for Special Olympics contenders and raising money to purchase books for local libraries, to name just two. An Internet audience then votes on which idea they like best. Whoever wins the vote gets funding from Pepsi to bring their ideas to life.

When Pepsi went digital, they shifted their focus to being a socially responsible brand. Then, backpedaling, they aggressively veered back toward being a lifestyle brand by focusing on music. Pepsi's campaigns include "Pepsi Pulse", a real-time visualization of social media conversations going on about Pepsi initiatives; "Pepsi X-Factor", a sponsorship website in collaboration with *X-Factor*, Simon Cowell's popular Fox program that competes with the Coke-sponsored *American Idol*, and "Pepsi SoundOff", a program that aims to create a virtual community based on social standing. Together, these disparate campaigns form a message that is difficult to discern.

In 2011, the marketing team "made a conscious decision to go aggressively back into music," says Frank Cooper, chief global consumer engagement officer at PepsiCo Beverages. "We have a rightful place in music."

Internet Pioneers live in a digital world where they are constantly inundated with lifestyle marketing guised as creative content. Being introduced to more of the same from a brand like Pepsi makes the brand's marketing efforts less memorable and engaging.

Both brands share well-established scholarship programs that award millions of dollars every year to worthy candidates. The Coca Cola Scholars Foundation, which gives annually to 1,400 college students, also has a Coca Cola Community College Academic Team, signaling their commitment to enable students of different backgrounds to succeed in the post-college world. Pepsi partners with institutions such as UNC, City College of New York, and Penn State to offer $10,000 scholarships to deserving students.

What is rare for Internet Pioneers and Internet Natives is having an experience that evokes innocent, unadulterated emotions, the best of which is happiness. With its "Happiness Machine," Coke manages to harness joy in their advertisements, while at the same time speaking intimately with a very diverse audience. The brand's focus on core values, along with Pepsi's inability to stay on course with a coherent brand identity, gives Coke the upper hand in the campus cola war. The lessons offer guidance for all marketers seeking to communicate with Internet Pioneers today and into the future, arguing for more emotionally-based campaigns and fewer traditional lifestyle marketing programs.

Hazards of College Marketing

One of the hazards of being a large company with many brands and a different marketing strategy for each product is the potential for values and messages in one campaign to contradict the messages of a sister brand's marketing.

In 2007, the Campaign for a Commercial Free Childhood (CCFC) denounced Unilever's Axe Campaign and pointed out the mixed messages that Unilever was sending to teens and young adults through the creatively conflicted Dove "Real Beauty" and Axe campaigns.

"Even as Unilever basks in praise for its Dove "Real Beauty" campaign, they are profiting from Axe marketing that blatantly objectifies and degrades young women."

~ Dr. Susan Linn
Director and Co-founder, CCFC

Unilever spokesperson Anita Larson defended the company in a *New York Times* article by saying that each marketing campaign is geared toward the specific brand and said that the Axe campaign was a spoof. "Unilever is a large global company with many brands in our portfolio," she said. "Each brand effort is tailored to reflect the unique interests and needs of its audience."

While the Axe campaign has been criticized, the outcome was successful. The campaign effectively captured the psyche of the target audience, and it communicated a positive message of enhanced self-esteem and confidence to young men.

With social media pervasive, marketers must be sensitive to new challenges created by it, as well as instant global communications. Coca Cola's successes have not been without setbacks, many of which have stemmed from social media campaigns questioning Coke's business dealings in countries where the company produces its products. College students across America have become involved in a campaign called "Killer Coke," which protests the corporation's actions. Launched on campuses in 2007, the campaign petitioned Smith, Oxford, Oberlin, Bard, Michigan State, and over 25 other colleges to terminate major contracts with Coke, in favor of introducing Pepsi onto campuses. On a few of the campuses, Coke products were banned entirely. The victory was especially sweet for Pepsi, which had been engaged in campus pouring wars since the early 1990s. In 2000, they had even filed an anti-trust lawsuit against Coca Cola for monopolizing the market for fountain-dispensed drinks in the United States. A federal judge dismissed the case.

In the highly politicized environment of early 2012, social media campaigns led Coca Cola, Pepsi, Kraft and other corporations to withdraw funding from the ALEC (American Legislative Exchange Council), which finances right-wing political organizations and initiatives. Social media will increasingly be a weapon used by Internet Pioneers to clearly communicate — and make purchase decisions based on — their political, moral and ethical beliefs. Marketers will need to be aware that their actions and policies domestically and around the world are an integral part of their brand messaging.

The Future: Internet Pioneers as Marketers

The single greatest threat to the traditional advertising business will be a failure to attract Internet Pioneers into the ad business.

The advertising and marketing business needs a radical overhaul, and Internet Pioneers can provide the necessary leadership. Internet Pioneers will be the first generation to enter the media and advertising businesses with the Internet in their DNA, and with an inherent understanding of how to reach consumers and communicate effectively via online, mobile and socially connected programs.

Over the next two decades, new innovative tactics that truly exploit the potential of the Internet will evolve as Internet Pioneers gain control over the marketing of major corporations, ad agencies and media companies.

These tactics will move the ad business in a different direction. They will focus on creative strategies tuned to online and mobile communications and Internet-based technologies rather than strategies designed for traditional media and especially for mass television.

It's a direction that will be more social and interactive, more engaging, more emotional, and more focused on building connections between the advertising messages and the content environment in which they appear. Marketing campaigns will depend on data and databases to target the right messages to the most receptive and potentially responsive audiences.

Advertising will travel from friend to friend as a part of recommendation engines, and advertising will be organized, curated and shared in the same way YouTube videos are today. TED.com has created the "Ads Worth Sharing" global initiative to identify and distribute messages that the curators at TED believe are worthy of attention for their creativity, message, relevance, controversy, etc.

Advertising will have direct commerce options embedded and activated instantly or when the consumer appears at a point of sale where the offer can be redeemed. Advertising will translate smoothly across multiple communications platforms.

Advertising will become more global as marketers recognize the potential of Internet communications, yet it will also serve consumers where they live, shop and travel. New digital strategies will displace local Pennysavers and Val-Pak coupon mailers. Local blog sites that serve their communities will expand and consolidate. These sites and apps will eventually dominate the market for consumer access to local information, services, merchant and restaurant recommendations and special offers.

As marketers begin to focus more on the Internet Native audiences and hire Internet Pioneers to manage advertising and marketing programs, completely new and unimagined relationships between marketers and consumers will evolve, altering the fundamental nature of advertising and communications.

Chapter 24:
The Future of the World as We Don't Know It

Anyone who was older than 25 in 2012 has little in common with the Internet Pioneers and Internet Natives born post-1991. While the world these post-Internet generations are inheriting is bewildering and may seem to some to be on a self-destructive downward spiral, my understanding of this new generation has given me a renewed and even optimistic outlook on the future.

But no matter how well we may understand the Internet Pioneers and Internet Natives, and no matter how much research we might do to learn more about them, we can only uncover and try to relate to the earliest stages of their evolution and future effects and influences.

Internet Pioneers are a transformative generation — bridging the gap between the "me" generations of the past several decades that have polarized almost all aspects of society and the "well balanced" generations that are emerging from the Internet culture. Internet Pioneers are, in that context, somewhat schizophrenic.

- They struggle with an awareness of the conflicts that have defined their youth, yet have an elevated consciousness and awareness of the need for a more balanced construct across all layers of human existence.

- They are focused on their day-to-day realities and challenges, yet also operate on a higher plane of social engagement.

- They are materialistic, yet not into material rewards.

- They are hard-working and hard-playing.

- They are conflicted about their roles, their wants, their needs and their goals. Yet they intuitively believe they are destined to achieve success and make a meaningful contribution to society.

- They believe in tolerance and acceptance, and that extends to a tolerance for those with whom they disagree. They expect equal tolerance of their lifestyles and opinions in return. Yet they are reluctant to become activists in support of their beliefs.

- They are funny and embrace humor, even politically incorrect humor that many may find offensive. But they are sensitive enough to understand when and where such humor is inappropriate.

- They are comfortable expressing their opinions and have little fear of authority, yet they are socially uncomfortable when put into roles outside their comfort zones.

- They are eager for assistance, support and guidance from those with more experience, but are convinced they have as much to offer as mentors as they do as mentees.

In my 1998 book *Reconnecting with Customers: Building Brands and Profits in The Relationship Age*, I wrote about the "Net-Generation," for whom I coined the term "N-Gen," calling them the "Engine" of the 21st century. I wrote then, and continue to believe, that "this generation is the most important generation in history — the most technologically savvy, educated, and economically powerful. This is a culturally diverse group to whom tolerance is not only important, it is natural. For the past several years, the number of immigrants entering the United States each year has surpassed the number of births, and this will continue for the next several years. Multiculturalism is far more apparent on MTV and Nickelodeon than it is on CBS."

I continued, "The N-Generation has far more influence over purchase decisions than preceding generations. It is the first generation that believes that its members are in control of technology, rather than technology controlling them. They do not sit passively in front of their television set. They interact. The percentage of kids who say it's 'in' to be online has jumped to 88 percent [in 1997]. The long sought-after 'killer app' is turning out to be the powerful N-Gen who perceive technology with a completely new set of perceptions, expectations, needs and issues. The killer app is the application of technology by a new generation defined by the Internet and computers to make connections and build relationships."

Looking back at my 1998 book in the context of writing this book, the two are a continuum, with a single core message: All the Internet-inspired inventions to date have been a precursor to the coming advances the Internet is inspiring and the extraordinary impact these advances will have on all aspects of culture and society.

The first wave of the "N-Gen" — the Internet Pioneers — are at the earliest stages of making their influence felt. They are an impressive group, and they will be up to the task of fulfilling their destiny to be the single most important generation of the past or next hundred years, even though they are the smallest — only 21.2 million.

When I began researching this group, I was concerned about whom I would discover. Would they prove to be a generation born into a society that elevates and honors false gods like Britney Spears and Paris Hilton; that has a shortened attention span brought on by a non-stop explosion of information, entertainment and constant social intrusion; a generation that seems to have little regard for traditional hierarchies or cultural mores? Would this generation have the chops to lead, inspire and guide society, or would they prove to be just a purposeless cohort group in the passing parade of humanity?

Of course, not all Internet Pioneers can be generalized with broad descriptions. They have more diversity than any generation of college-age youth that has preceded them — a larger percentage of them are Hispanic, Black and Asian. There are more Muslims among them. There are more openly gay 17- to 21-year-olds than ever before. They are at the front edge of a wave of diversity descending on America. Fifty-nine percent of college students in 2012 are female, and that disproportionate share will increase for at least the next decade, with the percent of graduate students even more weighted toward females. The effect of greater diversity in the general population and the population moving into their adult years will be game-changing — altering the culture and the strategic foundations of corporations, politics, education, the arts, media, advertising and almost every career category.

When asked: "What's the Future?" Internet Pioneers are likely to respond, "I Don't Know." But then they will explain to you how concerned they are about political dissension and social upheaval. Interventionist military politics are anathema to most, but they understand the nuances of international engagement. Economic collapse has been the norm throughout their lives, and the appeal of Wall Street is leveraged with a concern about income equality. The debates over global climate change, abortion, gay marriage and "Don't Ask Don't Tell," health care, gun control, education, unions and taxes are depressing. They want to move on from the partisan debates that polarize society. They want solutions, not controversies.

Internet Pioneers are the most aware generation ever, and they are committed to moving their lives forward, becoming productive adults and contributing in meaningful ways to society and to their communities — whether those communities be in their neighborhoods or online and global. But they remain weighted down with the baggage of generations before them who have led the nation to the brink of economic, political and social bankruptcy. Their first task will be to shed that baggage and refocus their energy on more positive and productive pursuits.

They are focused on their futures and welcome the prospect (eventual) of marriage and families. But they are unschooled in the basic foundations of one-to-one human relationships and have become overly dependent on technology to manage relationships in ways older generations truly cannot fathom.

We have no way of knowing how this new reality will be manifested and how relationships will evolve. From corporate human resource managers to educators to therapists to dating site executives, the relationship implications for Internet Natives need to be studied, interpreted and understood. But even then, the ability of those who grew up as part of pre-Internet generations will be of limited value in relating to and addressing the needs of Internet Natives and the problems and issues they are facing. It will be a mistake to try to anticipate the future problems of Internet Pioneers and Internet Natives or the solutions to these problems. Our traditional approaches, perceptions, beliefs and experiences are very different from theirs.

Pre-Internet generations — X-Gens and Y-Gens — will remain the most visible and powerful influences in society for at least the next two decades. But, inevitably and sadly, there will also be more disclosures about illegal, immoral and unethical actions of these generations, as well as conflicts, controversy and polarization that will further disconnect them from Internet Pioneers.

From Henry Kissinger's secret trip on Air Force One to China in 1970 to the election of Barack Obama, the world has been on a roller coaster ride of change and disruption. Internet Pioneers are at the forefront of a movement that will set a new stabilizing course for humanity, but it will take decades before their true influence and importance will be fully recognized and understood.

My goal with this book has been to share insights on the transformational effect on society resulting from the development of the Internet and the period of literally and virtually mind-altering advances that interconnectivity will lead to over the next few decades.

My study of Internet Pioneers — the small generation of today's college students born between 1991 and 1995 — provides a unique perspective on these coming advances and shifts in society, culture and all aspects of human interaction.

I hope I have shared a positive perspective, ultimately one of hope and even excitement that we will, indeed, be in good hands. Internet Pioneers are a generation I'm prepared to depend on to lead us into a period when reasonable minds and attitudes will prevail; when polarized segments of society will begin an inexorable move toward mutual understanding and acceptance; when human rights and human empowerment will prevail; when economic disparity will be rebalanced; when religious, ethnic and humanistic diversity will be embraced; and when the Internet will prove to have been one of the greatest and most positive transformational innovations and advances in history.

To provide some focused perspective to how Internet Pioneers may influence society, culture and relationships, here are a few personal perspectives and predictions for the future:

Relationships

The emphasis on "hook ups" during their college days assures a generation that is sexually liberal and liberated but that ultimately values relationships and marriage. They will come late to marriage and families, but divorce rates will decline. Internet Pioneers are open to gay marriage and will be active advocates for assuring full gay rights in society and the workplace. The hook up culture will extend across many aspects of their lives, as Internet Pioneers resist long-term commitments and entanglements, from their jobs to brand preferences. But once committed, they are fully engaged and actively involved, and willing to use the social tools available to them to communicate their support.

Women's Rights

Almost 60 percent of college graduates among Internet Pioneers will be women, and a larger percentage of graduate degrees will be granted to women. They are career-oriented and will be marrying and starting families later than previous generations. They are also more likely to stay in their jobs after having children and will find ways to achieve balance in their lives. As they begin their careers, they will connect with accomplished women mentors. A process of mutual upward and downward mentoring will assure that younger women will be better prepared to achieve success. Already successful women will have young coaches to help them adapt to, relate to, and embrace Internet Pioneers and the new approaches they will bring to all aspects of work and culture. While male Internet Pioneers are also open to similar relationships, their older colleagues are less evolved in their receptivity to younger men as mentors to them, and are less able to serve as effective mentors. Women will gain more power, responsibility, authority and dominance in a broad cross-section of corporations, institutions, government bodies and non-profit organizations.

Religion

Tolerance is a priority among Internet Pioneers. Religious dogma that is founded on intolerance will be less accepted or embraced as this group begins building their families and searching for religious affiliation. Offshoot congregations that embrace a more inclusive approach will evolve out of doctrinaire religions. Spirituality and a focus on the relevance and meaning of an afterlife in our present lives will gain importance. Internet congregations will become more prominent, as religious leaders emerge from websites, YouTube videos, and mobile apps.

Diversity

Internet Pioneers are at the front edge of a wave of ethnic, cultural and gender diversity in America. They are a global generation that views diversity and equality as the norm, not an ideal to be fought for (and against) as it has been by previous generations. They bring to their relationships, the workplace and their communities a set of fundamental beliefs about equal rights. They accept and embrace diversity and are far more color blind than earlier generations. To them, fair pay is common sense and the importance of work/life balance is understood. While it may take decades for these beliefs and attitudes to become the norm in American society, Internet Pioneers will be at the forefront of advancing and furthering the cause of diversity in all aspects of life.

Education

Internet Pioneers have grown up in a dysfunctional educational system. They fundamentally value school and had many qualified teachers. Yet, with a few exceptions, their schools and education remain embedded in 19th-century models with little relevance to the basic needs most Internet Pioneers will require as they graduate from college. This first generation of Internet Natives will become activists in restructuring education to embrace technology, connectivity and collaboration. Many of them will work as professionals and volunteers in educational systems to re-introduce a focus on the arts, physical activity, languages, interpersonal skills, and preparatory training for the jobs of the future, especially related to technology.

Politics

Internet Pioneers are most likely to support candidates for political office who advocate individual rights including abortion, gay marriage, medical marijuana, limited gun control; clearly defined economic policies that do not overly advantage the already wealthy; smaller government; a strong but controlled military with a non-interventionist agenda; and a reduction of the dominance of the military-industrial complex. They are likely to emerge as a powerful voting bloc, with a large percentage planning to vote in both presidential and general elections. They instinctively embrace multiculturalism and will be more likely than preceding generation to vote without consideration of gender, ethnic or sexual inclinations of the candidates. Morality and ethics, however, will be important concerns.

Television and Media

Internet Pioneers will embrace interactivity and naturally incorporate two-screen activities into their television viewing patterns. They will be less engaged with television overall, and will gravitate toward programs that embrace a tolerant and inclusive perspective on society. Entertainment and variety programs will appeal to Internet Natives, as will soap-opera style content across multiple platforms. They are not only Internet Natives, but YouTube natives, and will naturally be comfortable with short-form content, amateur videos, commenting and sharing. "TV" programs will be most successful when they evolve as brands that extend across multiple platforms, incorporate gaming, commerce and social applications, attract a large fan base and appeal to a loyal core audience. Gaming will be an embedded part of the media culture.

Music

The music industry will evolve further and further away from the "album" construct and toward one-hit wonders. Talent and the music industry will measure each new release based on its stand-alone hit potential, as packaging multiple songs around one or two hits becomes more and more challenging. Touring will be the most important financial opportunity, although prices will need to be kept low and venues comparatively small, except for the very few groups that can fill Madison Square Garden. Since most of those performers established their careers in the 60s and 70s, the current dependence of the music industry on scalable tours will erode. The music industry's continued focus on large corporate studios will be all but gone within another decade, and the new powers will be the leading digital distributors: Vevo, Pandora, Spotify, Clear Channel, Radio.com and others that will evolve.

Community, Culture and Commerce

There have been several articles and blogs comparing the development of the Internet to the invention of the automobile. While the car was a great invention with huge value, its greatest contributions were the changes in society it enabled. People became mobile and moved around the country, fundamentally shifting the nation's economic foundation. The car enabled people to move from the city — near their work and families — to the suburbs where they could afford a home and land. The car was at the foundation of empowering and enabling these societal and economic shifts. We did not know at the time how the suburbs would ultimately evolve and could not have envisioned thousands of malls and millions of strip centers, the expansion of highways and local roads, or the resulting years of urban blight. And we can only try to envision how the Internet and Internet Pioneers will alter community, commuting, commerce and connectivity as we know them today. The Internet, like the automobile, is spawning a plethora of innovations that will unlock potential as unimaginable to many of us as the advances spurred by the combustion engine and car were to their first users.

Business

Amazon was launched in 1994, the same year that FedEx became the first to offer online package tracking. Netflix, Google, and PayPal all were launched in 1997 and 1998. Napster, the very first peer-to-peer file-sharing program, was first released in 1999. The Internet has jumped from computers to mobile devices, televisions, airplanes, cars, and medical implants. It has led to dramatic changes in the way people share information, communicate with each other, do business, and generally live their lives. It has diffused itself through almost every device and electronic product in use today. All this took less than twenty years. The Internet is spawning a plethora of business innovations that will unlock potential of undreamed-of proportions. The Internet and computing have revolutionized transportation, not of material goods, but of information, social connectivity and entertainment. Internet Pioneers and online/mobile connectivity will be important forces behind a refocusing of corporate priorities that will place more emphasis on social and cultural responsibility. While profit will always be the motivating focus of business, Internet Pioneers will bring to business a new sense of ethics, morality, equality and economic fairness.

With the introduction of the Internet browser in 1993 and the subsequent years of innovation, the global pace of life and the inter-connectedness of individuals, groups, countries and corporations have been completely changed forever. The first generation of online natives is guiding us across the chasm from the Pre- to the Post-Internet Age. As the Internet becomes an increasingly embedded part of our lives, every one of us becomes an Internet Pioneer, struggling to adapt to a new world.

Addendum

Acknowledgements

With gratitude and thanks to all those who supported me in so many ways during the preparation for, writing and marketing of this book. Mere mention cannot do justice to the contributions many of you have made, and I'm certain there are many who deserve mention but who are unintentionally not included.

To Maryann Teller, my chief operating officer for the past 21 years. To my family: Gert Myers; Norah, Isabelle and Claire Burden; Ariele Myers Tritt; Dori, Leo and Jonah Tritt; Andy and Dominique Myers; Dan Myers and Janie Nutter; Sandy Adirondack. To Shelly Palmer, York House Press, Penelope Holt, Sheila Parsonson and Oriana Magnera for their guidance and editing. To Stuart Sandhaus and to Ipsos/OTX, Bruce Friend and Nancy Meyer for their research support. To the researchers, writers and editors at Contently.com and WriterAccess.com. To all those interviewed for this book who shared their perspectives, insights and understanding. To Gerry Laybourne for her support and amazing contributions to the Internet Pioneer generation. To the extraordinary women of the Women in Media Mentoring Initiative, several of whom have been both supportive and inspirational, especially Persia Tatar, Samantha Dascher, Lara Designor, Olga Casabona, Lisa Shalett, Allie Kline, Blair Cobb, Bonnie Kintzer and Katharine Panessidi. The Newhouse School family, especially Dean Lorraine Branham, Lynn Vanderhoek, Ed Wise and Kelly Jean Brown. Dean Mary Brabeck of the NYU Steinhardt School. Paul Adams and Carolyn Everson of Facebook. To David Houle, a long-time great friend and collaborator. To all my friends and colleagues at Caffe Cielo, especially Larry Divney, Gumby and Joe. To the Fast Lane and the Captains of Cable. To my talented colleagues at Cinelan. Plus to Debra Sharon Davis, Andy Batkin, Delaney Porter, Kitty Barnes, Eric Walpert, Joyce Tudryn, Dave Morgan, Alan Brown and Alan Elkin, Greg Coleman, Arianna Huffington, Michael Kassan, Dave Poltrack, Sir Martin Sorrell, Nick Brien, and Ian Wishingrad.

Special thanks to the subscribers to my reports and all those who have supported me throughout my career in the media, marketing, advertising, entertainment and financial industries. Finally, and most importantly, thanks to the Internet Pioneers who have not only inspired me but who will prove to be an inspiration to many future generations.

Myers Survey of Internet Pioneers

Survey conducted online in July/August 2011 by Media Advisory Group and Ipsos/OTX. Survey included a representatively balanced geographic, ethnic, gender sample of 1,000 U.S. high school and college students aged 17 to 21. (Slight over-representation of New York State and California respondents.) Respondents were screened based on being currently in college or planning to attend college. Respondents were required to complete the full survey and received compensation in the form of credits toward product purchases and prizes. In-person interviews were completed separately by several researchers.

Except for "political persuasion," percentages include only those who expressed an opinion and do not include those who did not respond or who did not select one of the opinions included.

When it comes to U.S. politics, I consider myself to be:

Liberal/Progressive:	22%
Moderate:	19%
Conservative:	17%
Libertarian:	1%
No Political Persuasion:	14%
Don't Know:	27%

I plan to vote in the Presidential Election:

(16% unsure excluded from the tabulation)

Yes:	88%
No:	12%
Yes — Politically Conservative:	96%
Yes — Politically Progressive/Liberal:	91%
Yes — Politically Moderate:	91%

While in college and after graduation, I expect to vote in political elections:

(13% unsure excluded from the tabulation)

Yes:	92%
No:	8%
Yes — Politically Conservative:	99%
Yes — Politically Progressive/Liberal:	94%
Yes — Politically Moderate:	94%

Regarding U.S. involvement in foreign wars, the position that best describes my position is:

It is important that the U.S. continues its current commitments but gets out soon	55%
Politically Conservative:	55%
Politically Progressive/Liberal:	66%
Politically Moderate:	60%

We should avoid all future military commitments	24%
Politically Conservative:	11%
Politically Progressive/Liberal:	22%
Politically Moderate:	21%

The threat of terrorism requires that we maintain a military presence overseas	21%
Politically Conservative:	34%
Politically Progressive/Liberal:	11%
Politically Moderate:	19%

My opinion on same sex marriage is:

I approve	57%
Politically Conservative:	25%
Politically Progressive/Liberal:	79%
Politically Moderate:	59%

My opinion on same sex marriage is:

I'm opposed but agree others should have the right	23%
Politically Conservative:	25%
Politically Progressive/Liberal:	17%
Politically Moderate:	29%

I disapprove	20%
Politically Conservative:	51%
Politically Progressive/Liberal:	3%
Politically Moderate:	12%

My opinion on freedom of choice vs. right to life is:

I believe a woman should have free choice to terminate a pregnancy if medically safe	53%
Politically Conservative:	30%
Politically Progressive/Liberal:	59%
Politically Moderate:	58%

Abortion should be illegal in some but not all instances	31%
Politically Conservative:	39%
Politically Progressive/Liberal:	4%
Politically Moderate:	7%

Abortion should be illegal in all instances	16%
Politically Conservative:	31%
Politically Progressive/Liberal:	16%
Politically Moderate:	35%

My opinion on income taxes is:

(Multiple choices allowed)

Only taxes on the wealthy and corporations should be increased	41%
Politically Conservative:	28%
Politically Progressive/Liberal:	59%
Politically Moderate:	40%

There should be a 'flat tax' (everyone pays the same percentage on their income)	35%
Politically Conservative:	42%
Politically Progressive/Liberal:	25%
Politically Moderate:	38%

Tax loopholes and temporary tax cuts only should be eliminated	26%
Politically Conservative:	25%
Politically Progressive/Liberal:	30%
Politically Moderate:	36%

Taxes are a necessary reality and we need more taxes	25%
Politically Conservative:	21%
Politically Progressive/Liberal:	40%
Politically Moderate:	26%

Income taxes should be eliminated and sales taxes increased to 20-30%	7%
Politically Conservative:	10%
Politically Progressive/Liberal:	2%
Politically Moderate:	9%

My opinion on income taxes is:

There should be no tax increases of any type	4%
Politically Conservative:	36%
Politically Progressive/Liberal:	13%
Politically Moderate:	23%

My opinion on health care is:

(Multiple choices allowed)

The government should support health care for all people	59%
Politically Conservative:	24%
Politically Progressive/Liberal:	82%
Politically Moderate:	59%

Health care programs are good as they are and should not be changed (survey conducted post-"ObamaCare")	21%
Politically Conservative:	31%
Politically Progressive/Liberal:	13%
Politically Moderate:	20%

Most forms of government funded health care should be eliminated	19%
Politically Conservative:	44%
Politically Progressive/Liberal:	5%
Politically Moderate:	21%

Government should provide health care only for those who need it	1%
Politically Conservative:	1%
Politically Progressive/Liberal:	0%
Politically Moderate:	0%
Government should provide health care only to legal citizens, not illegal immigrants	0%

My opinion on Medicare is:

I'm opposed to Medicare health benefits for my generation being reduced and delayed to an older age	64%
Politically Conservative:	54%
Politically Progressive/Liberal:	73%
Politically Moderate:	63%
I don't mind Medicare health benefits being reduced and delayed for those in my generation	36%
Politically Conservative:	46%
Politically Progressive/Liberal:	27%
Politically Moderate:	38%

My opinion on global climate change is:

It is important and I support environmental issues	32%
Politically Conservative:	19%
Politically Progressive/Liberal:	46%
Politically Moderate:	39%

It's important but I'm not personally engaged	28%
Politically Conservative:	24%
Politically Progressive/Liberal:	22%
Politically Moderate:	31%

It's critically important and I'm passionate about the environment	20%
Politically Conservative:	14%
Politically Progressive/Liberal:	25%
Politically Moderate:	19%

I haven't seen enough proof that it's real	15%
Politically Conservative:	34%
Politically Progressive/Liberal:	5%
Politically Moderate:	7%

It's not that important but I believe it's real	5%
Politically Conservative:	9%
Politically Progressive/Liberal:	2%
Politically Moderate:	4%

My opinion about the legalization of marijuana with a medical prescription is:

I support it but don't really care	36%
Politically Conservative:	30%
Politically Progressive/Liberal:	46%
Politically Moderate:	35%

I'm all for it	25%
Politically Conservative:	15%
Politically Progressive/Liberal:	33%
Politically Moderate:	23%

I'm opposed to it	22%
Politically Conservative:	34%
Politically Progressive/Liberal:	14%
Politically Moderate:	25%

I think it would be dangerous	18%
Politically Conservative:	22%
Politically Progressive/Liberal:	7%
Politically Moderate:	17%

My opinion on gun control is:

There should be strict gun control enforcement	33%
Politically Conservative:	26%
Politically Progressive/Liberal:	37%
Politically Moderate:	41%

My opinion on gun control is:

There should be strict gun control enforcement	33%
Politically Conservative:	26%
Politically Progressive/Liberal:	37%
Politically Moderate:	41%

Owning all guns is ok but not carrying them in public	24%
Politically Conservative:	22%
Politically Progressive/Liberal:	24%
Politically Moderate:	25%

Some guns should be legal but automatic weapons need to be illegal	17%
Politically Conservative:	21%
Politically Progressive/Liberal:	19%
Politically Moderate:	15%

Everyone should have the right to own guns and have guns in public	15%
Politically Conservative:	26%
Politically Progressive/Liberal:	7%
Politically Moderate:	11%

All guns should be restricted to law enforcement officials only	11%
Politically Conservative:	6%
Politically Progressive/Liberal:	13%
Politically Moderate:	11%

When it comes to the economy of the U.S., I believe:

It will get better in the next four years   35%

Politically Conservative:	28%
Politically Progressive/Liberal:	45%
Politically Moderate:	41%

It will get worse in the next four years   31%

Politically Conservative:	40%
Politically Progressive/Liberal:	26%
Politically Moderate:	22%

It will stay the same for the next four years   17%

Politically Conservative:	14%
Politically Progressive/Liberal:	16%
Politically Moderate:	22%

I'm panicked about the U.S. economy   18%

Politically Conservative:	18%
Politically Progressive/Liberal:	13%
Politically Moderate:	15%

When it comes to the global economy, I believe:

The global importance and power of the U.S. economy will become considerably less important in the next four years	24%

The global importance and power of the U.S. economy will become somewhat less important in the next four years	24%

The U.S. will remain the most important and powerful economy into the foreseeable future	24%
Politically Conservative:	25%
Politically Progressive/Liberal:	22%
Politically Moderate:	21%

The global importance and power of the U.S. economy has already become less important and will continue to decline	19%
Politically Conservative:	18%
Politically Progressive/Liberal:	18%
Politically Moderate:	15%

I'm panicked about the whole global economy and believe the U.S. will sink with it	9%

Definition of Millennials/Generation Y

From Wikipedia, The Free Encyclopedia
http://en.wikipedia.org/wiki/Millennials
(Redirected from Millennials)

This article is about the demographic cohort (a group of subjects with a common defining characteristic) following Generation X. For other uses, see Generation Y (disambiguation).

Generation Y, also known as the ***Millennial Generation*** (or ***Millennials***), ***Generation Next***, ***Net Generation***, or ***Echo Boomers***, describes the demographic cohort following Generation X. There are no precise dates for when the Millennial generation starts and ends, and commentators have used birth dates ranging somewhere from the mid-1970s to the early 2000s. Members of this generation are called Echo Boomers, due to the significant increase in birth rates through the 1980s and into the 1990s, and because many of them are children of baby boomers. The 20th century trend toward smaller families in developed countries continued, however, so the relative impact of the "baby boom echo" was generally less pronounced than the original boom.

Characteristics of the generation vary by region, depending on social and economic conditions. However, it is generally marked by an increased use and familiarity with communications, media, and digital technologies. The effects of this environment are disputed.

Terminology

The *Generation Y* first appeared in an August 1993 *Ad Age* editorial to describe teenagers of the day, which they defined, at that time, as separate from Generation X, and then aged 12 or younger (born after 1981), as well as the teenagers of the upcoming ten years. Since then, the company has sometimes used 1982 as the starting birth year for this generation. "Generation Y" alludes to a succession from "Generation X."

The name "Echo Boomers" refers to the size of the generation and its relation to the Baby Boomer generation.

Authors William Strauss and Neil Howe have been influential in defining American generations in their book *Generations: The History of America's Future, 1584 to 2069* (1991). Their generational theory is frequently cited in books and articles on the subject. Howe and Strauss maintain that they use the term *Millennials* in place of *Generation Y* because the members of the generation themselves coined the term, not wanting to be associated with Generation X. Almost a decade later, they followed their large study of the history of American demographics with a book devoted to the new generation, titled *Millennials Rising: The Next Great Generation* (2000). In both books, William Strauss and Neil Howe use 1982 and 2001 as the start and end years of the generation, respectively. They believe that the coming of age of year 2000 high school graduates sharply contrasts with those born before them and after them due to the attention they received from the media and what influenced them politically.

According to the authors' 1997 book, *The Fourth Turning,* modern history repeats itself every four generations; approximately 80–100 years. The authors of the book mention that the four-cycles always come in the same order. The first one, the *High cycle*, occurs when a new order or human expansion is developed, replacing the older one. The next cycle is called the *Awakening*. More spiritual than the previous, this is a time of rebellion against the already established order. The third cycle is known as the *Unraveling*, when elements of individualism and fragmentation take over society, developing a troubled era which leads directly to the *Fourth Turning*, an era of crisis dominating society during which a redefinition of its very structure, goals, and purposes is established.

Each generation has its archetypes, the four having the following one defined as: *Prophet, Nomad, Hero,* and *Artist.* According to the aforementioned book, Millennials belong to the Hero category, featuring a deep trust in authority and institutions; being somewhat conventional, but still powerful. They grew up during an *Unraveling* cycle with more protections than the previous generation (Gen X). They are heavily dependent on team work, and thus, when they come of age, turn into the heroic team-working young people of a Crisis. In their middle years, they become the energetic, decisive, and strong leaders of a *High* cycle; and in old age, they become the criticized powerful elders of an *Awakening* cycle. Another previous generation that belongs to this category is The Greatest Generation (1916–1924).

One author, Elwood Carlson, locates the American generation, which he calls "New Boomers," between 1983 and 2001, because of the upswing in births after 1983, finishing with the "political and social challenges" that occurred after the terrorist acts of September 11, 2001, and the "persistent economic difficulties" of the time.

In Australia, there is much debate over the dates of Generation Y — that is, when "Gen Y" began, and the "cut-off" period. It is generally accepted, however, that the first "Gen Y" members were born in 1982. Though some sources use the date range 1982-1995 for the generation, many, including the Australian Bureau of Statistics, use 1982-2000.

In Canada, 1982 is generally thought to be the starting birth year for Generation Y, ending in the mid-1990s or 2000, sometimes even as late as 2004.

Like members of Generation X, who are heavily influenced by the advent of MTV, early members of Generation Y are also sometimes called the MTV Generation. This term can also be a catch phrase for youth of the late 20th century, depending on the context.

Jean Twenge, author of the 2007 book *Generation Me*, considers Generation Y along with later Xers to be part of a generation called Generation Me. This is based on personality surveys that showed increasing narcissism among this generation compared to Boomers when they were teens and twentysomethings. She questions the predictions of Strauss & Howe that this generation would come out civic-minded, citing the fact that when the War on Iraq began military enlistments went down instead of up.

Twenge attributes confidence and tolerance to this generation, as well as a sense of entitlement, narcissism and rejection of social conventions.

Fred Bonner believes that much of the commentary on the Millennial Generation may be partially accurate, but overly general and that many of the traits they describe apply primarily to "white, affluent teenagers who accomplish great things as they grow up in the suburbs, who confront anxiety when applying to super-selective colleges, and who multitask with ease as their helicopter parents hover reassuringly above them." Other socio-economic groups often do not display the same attributes commonly attributed to Generation Y. During class discussions, he has listened to black and Hispanic students describe how some or all of the so-called seven core traits did not apply to them. They often say the "special" trait, in particular, is unrecognizable. "It's not that many diverse parents don't want to treat their kids as special," he says, "but they often don't have the social and cultural capital, the time and resources, to do that."

Demographics

Experts differ on the actual start date of Generation Y. Some sources use starting dates as early as 1976. Other sources use 1978, 1980, or 1982. Generation Y is the group generally considered to be the last generation of children wholly born in the 20th century. And while 1982 is a fairly common start date, some sources use even later dates. Sources citing 1982 mark the end the generation either in the early or mid-1990s or the early 2000s, with 1982-1995 and 1982-2000 as common ranges. Today, there are approximately 80 million Echo Boomers.

Generation Y has a tendency to be more culturally liberal with many supporting modern yet historically more liberal views in general as well as various other politically liberal stances, but, in spite of the new dominant liberal growth, a growing number of new youth clubs and groups have been created in developed countries (such as the US, UK, Japan, Australia and Italy) to take the task of promoting and preserving conservative views and religious beliefs (i.e. the rapid growth of nondenominational churches by gen-Yers), such as free market principles and "socially conservative" behavior (i.e. abstinence from drug experimentation, underage drinking and premarital sex). Since the 2000 U.S. Census which allowed persons to select more than one racial group, "Millennials" in abundance have asserted their right to have all their heritages respected, counted and acknowledged.

Generation Y'ers are largely the children of the Baby Boomers. Younger members of this generation have parents that belong to Generation X, and some older members have parents that are members of the Silent Generation.

There are different views regarding Generation Y. When the term originated in 1993, it referred to teenagers aged 13 to 19 at the time (born between 1974 and 1980) with "more to come over the next 10 years". Here is a verbatim reprint of the actual *Advertising Age* op ed. of August 30, 1993 — the above erroneous information notwithstanding:

"That cynical, purple-haired blob watching TV, otherwise known as Generation X, has been giving marketers fits for a long time. He doesn't respond to advertising, isn't brand-loyal and probably doesn't have much discretionary income, i.e. a job. But help is on the way. Following this angry young adult generation is a group of teens-agers who are leaving Generation X at the gate. There are 27 million of these 13- to-19-year-olds spending $ 95 billion a year, and both numbers will rise in the next 10 years. As our headline last week pointed out, this group is interested in *real life, real solutions*.

"Teens care — about AIDS, race relations, child abuse and abortion. But instead of saying, *I got screwed*, they say, *What am I going to do about it?* They like to volunteer and they respond to marketers who they can believe are helping make the world better. There are other differences with Generation X. Male teens read and don't spend all their time in front of the TV. A Roper survey showed that 83% of male teens read a major magazine at least once every four weeks, and 43% subscribe to a magazine. Comic books and place-based media are good ways to reach teens. If they're over 16, they listen to radio.

"OK, they like to shop for price and dump a brand if it gets costly. In personal care products especially, teens look for bargains. But Jane Grossman, Seventeen publisher, says they *love brands* and *trust advertising more than any other group.*

"That advertising can address them honestly and seriously without their tuning out. The Gap, Reebok and Bausch & Lomb are but three of the marketers that speak to teens without condescending to hip-hop language to do it. And they are reaping the benefits, proving again there are no smarter consumers than our average teen-agers, and no smarter marketers than those who speak honestly to them."

Economy

Economic prospects for the Millennials have worsened due to the late-2000s recession. Several governments have instituted major youth employment schemes out of fear of social unrest due to the dramatically increased rates of youth unemployment. In Europe, youth unemployment levels are very high (40% in Spain, 35% in the Baltic states, 19.1% in Britain and more than 20% in many more). In 2009 leading commentators began to worry about the long term social and economic effects of the unemployment. Unemployment levels in other areas of the world are also high, with the youth unemployment rate in the U.S. reaching a record level (19.1%, July 2010) since the statistic started being gathered in 1948. In the United States the economic difficulties have led to dramatic increases in youth poverty, unemployment, and the numbers of young people living with their parents. It has been argued that this unemployment rate and poor economic situation has given Generation Y a rallying call with the 2011 Occupy Wall Street movement. In Canada, unemployment amongst youths aged 15 to 24 years of age in July 2009 was 15.9%, the highest it had been in 11 years.

Generation Y who grew up in Asian countries show different preferences and expectations of work to those who grew up in the US or Europe. This is usually attributed to the differing cultural and economic conditions experienced while growing up.

The Millennials are sometimes called the "Trophy Generation", or "Trophy Kids," a term that reflects the trend in competitive sports, as well as many other aspects of life, where mere participation is frequently enough for a reward. It has been reported that this is an issue in corporate environments. Some employers are concerned that Millennials have too great expectations from the workplace. Studies predict that Generation Y will switch jobs frequently, holding far more than Generation X due to their great expectations. To address these new challenges, many large firms are currently studying the social and behaviorial patterns of Millennials and are trying to devise programs that decrease intergenerational estrangement, and increase relationships of reciprocal understanding between older employees and Millennials, while at the same time making Millennials more comfortable. The UK's Institute of Leadership & Management researched the gap in understanding between Generation Y recruits and their managers in collaboration with Ashridge Business School. The findings included high expectations for advancement, salary and for a coaching relationship with their manager, and suggested that organisations will need to adapt to accommodate and make the best use of Generation Y. In an example of a company trying to do just this, Goldman Sachs conducts training programs that use actors to portray Millennials who assertively seek more feedback, responsibility, and involvement in decision making. After the performance, employees discuss and debate the generational differences they have seen played out.

Peter Pan Generation

This generation is also sometimes referred to as the *Boomerang Generation* or *Peter Pan Generation*, because of the members' perceived penchant for delaying some rites of passage into adulthood, longer periods than most generations before them. These labels were also a reference to a trend toward members living with their parents for longer periods than previous generations.

As a group, Generation Y are said to be much closer to their parents than their parents' generation, the Baby Boomers were. While 40% of Baby Boomers in 1974 claimed they would be "better off without their parents" according to one study, 90% of Generation Y'ers claimed to be "extremely close" to their parents in another study. Most also claim that the older generations had better morals. Generation Y also saw the highest divorce rates of their parents, was the highest amount of children in foster care programs, and the highest amounts of recorded child abuse cases in U.S. history.

According to Kimberly Palmer, "High housing prices, the rising cost of higher education, and the relative affluence of the older generation are among the factors driving the trend." However, other explanations are seen as contributing. Questions regarding a clear definition of what it means to be an adult also impacts a debate about delayed transitions into adulthood. For instance, one study by professors at Brigham Young University found that college students are more likely now to define "adult" based on certain personal abilities and characteristics rather than more traditional "rite of passage" events. Dr. Larry Nelson, one of the three Marriage, Family, and Human Development professors to perform the study, also noted that some Millennials are delaying the transition from childhood to adulthood as a response to mistakes made by their parents. "In prior generations, you get married and you start a career and you do that immediately. What young people today are seeing is that approach has led to divorces, to people unhappy with their careers ... The majority want to get married [...] they just want to do it right the first time, the same thing with their careers."

Diversity

Internet Pioneers are at the front edge of a wave of ethnic, cultural and gender diversity in America. They are a global generation that views diversity and equality as the norm, not an ideal to be fought for (and against) as it has been by previous generations. They bring to their relationships, the workplace and their communities a set of fundamental beliefs about equal rights. They accept and embrace diversity and are far more color blind than earlier generations. To them, fair pay is common sense and the importance of work/life balance is understood. While it may take decades for these beliefs and attitudes to become the norm in American society, Internet Pioneers will be at the forefront of advancing and furthering the cause of diversity in all aspects of life.

Religion

In the United States, Generation Y has a slightly lower level of religiosity to older generations, and they are more likely to be skeptical of religious institutions. A 2005 study looked at 1,385 people aged 18 to 25 and found that over half of those in the study said that they pray regularly before a meal. A third said that they talked about religion with friends, attend places of worship, and read religious materials weekly. Twenty-three percent of those studied did not identify themselves as belonging to a religious affiliation.

Communication and Interaction

The Millennial Generation (or Gen Y), like other generations, has been shaped by the events, leaders, developments and trends of its time. The rise of instant communication technologies made possible through use of the Internet, such as email, texting, and IM and new media used through websites like YouTube and social networking sites like Facebook, MySpace, and Twitter, may explain the Millennials' reputation for being somewhat peer-oriented due to easier facilitation of communication through technology (Rock and soul for baby boomers, grunge, techno/rave and hip hop for Generation X). The 2000s produced no new, epoch-defining music genres, unlike past decades. Instead genres such as hip hop and R&B built incrementally on where they were in the 90's. Autotune has been cited as the decade's sole musical innovation. Many have cited the spread of information technology, from YouTube to iTunes, to file sharing blogs, as having increased the presence of the past in individuals lives because of the range of content that can be accessed. As a result, Generation Y has revived styles of past decades without actually creating anything new.

Now indie rock of the early 2000s has been attributed to Generation Y, as has the group Radiohead.

Expression and acceptance has been highly important to this generation. In well-developed nations, several cohorts of Generation Y members have found comfort in online games such as MMORPGs and virtual worlds like *World of Warcraft* and *Second Life*. Flash mobbing, Internet memes, and online communities have given some of the more expressive Generation Y members acceptance, while online pen pals have given the more socially timid individuals acceptance as well.

There is a trend among Millennials to choose urban, or gentrified neighborhoods, as their preferred living situations.

Digital Technology

In their 2007 book, authors Junco and Mastrodicasa expanded on the work of Howe and Strauss to include research-based information about the personality profiles of Millennials, especially as it relates to higher education. They conducted a large-sample (7,705) research study of college students. They found that Next Generation college students, born between

1982–1992, were frequently in touch with their parents and they used technology at higher rates than people from other generations. In their survey, they found that 97% of these students owned a computer, 94% owned a cell phone, and 56% owned an MP3 player. They also found that students spoke with their parents an average of 1.5 times a day about a wide range of topics. Other findings in the Junco and Mastrodicasa survey revealed 76% of students used instant messaging, 92% of those reported multitasking while instant messaging, 40% of them used television to get most of their news, and 34% of students surveyed used the Internet.

In June 2009, Nielsen released the report, "How Teens Use Media" which discussed the latest data on media usage by generation. In this report, Nielsen set out to redefine the dialogue around media usage by the youngest of Generation Y, extending through working age Generation Y and compared to Generation X and Baby Boomers. One of the more popular forms of media use in Generation Y is through social networking. In 2010, research was published in the Elon Journal of Undergraduate Research which claimed that students who used social media and decided to quit showed the same withdrawal symptoms of a drug addict who quit their stimulant.

Cultural Identity

Some have argued that the Millennials have "moved beyond" the ideological battles spawned by the counterculture of the 1960s, which persisted through the 1990s in the form of the culture wars.[87] This is further documented in Strauss & Howe's book titled *Millennials Rising: The Next Great Generation,* which describes the Millennial generation as "civic minded," rejecting the attitudes of the Baby Boomers and Generation X. Generation Y'ers never truly rebelled against their parents, unlike prior generations, often enjoying the same music, movies and products as their parents.

Generation Y has been described in a *New York Times* article as entrepreneurial and, "a 'post-emotional' generation. No anger, no edge, no ego." The hipster has been reluctantly accepted by members of the generation as a representative image. The social form of the small business has been cited as taking the place of the commune, and all social forms such as music, food, and good works have been expressed in those terms. However the article also says, "These movements always have an economic substrate. The beatniks and hippies — love, ecstasy, transcendence, utopia — were products of the postwar boom. The punks and slackers and devotees of hip-hop — rage, angst, nihilism, withdrawal — arose within the long stagnation that lasted from the early '70s to the early '90s. The hipsters were born in the dot-com boom and flourished in the real estate bubble."

Google's One-Size-Fits-All Privacy Policy

(Reprinted from Google's Website/Privacy Policy, April, 2012)

There are many different ways you can use our services — to search for and share information, to communicate with other people or to create new content. When you share information with us, for example by creating a Google Account, we can make those services even better — to show you more relevant search results and ads, to help you connect with people or to make sharing with others quicker and easier. As you use our services, we want you to be clear how we're using information and the ways in which you can protect your privacy.

Our Privacy Policy explains:

- What information we collect and why we collect it.

- How we use that information.

- The choices we offer, including how to access and update information.

We've tried to keep it as simple as possible, but if you're not familiar with terms like cookies, IP addresses, pixel tags and browsers, then read about these key terms first. Your privacy matters to Google so whether you are new to Google or a long-time user, please do take the time to get to know our practices — and if you have any questions contact us.

Information we collect

We collect information to provide better services to all of our users — from figuring out basic stuff like which language you speak, to more complex things like which ads you'll find most useful or the people who matter most to you online.

We collect information in two ways:

• **Information you give us.** For example, many of our services require you to sign up for a Google Account. When you do, we'll ask for personal information, like your name, email address, telephone number or credit card. If you want to take full advantage of the sharing features we offer, we might also ask you to create a publicly visible Google Profile, which may include your name and photo.

• **Information we get from your use of our services.** We may collect information about the services that you use and how you use them, like when you visit a website that uses our advertising services or you view and interact with our ads and content. This information includes:

• **Device information.** We may collect device-specific information (such as your hardware model, operating system version, unique device identifiers, and mobile network information including phone number). Google may associate your device identifiers or phone number with your Google Account.

• **Log information.** When you use our services or view content provided by Google, we may automatically collect and store certain information in server logs. This may include:

> • Details of how you used our service, such as your search queries
>
> • Telephone log information like your phone number, calling-party number, forwarding numbers, time and date of calls, duration of calls, SMS routing information and types of calls.
>
> • Internet protocol (IP) address.
>
> • Device event information such as crashes, system activity, hardware settings, browser type, browser language, the date and time of your request and referral URL.
>
> • Cookies that may uniquely identify your browser or your Google Account.

• **Location information.** When you use a location-enabled Google service, we may collect and process information about your actual location, like GPS signals sent by a mobile device. We may also use various technologies to determine location, such as sensor data from your device that may, for example, provide information on nearby Wi-Fi access points and cell towers.

- **Unique application numbers.** Certain services include a unique application number. This number and information about your installation (for example, the operating system type and application version number) may be sent to Google when you install or uninstall that service or when that service periodically contacts our servers, such as for automatic updates.

- **Local storage.** We may collect and store information (including personal information) locally on your device using mechanisms such as browser web storage (including HTML 5) and application data caches.

- **Cookies and anonymous identifiers.** We use various technologies to collect and store information when you visit a Google service, and this may include sending one or more cookies or anonymous identifiers to your device. We also use cookies and anonymous identifiers when you interact with services we offer to our partners, such as advertising services or Google features that may appear on other sites.

How we use information we collect

We use the information we collect from all of our services to provide, maintain, protect and improve them, to develop new ones, and to protect Google and our users. We also use this information to offer you tailored content — like giving you more relevant search results and ads.

We may use the name you provide for your Google Profile across all of the services we offer that require a Google Account. In addition, we may replace past names associated with your Google Account so that you are represented consistently across all our services. If other users already have your email, or other information that identifies you, we may show them your publicly visible Google Profile information, such as your name and photo.

When you contact Google, we may keep a record of your communication to help solve any issues you might be facing. We may use your email address to inform you about our services, such as letting you know about upcoming changes or improvements.

We use information collected from cookies and other technologies, like pixel tags, to improve your user experience and the overall quality of our services. For example, by saving your language preferences, we'll be able to have our services appear in the language you prefer. When showing you tailored ads, we will not associate a cookie or anonymous identifier with sensitive categories, such as those based on race, religion, sexual orientation or health.

We may combine personal information from one service with information, including personal information, from other Google services — for example to make it easier to share things with people you know. We will not combine DoubleClick cookie information with personally identifiable information unless we have your opt-in consent.

We will ask for your consent before using information for a purpose other than those that are set out in this Privacy Policy.

Google processes personal information on our servers in many countries around the world. We may process your personal information on a server located outside the country where you live.

Transparency and choice

People have different privacy concerns. Our goal is to be clear about what information we collect, so that you can make meaningful choices about how it is used. For example, you can:

- **Review and control** certain types of information tied to your Google Account by using Google Dashboard.

- **View and edit** your ads preferences, such as which categories might interest you, using the Ads Preferences Manager. You can also opt out of certain Google advertising services here.

- **Use our editor** to see and adjust how your Google Profile appears to particular individuals.

- **Control** who you share information with.

- **Take information** out of many of our services.

You may also set your browser to block all cookies, including cookies associated with our services, or to indicate when a cookie is being set by us. However, it's important to remember that many of our services may not function properly if your cookies are disabled. For example, we may not remember your language preferences.

Information you share

Many of our services let you share information with others. Remember that when you share information publicly, it may be indexable by search engines, including Google. Our services provide you with different options on sharing and removing your content.

Accessing and updating your personal information

Whenever you use our services, we aim to provide you with access to your personal information. If that information is wrong, we strive to give you ways to update it quickly or to delete it — unless we have to keep that information for legitimate business or legal purposes. When updating your personal information, we may ask you to verify your identity before we can act on your request.

We may reject requests that are unreasonably repetitive, require disproportionate technical effort (for example, developing a new system or fundamentally changing an existing practice), risk the privacy of others, or would be extremely impractical (for instance, requests concerning information residing on backup tapes).

Where we can provide information access and correction, we will do so for free, except where it would require a disproportionate effort. We aim to maintain our services in a manner that protects information from accidental or malicious destruction. Because of this, after you delete information from our services, we may not immediately delete residual copies from our active servers and may not remove information from our backup systems.

Information we share

We do not share personal information with companies, organizations and individuals outside of Google unless one of the following circumstances apply:

- **With your consent:** We will share personal information with companies, organizations or individuals outside of Google when we have your consent to do so. We require opt-in consent for the sharing of any sensitive personal information.

- **With domain administrators:** If your Google Account is managed for you by a domain administrator (for example, for Google Apps users) then your domain administrator and resellers who provide user support to your organization will have access to your Google Account information (including your email and other data). Your domain administrator may be able to:

- Vew statistics regarding your account, like statistics regarding applications you install.

- Change your account password.

- Suspend or terminate your account access.

- Access or retain information stored as part of your account.

- Receive your account information in order to satisfy applicable law, regulation, legal process or enforceable governmental request.

- Restrict your ability to delete or edit information or privacy settings.Please refer to your domain administrator's privacy policy for more information.

- **For external processing:** We provide personal information to our affiliates or other trusted businesses or persons to process it for us, based on our instructions and in compliance with our Privacy Policy and any other appropriate confidentiality and security measures.

- **For legal reasons:** We will share personal information with companies, organizations or individuals outside of Google if we have a good-faith belief that access, use, preservation or disclosure of the information is reasonably necessary to:

- Meet any applicable law, regulation, legal process or enforceable governmental request.

- Enforce applicable Terms of Service, including investigation of potential violations.

- Detect, prevent, or otherwise address fraud, security or technical issues.

- Protect against harm to the rights, property or safety of Google, our users or the public as required or permitted by law.

We may share aggregated, non-personally identifiable information publicly and with our partners — like publishers, advertisers or connected sites. For example, we may share information publicly to show trends about the general use of our services.

If Google is involved in a merger, acquisition or asset sale, we will continue to ensure the confidentiality of any personal information and give affected users notice before personal information is transferred or becomes subject to a different privacy policy.

Information security

We work hard to protect Google and our users from unauthorized access to or unauthorized alteration, disclosure or destruction of information we hold. In particular:

- We encrypt many of our services using SSL.

- We offer you two step verification when you access your Google Account, and a Safe Browsing feature in Google Chrome.

- We review our information collection, storage and processing practices, including physical security measures, to guard against unauthorized access to systems.

- We restrict access to personal information to Google employees, contractors and agents who need to know that information in order to process it for us, and who are subject to strict contractual confidentiality obligations and may be disciplined or terminated if they fail to meet these obligations.

Application

Our Privacy Policy applies to all of the services offered by Google Inc. and its affiliates, including services offered on other sites (such as our advertising services), but excludes services that have separate privacy policies that do not incorporate this Privacy Policy.

Our Privacy Policy does not apply to services offered by other companies or individuals, including products or sites that may be displayed to you in search results, sites that may include Google services, or other sites linked from our services. Our Privacy Policy does not cover the information practices of other companies and organizations who advertise our services, and who may use cookies, pixel tags and other technologies to serve and offer relevant ads.

Enforcement

We regularly review our compliance with our Privacy Policy. We also adhere to several self regulatory frameworks. When we receive formal written complaints, we will contact the person who made the complaint to follow up. We work with the appropriate regulatory authorities, including local data protection authorities, to resolve any complaints regarding the transfer of personal data that we cannot resolve with our users directly.

Changes

Our Privacy Policy may change from time to time. We will not reduce your rights under this Privacy Policy without your explicit consent. We will post any privacy policy changes on this page and, if the changes are significant, we will provide a more prominent notice (including, for certain services, email notification of privacy policy changes). We will also keep prior versions of this Privacy Policy in an archive for your review.

References and Sources

Chapter 3

http://www.cisco.com/en/US/netsol/ns1120/index.html

Chapter 4

http://www.drfranwalfish.com/http://abcnews.go.com/Technology/hook ups-casual-sex-common-college-students-meaning-term/story?id=14565942

http://yourlife.usatoday.com/sex-relationships/dating/story/2011/03/More-hook ups-on-campuses-but-more-virgins-too/45556388/1,

http://www.time.com/time/magazine/article/0,9171,1989124,00.html

http://www.cnn.com/2011/08/04/living/married-college-students/index.html

http://www.usatoday.com/news/health/2007-12-12-porn-study_N.htm

http://news.byu.edu/archive07-Dec-porn.aspx

http://www.azcentral.com/ent/pop/articles/0323pr0n0323.html

http://www.socialcostsofpornography.org/Bridges_Pornographys_Effect_on_Inter-personal_Relationships.pdf

http://books.google.com/books?id=xQUUuxaN3esC&pg=PA3&lpg=PA3&dq=how+has+Internet+use+changed+gender+roles&source=bl&ots=EQaJRWRWqh&sig=ovq3ZnNdAp_lA9KBmXOWjac6h5g&hl=en&sa=X&ei=hFMTT_SBB4bA2gXw6ZyDCg&ved=0CDcQ6AEwAzgK

http://www.scientificamerican.com/article.cfm?id=the-sunny-side-of-smut&page=2

Chapter 5

http://tobaccodocuments.org/ads_pm/205.850.0255.html

http://www.rochester.edu/sba/suffragetimeline.html

http://www.catalyst.org/publication/211/firsts-for-us-womenhttp://money.cnn.com/magazines/fortune/fortune500/2011/womenceos/

http://www.bls.gov/spotlight/2011/women/

http://books.google.com/books/about/The_young_lady_s_counsellor.html?id=DXICAAAAYAAJ

http://rd.springer.com/article/10.1007/BF01548175

http://www.bls.gov/spotlight/2011/women/

http://www.phoenixpubliclibrary.org.subdbs.phoenixpubliclibrary.org:2048/web-check.jsp?atz=http://search.ebscohost.com.subdbs.phoenixpubliclibrary.org:2048/login.aspx?direct=true&db=a9h&AN=31842135&site=ehost-live&scope=site

http://www.bsos.umd.edu/socy/vanneman/papers/CotterHV10.pdf

http://www.phoenixpubliclibrary.org.subdbs.phoenixpubliclibrary.org:2048/web-check.jsp?atz=http://search.ebscohost.com.subdbs.phoenixpubliclibrary.org:2048/login.aspx?direct=true&db=a9h&AN=31842135&site=ehost-live&scope=site

http://www.ojp.usdoj.gov/newsroom/events/pdfs/apa_report.pdf

http://www.guardian.co.uk/music/2010/sep/17/lady-gaga-feminist-icon

http://msmagazine.com/blog/blog/2010/03/11/is-lady-gaga-a-feminist-or-isnt-she/

http://bitchmagazine.org/post/lady-gaga-im-not-a-feminist-i-hail-men-i-love-men

http://opinionator.blogs.nytimes.com/2010/06/20/lady-power

http://fullcomment.nationalpost.com/2011/03/07/tasha-kheiriddin-feminisms-second-wave-hangover/

http://www.biography.com/tv/classroom/womens-history-inspirations

Chapter 6

http://www.childtrends.org/Files/Child_Trends-2010_09_27_RB_Spirituality.pdf

http://commons.trincoll.edu/aris/files/2011/08/ARIS_Report_2008.pdf

Chapter 10

http://www.kahnacademy.org/

Chapter 11

http://www.theatlantic.com/entertainment/archive/2011/08/the-genius-of-doug-rugrats-and-ren-stimpy-20-years-later/243437/

http://articles.latimes.com/2011/oct/02/entertainment/la-ca-mtv-research-20111002/2

http://www.broadcastnow.co.uk/comment/the-editor/still-rocking-after-30-years/5030507.article

http://latimesblogs.latimes.com/gossip/2011/04/nicole-polizzi-snooki-rutgers-32000.html

http://www.nj.com/news/index.ssf/2011/09/gov_christie_vetoes_jersey_sho.html

http://publicmind.fdu.edu/2011/snooki/

http://www.upiu.com/culture-society/2011/03/16/The-Affect-The-Jersey-Shore-Has-on-College-Students/UPIU-315.130.0302709/

http://www.mtvu.com/about/mtvu/

http://www.prnewswire.com/news-releases/president-clinton-announces-mtv-and-college-board-collaboration-on-first-ever-social-media-tool-for-financial-aid-119181474.html

http://www.viacom.com/ourbrands/medianetworks/mtvnetworks/Pages/default.aspx

http://www.*forbes*.com/sites/greatspeculations/2011/02/07/jersey-shore-puts-mtv-viacom-into-great-situation/

http://adage.com/article/trending-topics/amc-s-walking-dead-eating-television-alive/230644/

http://splashpage.mtv.com/2011/10/25/walking-dead-zombie-walk-new-jersey/

http://www.kansascity.com/2011/10/24/3226460/a-lively-time-on-walking-dead.html

http://www.slate.com/articles/arts/culturebox/2011/10/zombies_the_the_zombie_boom_is_inspired_by_the_economy_.html

http://www.nytimes.com/2010/12/05/arts/television/05zombies.html

Chapter 12

http://k-otix.com/index.php/2005/10/13/the-c-i-g-a-c-mixtape/

http://youtu.be/2elYnsqG-MMChapter 13

http://www.youtube.com/watch?v=_JmA2ClUvUY

http://www.youtube.com/watch?v=0Bmhjf0rKe8

Chapter 14

http://www.apa.org/news/press/releases/2000/04/video-games.aspx

http://www.pbs.org/kcts/videogamerevolution/impact/myths.html

http://www.suntimes.com/lifestyles/easy/7806663-423/playing-scrabble-social-media-style.html

http://children.webmd.com/news/20040702/video-games-tv-double-childhood-obesity-risk

http://www.digitaltrends.com/gaming/new-study-links-increased-creativity-to-video-games/

Chapter 17

http://en.wikipedia.org/wiki/Anti-consumerism

2http://knowyourmeme.com/memes/demotivational-posters

Chapter 19

http://www.wikipedia.org/

http://www.wikileaks.org/

http://www.yelp.com/

http://www.huffingtonpost.com/

http://www.smalltalk.org/

http://www.c2.com/cgi/wiki?PortlandPatternRepository

http://socialmediatoday.com/index.php?q=SMC/46766

http://www.nytimes.com/2008/09/07/magazine/07awareness-t.html?_r=1&pagewanted=1

http://pbworks.com/

http://www.wikispaces.com

http://docs.google.com/

http://wikileaks.org/

http://wikileaks.org/About.html

http://www.bostonherald.com/news/national/general/view/20111219defense_in_
wikileaks_case_claims_lax_computer_security_in_iraq/

http://ireport.cnn.com/

http://contributor.yahoo.com/

http://www.yelp.com/

http://www.kaboodle.com/

Chapter 21

http://www.mediabizbloggers.com/shelly-palmer-report/Google-Skynet-Yikes-Shelly-Palmer.html

Chapter 23

http://www.slate.com/id/2301427/

http://www.usatoday.com/money/advertising/2010-10-03-marketing-to-college-students_N.htm

http://www.time.com/time/video/player/0,32068,767.062.72001_1978837,00.html

http://www.forbes.com/sites/wendytanaka/2010/12/15/names-you-need — to-know-haul-video/

http://www.jcpenney.net/Media/Media-Room/Press-Releases/jcpenney-News/Teens-Create-a-Haul-Nation — This-Back-To-School-S.aspx http://www.youtube.com/user/juicystar07?ob=4&feature=results_main

http://www.youtube.com/user/AllThatGlitters21?ob=0&feature=results_main

http://www.mryouth.com/

http://www.focusforwardfilms.com

http://topics.nytimes.com/top/news/business/companies/hewlett_packard_corporation/index.html?inline=nyt-org

http://www.youtube.com/watch?v=hibyAJOSW8U

http://www.marketingvox.com/dove_evolution_goes_viral_with_triple_the_traffic_of_super_bowl_spot-022944/_

http://www.youtube.com/watch?v=epOg1nWJ4T8

http://www.youtube.com/watch?v=XkFPN1WYi3E&feature=player_embedded

http://www.mobilemarketer.com/cms/news/advertising/9412.html

http://www.businessinsider.com/axe-advertising-unilever-brandwashed-2011-10

http://www.youtube.com/watch?v=aYywiQ3-6To

http://www.youtube.com/watch?v=lqT_dPApj9U

http://mashable.com/2010/07/21/coke-happiness-machine/

http://www.coca-cola.com/music/en_ZA/portal/index.html

http://www.thecoca-colacompany.com/dynamic/press_center/2010/12/expedition-206-finale.html

http://www.spadre.com/cocacolabeach.htm

http://www.mycoke.com/jsps/college/faqs

http://www.refresheverything.com/

http://www.pepsipulse.com/

http://www.pepsipulse.com/

http://www.pepsisoundoff.com/

http://content.usatoday.com/topics/topic/Frank+Cooper

https://www.coca-colascholars.org/

http://www.collegescholarships.org/scholarships/companies/pepsi.htm

http://www.nytimes.com/2007/10/15/business/media/15axe.html?_r=2&ex=135.018.7200&en=85b572dfe3df0e72&ei=5088&partner=rssnyt&emc=rss&oref=slogin&oref=slogin

http://killercoke.org/

Additional References and Sources

Relationships and Sexism

Braithwaite, Scott. "Romantic Relationships and the Physical and Mental Health of College Students." *Personal Relationships*. Vol. 17, issue 1, pp. 1–12. March 2010.

"Infographic: Evolving Attitudes About Interracial Marriage." *GOOD Magazine*. http://good.is/post/infographic-evolving-attitudes-about-interracial-marriage/

Rouleau, Tanya. "Attitudes About Stay-At-Home Fathers." http://www.unh.edu/sociology/media/pdfs-journal2010/TanyaRouleau.pdf"

Statistics About Stay-at-Home Dads." Seattle Stay-At-Home Dads. Web. 20 Jan. 2012. http://www.seattledads.org/node/34.

US Census Bureau. Number, Timing and Duration of Marriages and Divorces:2009. http://www.census.gov/hhes/socdemo/marriage/data/sipp/2009/tables.html

Lewis, K. & Burd-Sharps, S. (2010). *The Measure of America 2010-2011: Mapping Risks and Resilience*. New York and London: New York University Press.

http://www.thefutoncritic.com/interviews/2011/01/03/interview-pretty-little-liars-executive-producers-i-marlene-king-and-oliver-goldstick-504304/20110103_pretty-littleliars/http://entertainment.gather.com/viewArticle.action?articleId=281.474.980901126http://entertainment.gather.com/viewArticle.action?articleId=281

Relationships

http://www.time.com/time/magazine/article/0,9171,1904147,00.html

http://factfinder2.census.gov/faces/tableservices/jsf/pages/productview.xhtml?pid=ACS_10_1YR_B12007&prodType=table

http://www.sciencedaily.com/releases/2011/07/110.725.190040.htm

http://yourlife.usatoday.com/sex-relationships/dating/story/2011/03/More-hook
ups-on-campuses-but-more-virgins-too/45556388/1

http://huntnewsnu.com/2010/11/Internet-networking-benefits-relationships/

Harry Potter

http://www.time.com/time/magazine/article/0,9171,1083935-2,00.html

http://www.metrosantacruz.com/metro-santa-cruz/05.23.07/harry-potter-0721.html

http://www.ew.com/ew/article/0,,20154416,00.html

http://www.mtv.com/news/articles/1572107/jk-rowling-talks-about-christian-imagery.jhtml

http://www.michiganlawreview.org/assets/pdfs/104/6/Barton.pdf

http://www.time.com/time/specials/2007/personoftheyear/arti-
cle/0,28804,1690753_1695388_1695436,00.html

http://www.guardian.co.uk/books/2009/sep/29/harry-potter-rowling-medal

http://www.theatlantic.com/entertainment/archive/2011/07/the-political-parable-of-
harry-potter/241946/

Sexuality

http://abcnews.go.com/Technology/hook ups-casual-sex-common-college-students-
meaning-term/story?id=14565942#.Tu_HrbLEFvI

http://www.usatodayeducate.com/staging/index.php/ccp/study-students-are-not-
hooking-up-as-much-as-you-might-think

http://www.psychologytoday.com/blog/partying-101/201106/getting-messed-hook-
the-role-alcohol-in-college-students-casual-sexual-enco

Education

http://nces.ed.gov/fastfacts/display.asp?id=80

http://www.macquil.com/articles/onlinemba.php

http://www.onlinelearningsurvey.com/reports/goingthedistance.pdf

http://www.washington.edu/lst/help/teaching_guides/collaboration

http://www.nj.com/news/index.ssf/2009/11/students_discovering_online

Women's Rights/Sexism

http://www.fordham.edu/halsall/women/womensbook.asp#North America

http://www.trinity.edu/mkearl/gender.html

http://www.crito.uci.edu/noah/HOIT/HOIT%20Papers/Gender%20Asymmetry.pdf

http://www.csa.com/discoveryguides/archives/gender.php

http://www.soc.duke.edu/~efc/Docs/pubs/Social%20Demography%20of%20Internet%20Dating.pdf

http://ritim.cba.uri.edu/wp2003/pdf_format/Wiley-Encycl-Internet-Usage-Gender-Final.pdf

http://yourlife.usatoday.com/sex-relationships/dating/story/2011/03/More-hookups-on-campuses-but-more-virgins-too/45556388/1

http://www.colostate.edu/Depts/SAHE/JOURNAL2/2003/CrossMorgan.html

http://www.cyberpsychology.eu/view.php?cisloclanku=200.906.1503&article=3

http://www.thenationalcampaign.org/resources/monster/MM_1.0.pdf

http://www.stanford.edu/class/pwr3-25/group2/pdfs/IM_Genders.pdf

http://pewresearch.org/pubs/1516/millennials-panel-two-millennials-media-information

Life, Liberty & Pursuit

Bennett, Lance, Wendi Pickerel, and Helen Jorgenson. *Culture Jams and Meme Warfare: Kalle Lasn, Adbusters and Media Activism*. Center for Communication and Civic Engagement, 2001.

Krupnick, Ellie. "Nancy Upton Wins American Apparel Contest, Has It Taken Away By Retailer." The Huffington Post. 14 Sept. 2011.

Lytle, Ryan. "Social Media Means More Than Salary to Some College Students." US News & World Report. 6 Dec. 2011.

Micheletti, Michele, and Dietlind Stolle. "Fashioning Social Justice Through Political Consumerism, Capitalism, And The Internet." *Cultural Studies* 22.5 (2008): 749-69.

Shore, Billy. "When Social Media and Social Justice Intersect." The Huffington Post. 13 July 2009.

Index

A

H

Shelly Palmer Digital Living Series

Shelly Palmer is a leading expert and widely published commentator on technology, media, and entertainment. The Shelly Palmer Digital Living Series brings you insightful works from the connected world's most interesting and provocative thought leaders.

Other titles in the Digital Living Series:

- *Overcoming the Digital Divide*, 2009, Shelly Palmer, Mike Raffensperger

- *Television Disrupted, Second Edition,* 2007, Shelly Palmer